HENRY GREEN : *Nine novels and an unpacked bag*

HENRY GREEN : *Nine novels and*

an unpacked bag : *by* JOHN RUSSELL

RUTGERS UNIVERSITY PRESS :

New Brunswick, New Jersey

The author acknowledges the kind permission of Henry Green and his publishers to quote from his nine novels and *Pack My Bag*: Hogarth Press, Ltd., London; E. P. Dutton and Company, Inc., New York; Macmillan Company, New York; Viking Press, New York.

Permission to quote has also been granted by Jonathan Cape, London, and Liveright Publishing Corporation, New York: *Travels in Arabia Deserta* by Charles M. Doughty (London, 1888; New York, 1931, Edward Garnett, ed.).
Columbia University Press, New York: *The Literary Symbol* by William York Tindall (1955).
Harcourt, Brace and Company, Inc., New York: "Burnt Norton" in *Four Quartets*, copyright, 1943, by T. S. Eliot—reprinted by permission of Harcourt, Brace and Company, Inc.; and *The Film Sense* by Sergei M. Eisenstein, translated and edited by Jay Leyda, copyright, 1942, 1947, by Harcourt, Brace and Company, Inc., and reprinted with their permission.
Hogarth Press, Ltd., London, and the Macmillan Company, New York: *The Novels of Henry Green* by Edward Stokes (1959).
Alfred A. Knopf, Inc., New York: *The Castle* by Franz Kafka, translated by Willa and Edwin Muir (1954); and "Owl's Clover" by Wallace Stevens, in *Opus Posthumous* (1957) and *The Man with the Blue Guitar* (1945).
Little, Brown and Company, Boston: *The Vanishing Hero* by Sean O'Faolain (1956).
New Directions, Norfolk, Connecticut: *Death on the Installment Plan* by Louis-Ferdinand Céline, translated by John H. P. Marks, copyright 1938 by Little, Brown and Company, Boston, reprinted by permission of New Directions.
Routledge and Kegan Paul, Ltd., London: *The Tightrope Walkers* by Giorgio Melchiori (1956).

Manufactured in the United States of America
by H. Wolff, New York
designed by *Robin Fox*

TO JONATHAN KISTLER

AUTHOR'S NOTE :

Until recently, Henry Green's elusive novels, the last of which appeared in 1952, have received scanty criticism. Last year, though, Edward Stokes's book on Green appeared, and meantime two others were being written—the present study, and one by Kingsley Weatherhead (in press). The three (Weatherhead's having appeared earliest, as a thesis) differ widely from each other, suggesting that Green's fiction is rich and challenging enough to encourage and survive many critiques. Among the citations I have made from critical commentaries on Green will be found only a few from Stokes and Weatherhead, because I did not read their work until after I had completed my own.

To five men in particular I owe thanks for having helped in the shaping of this book—to Horace Hamilton of Rutgers University, who saw it through every stage, to James Hall of the University of Washington (who introduced me to Green), and to Francis Fergusson, Paul Fussell, and Arthur Young, all of Rutgers, who gave me both encouragement and solid criticism. For encouragement without criticism I have my family to thank—and for a special kind of enthusiasm (when he heard of the project, he got hold of and read all of Henry Green's books), a friend, Leonard Kaplan.

John Russell

July 1960
Columbia, South Carolina

CONTENTS :

HENRY GREEN : *Nine novels and an unpacked bag*

ONE : *A wedge into Green's world*

Henry Green, the pseudonymous English writer whose nine novels
and autobiography were published between 1926 and 1952, was born
in 1905, the third son of a wealthy Midlands industrialist. "Children
in my circumstances," Green once wrote, "are sent away to boarding
school. I went at 6¾ and did not stop till I was twenty-two, by
which time I was at Oxford. . . ." [1] In progressing from private
school to public school to the university, Green was following the
regimen of other young men of his class; but instead of taking a degree at Oxford, he left at the end of his second year and went to
Birmingham to work as a laborer in the family factory. He emerged

eventually as managing director of the enterprise (his company makes distillery equipment), and at present directs company operations from the central office in London.

With the exception of his partly autobiographical first novel, *Blindness* (1926), begun at Eton and published while he was still at Oxford, Green wrote his books during a period in which he was committed to the exigencies of business—or to those of war. His novels reflect his experience, and so are involved with subject matter common to many writers of the thirties and forties. To characterize them in order after *Blindness,* the novels *Living* (1929) and *Party Going* (1939) are both in a sense proletarian novels; *Caught* (1943) and *Loving* (1945), continuing to juxtapose social classes, are novels of the British Isles in World War II; *Back* (1946), the story of a returning veteran, is a war novel in which for the first time Green confines himself to a single social class; and *Concluding* (1948), *Nothing* (1950), and *Doting* (1952) deal with repercussions of a postwar Welfare State on individuals and society.

Though in subject matter the novels of this businessman-author seem conventional enough, his real affinities are with the major artists of the generation preceding his own, who dedicated themselves to literature and art, and who have been responsible for the technical innovations that have been hallmarks of fiction and poetry in the early twentieth century. Like another businessman, Wallace Stevens, he has been concerned first with the problem of expression. His published theories of art and communication, while meager in quantity, are aesthetic in purport and elevate the work of art as communicator of the ineffable.[2] He is a symbolist. And as a "terrorist of language" (the phrase is Philip Toynbee's [3]), Green follows the great experimenters of the first quarter of the century—Mann, Joyce, Gertrude Stein, Lawrence, Virginia Woolf.

Before making any attempt to place Green among other writers, we should perhaps open the special door into his world that is provided by his one work of nonfiction, the self-portrait *Pack My Bag* (1940). Green wrote this book because he felt the approaching war to be a personal nemesis. He thought he had no time to rework material "directly personal" into novel form, and that he could only "turn to what first comes to mind and that must be how one changed from boy to man . . ." (p. 5). But he did not go on to search through his past introspectively, and instead submitted to many strictures in composing this factual book. These strictures provide a key to his purposes and attitude as a novelist, with respect to both the way he combines his materials and the way he customarily views his characters.

If the reader of this book were to expect a kind of carefully stowed bag of remembrances and self-evaluations, he would discover that Green left the bag unpacked. Notably unaccounted for are the ten years prior to 1938, the year he began the book. He mistrusted his ability to gain perspective over events even ten years distant in time. What he charts within the arbitrary time span—a boy's progress through three educational environments to the "real" life of the "outside" world—shows how seriously he took the matter of perspective. For his review of his life is generalized. Hardly any proper names are mentioned. Refreshingly, *Pack My Bag* hardly touches on the boy's relationship with his parents. Perhaps the reason that the anonymous boy blends into one large anonymous group is lodged in Green's belief that "little boys hardly ever think about themselves as everyone else does all the time" (p. 25). Certainly a faithfulness to this perception keeps him emotionally uninvolved with that figure of the past during its growing pains.

Green's ability to detach himself from the boy in the self-portrait promotes its main relationship with most of his novels; for the self-portrait deals with the most commonplace experiences. They are often frenetic but never crucial; that is to say, none of the situations is relevant in terms of marking character indelibly. Yet though he has no traumatic experiences, no drastic accounts of parent-child friction, no serious privations or serious rebellions to report, in *Pack My Bag* as in the novels he has the sensitivity to make low-key emotional experience sharply felt.

Green is remarkably sensitive to human beings' needs, though aware that it is potentially dangerous to have longings and needs fulfilled. This ambivalence is the touchstone of his attitude as a novelist. In *Pack My Bag* it is the urgencies of the young he realizes.

—of the little boy wonderstruck by the "treasure and menaces" hidden behind a coal-cellar door (p. 5); of the bigger boy, lured yet appalled by the treasure and menace in sex, in drink, in war. As an adolescent, Henry's muted awareness of sex mystifies him, and because of this, terrifies him. Yet the account of a headmaster's bungling attempt at sex education (in Green's last year at private school, age about twelve) ends characteristically on a "no matter" note: "I was left, in no wise the worse for not knowing, in a void of unmentionables, or as they say all at sea" (p. 37).

Green is not so much shrugging here as emphasizing his belief that questions are often best left unanswered. He is also implying that if needs are to be fulfilled, they must be replaced by other stirrings and strivings that make for individual dissatisfaction and distress. Many times in *Pack My Bag* he observes that a too-easy fulfillment, of the need for praise, say (which can be satisfied for the athlete), is likely to arrest the individual's growth, whereas dissatisfaction forces another boy to struggle up to another level. This unruffled view of struggle and insecurity carries over into his fiction (in the treatment of factory life in *Living*, for instance), but a second, more clinical insight into the workings of people's minds does make him shrug in the case of characters who thwart themselves from attaining objectives by creating their own terrors (as almost all of Green's rich people do). The best example of this insight in *Pack My Bag* comes from Green's account of the legend of the Mons angels, who were supposed to have appeared on the Allies' behalf in France in World War I.

Green was at boarding school at the time, and when the tribal chieftain of a headmaster accepted these angels as fact, the boys began to keep vigils for them. "It was typical of our society," says Green, "that when our elders believed these angels had been seen at Mons we believed we had seen them for ourselves. Even more typical we did not suppose they came to protect us, we were afraid of them, horribly afraid" (p. 45).

Two actions are involved here. The mind had first to foster the mystery ("we believed we had seen them"), and then, to terrorize itself, had to *deny* the legend (for the angels were good). It is as if the mind will make mysteries at all costs, then demand that what is unknown be threatening. Green describes this waywardness as "typical," and such self-intimidation is a staple of his fiction.

In the two incidents just described, which help form one of the book's motifs, sex and war are felt as presences by schoolboys, but remain uncomprehended. Though the boys are frightened, they are also infatuated with the mysteries. Many a time in *Pack My Bag* one sees them in silhouette as they listen attentively to the sound of cannon reaching their dormitory from across the Channel; or one is made privy to their furtive, compulsive keyhole-spying, as when Green tells of a boy who had kept nightly watch on a maid's room across the way. "Their windows were some way apart," he says, "there was almost nothing he could make out except the glint of flesh. . . . And yet, if he had been closer, if she had undressed in his room, he would almost certainly have been appalled" (pp. 121–122).

Being so susceptible to fear, this boy and others like him had to allow their curiosity to go ungratified, or only partially gratified. "I would not have it any other way," says Green of this necessity (p. 124). Not that he denies the poignancy of the situation. As he says in another place, the child differs from the adult by "not being able to avoid [the] wonder, as we can now dismiss things we have not seen . . ." (p. 116). But what is important to him is that as wonder subsides—when sex, for example, descends to the commonplace—people begin to profiteer, or to stagnate. Typical is the comment upon some men in "the harvest festival of their thirties," whom young Henry meets: "They appeared to be on too good terms with themselves . . ." (p. 174).

This is the fearful thing that may happen, when the quandaries pass. Harvests are fast gathered, the daily round of bread is baked —and goes stale. Satiety is more damaging than anything else in Green's novels; people who reach that state are forced to invent phobias. This explains what critic James Hall sees as the recurrent paradox in Green's books, "that people who, by some going standard, ought not to be enjoying life are enjoying it and that other people who ought to be enjoying it are not." [4]

Green's recognition that the anticipated fulfillment of a desire fails to correspond with the real fulfillment is the mark of a highly unromantic intelligence. It enables him to rest easy, in a sense, when his characters are dogged with menaces or grope after mislabeled treasure; because being hounded, or being wonderstruck, is better than being disenchanted. Also prevalent in his fiction is the theme in *Pack My Bag* that sheer discontent can force a person to gain in strength and vision and expansiveness. As Green put it once, "questions unresolved stay in mind" (p. 35). The statement throws much light on those fictional practices of his which harass the reader because things remain unexplained.

Not only does *Pack My Bag* help to show Green in some of his characteristic stances but also it is valuable in explaining the genesis and content of his work. Two of his early experiences are particularly worth mentioning because they have bearing on the content of all his fiction. They concern his first awareness of class barriers reared on specious grounds, and his first knowledge of sharing experience with others, or of being sundered from them and made what he calls "an albino."

During World War I, the manor house of Henry's family was converted into a hospital for wounded officers, and the eleven-year-old observed at first hand the disparity in manners between his family and the generally low-bred officers. The behavior of these men was so uncouth that the senior officer had to take measures to prevent abuses of hospitality. "In this way," says Green, "manners were ruled by discipline and so they became something else, bad manners became an offence against authority and in this way at once came near to what I knew at my private school" (p. 69).

The significance of his relating military and school discipline rests in the youth's grasp of the foundation of manners. If regimen is their source, it occurs to the boy that his own class may be impeccable only because its members have been subjected to the same pressures earlier, and for more extended periods. His apprehending this possibility led young Henry to evaluate his elders during wartime. Those frantic officers who, convalescent, swam rivers to get to girls, were only obeying crude instincts of self-preservation; and members of the "trained up" class who gave them hospitals were really doing nothing more, although their instincts may have been blurred by refinements. "In the war," said Green, "people in our walk of life entertained all sorts and conditions of men with a view to self-preservation, to keep the privileges we set such store by, and which are illusory, after those to whom we were kind had won the war for us" (p. 68).

The privileges he mentions are, of course, those of class boundaries and all they entail, boundaries staked out on the theory that manners determine real differences between groups. The "forced atmosphere" of war, placing the bumpkin officers in sight of the wellborn among other things, gave opportunities "to every child," says Green, "to see the cracks in the façade people put up before children in my circumstances" (p. 75). The four novels that follow *Blindness—Living, Party Going, Caught,* and *Loving*—all chisel into the cracks in the façade; and only in *Caught,* at the cost of deep suffering, is a member of the privileged class able to make a meaningful commitment to members of a lower class.

The other important experience of Green's youth has to do with the problem of communion and alienation. It is best illustrated in *Pack My Bag* by two episodes, one at the country house hospital and the other some years later at Eton. The former exemplifies one of the emotional bulwarks of the book—Green's belief that bonds forged between persons impel growth as no other force can. It concerns an Australian soldier, ruined by the war, whom Henry's mother tended, and who later committed suicide aboard the ship that was taking him home. When it seemed this man was getting better, he asked Henry to go bicycling with him:

> We got to where the road goes round the church and then we came back. He was soon wobbling but he would not get off to rest until when we got into the drive he could just get off his bike and zig zag into the house not wishing I suppose that I should see him fall. He was up again in four days . . . but it damaged me . . . because it was not until then I realized by sharing it with him, how hopelessly far gone he was. (p. 67)

The bike trip, which happened to him, was able to touch Henry's feelings. But at Eton, when he was notified one day of an accident to his parents in Mexico, he could but pantomime feelings. Ensuing guilt made him self-estranged. Soon afterwards he blurted out to a friend that his parents were not expected to live, whereupon "a wall was built between us by my news, his eyes grew blank and he went off at once leaving me an albino again . . . what I told him separated us because it was outside his experience and so was awkward . . . something to be dodged" (pp. 146–147).

The possibilities of sharing with or being sundered from others, illustrated in these episodes as deriving from certain accidental kinds of experience, help shape the content of Green's novels. This is especially true of the six novels before *Concluding* (in which book, as we shall see, his art seems to undergo a change). In *Living, Party Going,* and *Loving,* novels that deal with ordinary, everyday mishaps, unplanned participation in concerted efforts enables people to share common experience, as did the boy on the bicycle trip. A tangible sense of union may be felt by members of a foundry team casting iron molds (in *Living*), or commuters on a fog-bound railway platform (in *Party Going*), or servants cohering into a sort of great family when their masters are away (in *Loving*). These people are not exactly aware that they are sharing situations. Although Green could single out occasions of emotional growth like the bicycle trip, he did say in another place, "we seldom learn directly; except in disaster, life is oblique in its impact upon people." [5] And this statement marks the difference, for him, between circumstances that permit common experience and those that cause estrangement.

Blindness, Caught, and *Back,* differing from the *-ing* novels, start from situations in which life's impact has been direct. They present characters separated from others because their losses (of eyesight, a wife, a leg) are outside the experience of their fellows—just as young Henry was made "an albino again" when news of disaster impinging on him alone estranged him from his schoolmates. Catharsis, "not a theme with much future," as Green said in 1950,[6] served him at the beginning and at the end of World War II, when he resolved *Caught* and *Back* by bringing their bereaved main characters out of alienation after prolonged suffering; it had served him also at the start of his career, when he similarly resolved *Blindness*.

Because all of Green's books deal with situations of communion and isolation, within and across boundaries of social class, I have emphasized experiences of his youth which bear on his fictional situations. Yet such experiences were sporadic, and meanwhile at Eton his fatuity prevented much real emotional growth. First he had adulated athletes, then peers ("I was a title snob"), and later, with the upperclassman's opportunity to make freer choices, he became a self-styled aesthete.

He began *Blindness* at Eton, and in this introspective book, devoid of humor, brought an indictment against himself. Through the *deus ex machina* of accidental blindness, John Haye, an Arts Society schoolboy like the author, is made to renounce his supercilious ways and to shed his self-conscious aestheticism. Taking its theme from *Crime and Punishment,* and its technique possibly from Joyce's *Portrait of the Artist as a Young Man,* this is Green's only derivative as well as his only humorless novel. Understandably, the young writer lacked experience; he did not gain much at Oxford. There he found himself something of a celebrity, on the eve of the success of his first novel, yet records that the increase in his liberty caused only renewed emulation (of the dons), all fresh advances being made toward a higher sophistication and sharper discrimination between sets. There, too, Green courted the rich, but at the same time, in the atmosphere of those middle twenties with their incipient labor movement, he wondered whether he had the right to an inherited fortune. The complex he developed, he says in *Pack My Bag,* "drove me to go to work in a factory with my wet podgy hands" (p. 195). From his experience as a common laborer, in the factory he would one day direct, came in 1929 his novel *Living.*

Recently, however, Green has said that between *Blindness* and *Living* he attempted another novel, to have been called *Mood.*[7] A few words about this attempt, which he apparently made while still at Oxford, may indicate how important his removal to Birmingham was to his development as a writer. In the passages he has published from *Mood,* a book that proposed to deal with the inner reveries of a girl named Constance, Green shows himself to have been even more derivative than in *Blindness*—one garden interlude, for example, seems to have come straight out of Mrs. Woolf's "Kew Gardens." Rather than quote at length from his extracts, it is more to the purpose to give his own reason for being unable to complete the work. He had become convinced that "to establish a girl, in this case Constance, in a static situation where nothing is happening to her except her thoughts and feelings, is an impossible project for the novelist and one which only a very young man, as I was then, would try for."

More interesting than the parallels with Mrs. Woolf are clues that Green was trying to relieve the stasis with methods derived from Lawrence. One furtive contact between Constance and a street-car conductor he refers to as "an obviously incompetent echo of D. H. Lawrence," but there is an even more revealing passage, in which Green fractures the "static situation" by dramatizing one of Constance's girlhood recollections. She and another girl are in a hay field, and drawn magnetically to its center. Running along each of the field's "long concentric rings," they are brought nearer and nearer "to the middle of this piece which had been mowed in a round"; when they reach the center they fall down, each giving "a faint cry," and nearby, as if in answer, "two horses, with a scream, bolted. They careered away, the wagon pitching, crashing behind them."

The allusions to muted sexuality are unimportant here; what is worth remarking is Green's sharp criticism of the passage. "Thus the worked up climax," he says, "which fails however well written, and thus the old trick by which the novelist, to be dramatic, casts his reader, or rather drags his reader back into that imaginary golden sunny adolescence spiked with simple fears."

A comment like this challenges probably the most prevalent cliché in modern fiction. Green made a similar, almost flippantly empirical remark in *Pack My Bag* when he said of childhood that "we are warned that what happened in those days, like the wilder wild animals, lies in wait, in ambush for when one has grown up. So they say, but it never does" (pp. 14–15). But when he was writing *Mood,* he was of course succumbing to the cliché. This was before he went to Birmingham, where his empiricism was forged.

Green went to Birmingham with no political prejudices such as those held by his Oxford contemporaries, Auden and Day Lewis. As he says in *Pack My Bag*, he found there "a new world which was the oldest" (p. 236), and it delighted him aesthetically. He spoke of "the deep, the real satisfaction of making something with [one's] hands," which he said was "more than sensual and . . . obviously the purest form of self-expression" (p. 240). And to his surprise he found among his fellow workers exuberance, gaiety, humor. Gayest of all were the old ones, having got to "that blessed state when you forever cease to give a damn" (p. 244). Above all, Green was captivated by his co-workers' interest in other people, in "crazy situations," an interest tempered by decent manners that always drew praise from him: "I had not yet met, and have not since, such concentration on human behaviour" (p. 239).

The book that came from this experience, built around a pseudo-family of working people held together by the old molder Craigan, poses conflicts between generations and between classes. It is permeated, says Walter Allen, by its author's "delighted sense of novelty." [8] The phrase exactly explains Green's capacity for absorbing social experience, and points to his affinities with Gertrude Stein. Her *Three Lives* is much like *Living,* and as bare of sociological or political implication.

With *Living,* Green quit the ways of introspection, as can be seen from his portrait of Dick Dupret, the factory owner's son into whose hands comes control of the Bridesley works. This young man, Green's counterpart, is unapologetically dumped from the novel far from its finish, after having served a basically structural purpose.

Green was married in 1929, and between 1931 and 1938 wrote *Party Going.* This was the only book on which he worked more than two years. He told Nigel Dennis that the novel about "my own circle in London" proved difficult to write because he was faced with "creating an abstract situation out of new conditions." [9] It is possible that Green siphoned too much life from *Party Going,* a book that imprisons a dozen or so chief characters in the amber of a railway station and adjacent hotel during four hours of a fog which delays all trains. Against static hotel room conversations held by the frustrated party-goers, Green places scenes of a restless, kinetic crowd in the station. Material so handled seemed to him most susceptible to the demands of art, inasmuch as it was problematical and impersonal. But this novel has an effect opposite that of *Living*— an effect of torpor. Sidestepping its images and motifs, one might be able to enjoy *Party Going* as conventional satire; but its humor is forced to coil back upon itself and to derive again and again from an unchanging desert of emotions. Very different are the three war novels which Green produced in 1943, 1945, and 1946. *Caught, Loving,* and *Back,* all structurally complex, are also totally engaging at the very first level of story telling.

The dialogue of these books is refurbished by Green's renewed contact with the lower classes. Before the outbreak of war he had joined the National Fire Service, and from 1939 to 1945, a gentleman in the ranks, he served with regular firemen and the conglomerate of butlers and clerks and cooks who fought fires during London's night blitzes. *Caught* is the story of the London Fire Brigade in 1940, and it is likely that the wartime milieu of London also provided Green with characters for *Loving* and *Back.*

Richard Roe, a "gentleman ranker," and the last of Green's characters who may be identified with their author, is the co-hero of *Caught.* But most of the plot of this book centers around the fire captain Pye, a newly promoted fireman who is caught in a terrible mesh of circumstances in the months just before the bombings begin. More important even than the plot is Green's evocation of waiting-before-crisis—for their inability to take any really decisive measures is what prompts the antic, fitful behavior of the men and women in this novel who wait to be bombed.

In *Loving,* a group of English servants maintain a crumbling Irish castle for their masters, while across the water England lies stricken by war. By removing his people spatially from danger, Green has made a comic novel out of the dissensions and collusions within the servant ranks, but the effect of the war reaches them nevertheless, in two ways: they are terror-stricken by rumors that an Irish underground association is in league with Hitler, and they are guilt-ridden by the very fact of their safety. Thus *Loving* illuminates an "emotional Black Hole of Calcutta," says Henry Reed, much as did *Party Going* and *Caught* before it.[10]

The effect of war is indirect in all of Green's war novels. Even in *Back,* the story of Charley Summers, who had lost his leg and been taken prisoner by the Germans, London is the locale, and Charley's readjustment is portrayed against the background of a diminished war and an increased round of rationing and bureaucratic control. In all three novels war is treated as much as a binding force as it is a sundering one, principally because the circumstances that make for alienation, in *Caught* and *Back,* arose before the novels begin. (Roe lost his wife, Summers his leg.) In their indirection, and in their odd faculty for enabling human beings to profit by their anxieties and privations, Green's war novels have the unconventional originality of *The Enormous Room*. All three, in fact, work upon the principle of confinement on which Cummings's book operated. The firemen are confined to their station, the servants to their castle, and Charley Summers not within a German prison camp but within himself.

Caught, however, written at the height of war, indicts women, who have been modified by the fear of impending war, and who have lost the feminine attributes that at least temporarily sustain men in the earlier novels. *Loving* and *Back* reimplant this capacity in their heroines, Edith and Nancy. But these are the last such heroines in Green's fiction. *Caught* then in a way looks forward to *Concluding;* for in this futuristic novel women are again changed by pressures from without.

An authoritarian state is the force that has modified the matrons and schoolgirls of *Concluding,* and thrown the burden for humane action onto the old scientist Rock. The state has rewarded Rock with a cottage, but the school principal Miss Edge wants to usurp the place since it is on school grounds. Rock also stands to lose the comfort of his old age, his granddaughter, whose heart has been captured by one of the tutors. When this old man's concern for his neurotic granddaughter and jeopardized cottage broadens to a concern for a missing schoolgirl, about whom no one else cares, *Concluding* begins to put forward a dark proposition that responsible civilization has at last succumbed to system. The theme is not new, but Green's treatment is radical, especially because what transpires this one summer day is not made clear. Mr. Rock's experiences, and those of his antagonist Miss Edge, verge on the hallucinatory; and seemingly evil figures like the old forester and the secretive girls may be harboring ordinary guilt or enjoying ordinary pranks. Nevertheless, three phenomena help guide the critic toward an analysis: the treatment of "modified" women; the attitude toward organic nature, long an emblem of instinctual vitality in Green's books, but in *Concluding* affected ominously by imagery suggesting mutations, actual sea changes, in nature; and the fact that neither resuscitative nature nor sympathetic, resourceful women appear in the last two novels, *Nothing* and *Doting*.

These last novels go back to *Party Going* for their materials, but the Mayfair set having been impoverished through postwar taxation, the submerged social protest that was in *Party Going* is gone. *Nothing* and *Doting* consist of dialogue scenarios set in hotels and restaurants and bedrooms (for food first, sex second, are the characters' chief pursuits). They also pit the generations against one another; men are pawns, and older women run roughshod over sweet young things when clashing interests impel them to take drastic action. As in *Party Going*, as in Waugh and Huxley, diversions are craved, but satisfactions usually denied. But perhaps because Green's middle-aged men are willing to settle for very little, and know how to make use of pleasure, not hoping for happiness—perhaps because of this, *Nothing* and *Doting* do not fail to delight, and skirt real gulfs of pessimism.

TITLES

Having given a sequential account of Green's work, I should like to relate his novels in another way by grouping them briefly according to their monolithic titles. Least enigmatic of these is *Blindness,* and this is Green's most reducible novel; yet it is like two others, *Caught* and *Back,* significantly enough because there is no *-ing* in the title.

It is dangerous, of course, to systematize the work or even the titles of a writer. *Nothing,* for example, is not a gerund as are Green's other *-ing*'s; still it deals with material as uncatastrophic as that in *Doting.* The point is that *Nothing* and the gerundive books take place only in the present, and do not confront their leading characters with catastrophes but rather threaten them with losses—not of life and limb, but of cottages, housekeepers, jobs, and extra lovers. Whatever tragedies they hold in wait are veiled and kept off in the distance; these are harrowing only insofar as the minds of the characters permit threats to stultify them, to interrupt their daily rounds. Meanwhile the favorite characters "carry on" in the face of oblique intimations of life's dangers; and when the *-ing* novels end, they insinuate that days to come will be much like days just gone.

Not so with *Blindness, Caught,* and *Back,* in which life and limb have been in jeopardy, and in which actual loss sustained by central figures results in crippling stasis. Life oppresses directly through disaster; the characters fly back to their pasts, misinterpret these, remain perplexed; the kinetic flow of *Living* and *Loving* is stoppered until the final pages of *Blindness, Caught,* and *Back.* Deep suffering then becomes the catalyst for emotional release and rescue. In these, the only books of Henry Green whose situations are resolved, the characters face prospects entirely different and essentially promising.*

Yet another distinction can be made, this time among the *-ing* novels. Again titles give an index to significant content. Going to parties, doing nothing, and doting are certainly inane enough pastimes; and the stock responses, the stylized routines in these conversation pieces, come to be as expected as the similarly stereotyped

* A coincidence that seems to refute my distinction here might, on investigation, appear to confirm it. It happens that *Back, Loving,* and *Nothing* all end with betrothals. But at the end of *Back* the fact that the hero is crippled has become nearly obliterated; in *Loving* and *Nothing,* the heroes' illnesses are almost morbidly accentuated at the end—Charley Raunce's dyspepsia, John Pomfret's diabetes.

exchanges of Restoration comedy. The public behavior of sophisticated people is fairly predictable of course—Green's comedies are
not wholly artificial. But one does sense in these books a rather more
obvious manipulation of character, and correspondingly increased
detachment on the part of the author. In *Party Going* the detachment derives probably from the abstract nature of the problem
Green set for himself in 1931; in *Nothing* and *Doting* it is felt
mostly through the curtailment of "terrorist" prose—of the welter
of images set free by an oddly visual imagination, and of syntax
that, expanding sinuously or wrenching even terse expressions out
of normal sequence, stirs with feeling the strongest of his thoughts
about people and their imbroglios. This kind of writing occurs in
Caught and *Back,* and also in *Living, Loving,* and *Concluding.* These
last titles suggest perhaps the most resistless of the problems with
which Green has been engaged in his writing—the problems of living, of loving, and of continuing to live and love, even in retrograde.
Living, Loving, and *Concluding* may be his most representative
books, because in them his sensibilities are balanced between compassion and satire. They are certainly his most dynamic books. They
strike between the stasis of bereavement and the frothiness of the
very frivolous, and partake glancingly of both.

GREEN AND THE TWENTIETH CENTURY NOVEL

Having already hinted of Green's affinities with the experimental
novelists of 1900 to 1925, I shall make only one or two comparisons
between him and other writers in the hope of widening the focus of
this introduction to his work. Since I shall next discuss his technique and style, it may suffice to mention here that writers like
Mann, Joyce, Forster, and Mrs. Woolf show the same concern for
contours of structure that is Green's most obvious artistic preoccupation. To their names should be added the name of Charles M.
Doughty, whose *Travels in Arabia Deserta* (1888) seems to have had
more influence than any other body of work on Green's prose style.

Green differs from the earlier experimental novelists chiefly in two ways: he prefers a scenic point of view, and he is unwilling to provide pasts for his characters. Never does Green allow the cast of thought of a single character to pervade a novel. In fact he is sparing in his record of even the glancing thoughts of his speakers. And never do we watch a character of Green's evolve through a lifetime, or even a significant portion of a lifetime. When his people do have pasts, they misread them; usually they have none, and often they have no interiors to which the reader is given direct access.

Although his tendency to concentrate on exterior behavior of characters is foreign to the methods of Joyce and Mrs. Woolf, Green's criteria remain aesthetic ones. In the dozens of short scenes into which his novels are split, his characters tend to compete or to form alliances, for the most part obliviously, that give an index to a balanced structural design. Speaking of his attempts to be selective and nonrepresentational, Green once said: "The Chinese classical painters used to leave out the middle distance." [11] He himself leaves out a middle distance—the analyzed minds and motives of his characters —and is enabled to work his figures into tableaux almost mathematically precise, and aesthetically satisfying. "We want to find out what's behind things, don't we?" says the budding novelist Terence, in Virginia Woolf's *The Voyage Out*. "Look at the lights down there scattered about anyhow. Things I feel come to me like lights. . . . I want to combine them. . . . I want to make figures." [12] This is at least a good part of what Green also wants to do.

As Green's figures are deployed through his slim, balanced novels, and shown responding to life at a "warm, tactile, pre-verbalized level," [13] a dissociation seems to become evident between him and his contemporaries. At least this is the case if we accept the useful generalization R. W. B. Lewis has made, in *The Picaresque Saint*, about representative writers of this century's "second generation." Lewis feels that writers like Camus, Silone, Faulkner, and Graham Greene, unable to find in art "a basis for sheer existence," forged for themselves, especially by creating roguish but saintly heroes who could immerse themselves in the tragic community of man, a "belief in the act of living . . . achieved by a desperate struggle. . . ." [14]

This belief, reflected through such spokesmen as Meursault and Isaac McCaslin, offers the dignity of man's endurance as a total and genuine compensation for remaining alive and positively engaged in an absurd universe.

Green's characters, in contrast, are neither reflective nor articulate enough to stand as his spokesmen. He is trying to make them come alive, but not for a philosophical purpose. If asked what he hopes to achieve in print, he always answers that he wishes what he writes to have a life of its own—and when pressed, admits that this "crux of the matter . . . like all hilarious things, is almost indescribable." [15] His words are equally irreducible when he says he writes to "get himself right," and calls such effort "a kind of solitary self-control" and "a kind of mental diarrhea. . . ." [16]

But if he finds his craftsmanship therapeutic, he makes no claims *in* his work for the supremacy of art. In this respect he differs from the "first generation" novelists who share his preoccupation with form. It is noteworthy that although we find no picaresque saints in his novels, neither do we find people of artistic sensibility—people like Charles Swann or Stephen Dedalus or Charles Strickland, "who bespoke their authors' conviction," as R. W. B. Lewis says, "that art was the one genuinely redemptive power of the day." [17]

This is a small point but may be significant. Roguish humanitarians may supplant artists in the works of second generation novelists, but there is a strong similarity between the two breeds: both are rebellious. Here is where the two generations seem most obviously to overlap. Self-exiled or cast out from society, the rogues continue where the artists left off to represent what Sean O'Faolain, in *The Vanishing Hero*, has called "the tradition of individualistic revolt against the order of nature and society which is so evident in all fiction in our time." [18]

Now Green's characters—perhaps because they are unreflective—do not revolt; or if they do, they are satirized as puerile fellows, like Bert Jones in *Living* or Raunce's Albert in *Loving*, who try to escape their own inadequacies. His best characters either hold tenaciously to what is theirs by fiat, or show themselves shrewdly capable, like

Raunce the butler, of feathering their nests on the sly while to all appearances observing regulations.

That Green regards individualistic revolt rather coolly is not due to a matter of principle but rather to a matter of temperament. Up to now I have avoided associating Green temperamentally with the writers with whom he has much in common as a technician. I have done this deliberately, because I think Green's addiction to form conceals a wit and temperament that connect him with English writers of a remoter tradition: with the Restoration dramatists and with prose writers of varying satiric intensity from Swift and Fielding to Sterne, Lewis Carroll, Samuel Butler, perhaps even Ronald Firbank. To these I should add the names of two more recent writers on the Continent who possibly influenced Green more directly: Kafka and Céline.

None of these writers (except Carroll) cares much for form; and among them there are large differences; but they are all tinged, it seems to me, with a kind of amused distrust in mankind that gives their work much of its gusto. This attitude allows for variety of feeling. Certainly Sterne's and Carroll's misanthropy is rosy compared with Céline's. But all, and Green with them, seem to admit man's incorrigibility, and in fact to build on that. They therefore tend to skirt the issue of man's predicament in a hostile universe. Their focus instead is upon man's mental and moral inadequacies, which render him a comic rather than a tragic figure.

Green's own reaction to man's inadequacies is quite a cheerful one. Fundamentally a pessimist, though, he does have a macabre streak, which possibly can be attributed to Continental influence. He has recently, for example, responded to a question about influence by confessing a "tremendous admiration for Céline." [19] In Céline's *Death on the Installment Plan,* a character pronounces this virtual motto: "To get a kick out of dying while he's busy bringing death nearer and nearer—that's Man all over, Ferdinand!" Throughout that book, Céline catalogues the most antic pastimes, that swell men's expectations wondrously—diving bell ventures, balloon ascents, motorcycle rides, perpetual motion schemes—only to punctuate every

activity uglily, as when young Ferdinand recounts the aftermath of
a day's ballooning:

> They rolled it all up. But it was a dreary wreckage that was
> left, badly scratched by the branches, a tattered mass lightly
> clinging together. . . . It had brought whole hedges with it,
> between its skin and the rigging. The boisterous salvagers,
> thrilled and enchanted, lifted Courtial shoulder-high and car-
> ried him off in triumph. . . . I, on the other hand, still had the
> lousiest part of the job to do. . . . I had to [urge] them on,
> by dint of the most ponderous repartee, to manhandle gratis
> and for love all these exhausting tons of junk . . . the gasbag
> torn to ribbons, the relics of this hideous catafalque, and to
> sling the whole of this garbage into the last car of all as the
> train pulled out.[20]

Such is Céline's method, the laborers' response to the repartee an
integral part of the exhausting scene; and such often do we find to
be Green's motto and method, in less boisterous terms, to be sure.
Raunce and the other servants of *Loving,* on one occasion of dinner-
time hilarity, all have a look of agony about them, but go on punish-
ing themselves by continuing to imitate a lisping man and bringing
on more laughter. At a middle-aged party in *Nothing,* the curled
and yellowed place card of a man long dead arrives mysteriously on
a table set for festivities; in that same book, Richard Abbot, about
to achieve sexual conquest, goes black in the face from an unac-
countable choking fit. But these intimations that they are dying on
an installment plan do not reach these characters, and they are only
momentarily discomfited. Hence, though Green concocts such macabre humor, he can also relish the tiny gains his people make, much
as Sterne and Butler relish the muddled progress of their characters.
Such people cannot help themselves or rid themselves of their preoccupations. Being thus incorrigible, they are not worth satire but
laughter—until one discovers that preoccupations and flagging
memories enable them to get along in an alien, uncompromising
world, and hence prove their boon as well as their limitation.

Because he takes a cheery view of man's limitations, there is small compassion in Green's work, but also little dismay. There is in fact exuberance. This is cloaked, though, and may not be sensed by some readers. His stringent observance of form does give his work a kind of chilliness which disguises his affinities with Sterne, at one extreme, and Céline, at another, so that his connection with Kafka is more readily apparent than with others I have listed as kindred spirits. No one book of Green's has the range and digressive diversity of a book of any of these men; but his nine novels taken together have that range, have shown him to be anything but predictable, and have kept him virtually unclassifiable.

Humorous though he may be, even in his comedies of manners Green's is not the hard, consistently funny satire of Waugh and Huxley. Implicit in their work is a wretchedness over the decay of old, stable forms (think of Brideshead's chapel, or Mark Rampion's "sane, harmonious Greek man" [21]) which argues that they do believe in attainable norms of behavior, hence their satire bites harder. But Green, "not outside, [but] inside the human zoo," as V. S. Pritchett has said,[22] sees no way out; consequently his ardor is nil, he does not inveigh. If there is one contemporary English satirist whom he does resemble, this is Anthony Powell, "a mellower Waugh," in William York Tindall's phrase.[23] Powell's *The Acceptance World* is not only like Green's last novels, *Nothing* and *Doting,* but contains in its title the flavor of acquiescence that distinguishes Green from Waugh and Huxley.

Being a non-Promethean in a Promethean age, and at the same time not a morally outraged satirist, Green resists being placed in a niche alongside other contemporary English novelists. His humor seems to derive from the rational, limited view of man prevalent in the eighteenth century; his near-morbid insistence that man threads an obstacle course to death, from the Continental writers I have named. That he should also be a symbolist is the most fascinating and perplexing thing about him, for there is an energy of passion in much of his symbolism. His work gives sporadic glimpses of a fructifying natural order, of beauty attending natural processes. He responds too, sometimes, to the beauty of artifice and mechanics—

to a juggler's legerdemain (in *Doting*), or a workman's operation of his lathe (in *Living*). Such responses, it would seem, overcome fairly austere intellectual checks. The difficult conversion of response to symbol could bring therapy to the man who has admitted he seeks it in self-expression. But if art consoles, so did talk console Dr. Johnson; to be steeped in misgivings and to seek consolation does not argue nihilism. At any rate, the rest of this book is designed to show that wholesome and positive attitudes may be constructed from Green's pessimism, just as such attitudes could coexist with Johnson's melancholia.

T W O : *Theory, technique, style*

THE FUNCTION OF THE ARTIFACT

Green's theories of art and communication, for the most part clarified between 1950 and 1952, were derived empirically. In 1927 and in 1939, when the General Strike and Hitler sent Green voluntarily among the lower classes, he received the "proletarian inspiration" he has considered essential to his development as a writer.[1] After the war he returned to the directorship of his business. But he has remained as gregarious as when he left Oxford. He has continued to believe, as he told Nigel Dennis, that the writer's duty is "to meet as many pedestrian people as possible and to listen to the most pedestrian conversation." [2]

Such conversation seems to serve Green in two ways as the prime ingredient of his art. Beyond his conviction that human beings spring from an unchanging mold and that their talk will reveal them, there is his savoring of talk as one catalyst—the best one—for promoting the mysterious potential people have for sharing. "The argument," he says, "is that we cannot go outside everyday life to create something between reader and writer in narrative. The communication between the two will be on a common or garden plane, but the mere exchange between two human beings in conversation is a mysterious thing enough. The mere fact that we talk to one another is man's greatest asset. That we talk to one another in novels, that is between complete strangers . . . is nothing less than miraculous if you once realise how much common experience can be shared. My plea is that we should not underestimate this. . . ." [3]

The real mystery of speech to Green is its ability to communicate that which is left unsaid. His formula runs something like this: Talk between characters, accompanied by action but not by commentary, creates those characters for the reader. By observing discrepancies between talk and action, the reader can get to know two things: what the characters are like and what they are really communicating to one another beneath the façade of ready speech. All this involves a conscious act of imagination on the reader's part, and the creation of life in his mind becomes in turn the medium of communication between author and reader. Just as talk between people establishes some sort of communion by what is left out, to be supplied by the listener, so that which is left out of a novel establishes similar rapport between creator and apprehender.[4] As V. S. Pritchett put it, in a defense of Green's theories, "more and more the contemporary novelist is oblique and relies upon the reader as upon some opposite number in a conspiracy." [5]

The collaborating reader is likely to be mired in discrepancies in Green's books. Many times he finds himself knowing no more about the characters than they do themselves. No one can say whether or not young Philip (in *Nothing*) is illegitimate. Nor is it clear whether or not Mrs. Grant (in *Back*) has been feigning amnesia. What is more, Green's people all carry different reports about one another.

And the forces that send them bumping about their uneasy worlds
are kept as nebulous and unanalyzed as the characters. Hence forces,
characters, events become different things to different readers, and
by being such they fulfill the function of nonrepresentational art:
they enable the artifact to become, as Green says, "all things to all
men, as a good novel . . . should." [6] Loose ends are functional in
another way, too. "And if the novel *is* alive," Green told Terry
Southern, "of course the reader will be irritated by discrepancies—
life, after all, is one discrepancy after another." [7]

Green's wish for a book to have a life of its own is a concept that
he feels is "indescribable." Nevertheless, he is steadfast on the point
—so much so that he tries at the end of a novel "to leave characters
alive enough to go on living the life they have led in the book. . . ." [8]
Ideally, for him, novels (as *Concluding* suggests) should be concluding, but not concluded. Beneath this logic lies the curiously romantic
expectation that the rapport between author and reader can be extended indefinitely by the book's afterlife.

Green's characters, those who "get along," come into rapport
mainly by participating in various concerted efforts; but most of the
time even these people are not communicants. Green will not falsify
experience when he formulates it. His people are mostly alone.
Those moments when common experience is shared occur sporadically in life, and are therefore sporadic in the novels. To a footman
in *Party Going,* from behind a barrier of luggage, appears a girl
who plants a kiss when he wishes it most, then vanishes. The rest of
the book gets along by humor, and that epiphany is likely to be
missed, though it is an approximate symbol for the whole meaning
of the book. But, in a paradoxical sense, while the novels in making
their way so often show characters alone or at cross purposes,
Green, if his art is successful, will be forging bonds between himself
and his readers. Even this sharing will be sporadic. Novels must repeatedly be made, for the artist cannot afford to be static any more
than the work of art can.

Green has said nothing publicly about the value of the artifact in
itself, although his practice reveals a formal preoccupation reaching
geometric exactitude. Before examining the place form has held in

his art from the beginning, we may turn to his account in *Pack My Bag* of his favorite sport, billiards, and detect an equivalent fascination with linear and angular patterns:

> . . . much of the charm lies in the green cloth under electric lamps with the three balls, two white, one red, going through movements geometrically exact while the slow score is chanted. A drop cannon which gathers them by the top cushion is a stroke so precise in the way the three widely separated balls are brought together within the span of the fingers of one hand, so leisurely but so inevitable when played right that silence is the tribute the ordered revolutions each must roll softly through, is the tribute this shot demands. (p. 177)

Nowhere else in Green's writing is the reverence for the thing completed, having followed its pattern, made so explicit. Something of this same fascination reappears in Green's last novel, *Doting,* which begins and ends with the magic air-cupolas of a juggler. The juggler's craft, artificial and formal, serves as invocation and valediction to the artificial activities so geometrically arranged in the novel.

Giorgio Melchiori, in his fine essay, "The Abstract Art of Henry Green," traces a development in Green's writing away from commitments to humane values, to culminate in *Nothing* and *Doting* with the superimposition of aesthetic norms, these marking out for the artist the only goals worthy of achievement.[9] It is true that *Nothing* and *Doting* are honed and fitted with precision, but I do not know if the aim of such carpentry is quite the same as the aim of the Cubists, to whom Melchiori compares Green. These artists "aimed at complete abstraction—a pattern of rigid geometrical figures creating abstract emotions through the intellect rather than the heart."[10]

For many reasons I cannot accept Melchiori's persuasion that Green derives from a growing obligation to pure form "the superimposed aesthetics which must absorb and annihilate reality."[11] Chronology would be my first argument. Green was an "unripe" aesthetician at Eton, and fled to a world of things and people he

has not since abjured. His fondness for the "aesthetics" of billiards
—which constitute a real equivalency to those of art—we discover
as early as 1940. More important, *Party Going* is designed like
Nothing and *Doting*. There are the same motiveless regroupings of
characters, the same innocuous dialogue. These three books may be
geometrically more proportionate than Green's other novels because
Green's aim is partly to reveal the stultification of his principals,
and a geometric scheme enables him to shuffle them into their places
predictably. Like billiard balls, they are volitionless. But taking
away their volition does not take away their lives. Green genuinely
understands these people as people, not as shapes out of which a
Cubist creates emotions through the intellect.

One reason I tend to disagree with Melchiori on the point of
Green's abstract art is that I feel it is right to put weight on Green's
public pronouncements, which came along between 1950 and 1952,
the years in which *Nothing* and *Doting* appeared. Green's stated
position makes it clear that communication is the end of art; what is
more, the communication "will be on a common or garden plane."
But for Melchiori to arrive at his conclusion, he is forced to cancel
out for Green that common or garden plane on which human beings
feel.

Green in 1940 had demanded of prose fiction essentially what he
demanded in 1950. "Prose," he had said, "should be a long intimacy
between strangers with no direct appeal to what both may have
known. It should slowly appeal to feelings unexpressed, it should in
the end draw tears out of the stone" (*Pack My Bag*, p. 88). Melchiori makes a questionable deduction when he interprets this definition.
"Green," he says, "seems to have started from the idea . . . that
there is a world of 'unexpressed feelings,' *beyond the common
human ones,* which have formed the material of earlier works of art
—feelings of an exquisitely aesthetic nature." [12] But Green seems
rather to mean inexpressible common feelings; he wants to appeal
to these, not to preempt others intellectually. All of the emotional
peaks in *Pack My Bag* are concerned with the experience, common
to all but ineffable, of "sharing situations." Henry bicycles with the

Australian soldier; schoolboys smoke at an unused gravel pit, going there "as if to an assignation . . ." (p. 141).

The intimacy between strangers that Green wishes art to engender depends upon the feelings aroused by such assignations and conspiracies. And if he proscribes "direct appeal to what both [writer and reader] may have known," it is because he does not wish his readers to read subjectively any more than he wishes to write that way—for then a collaboration would be precluded. Hence he resorts often to situations steeped in myth and fantasy, yet retains verisimilitude of surface action and infuses into his work themes that are most mundane.

Concerned as he is with Green's abstract manipulation of scenes and characters, Melchiori passes over two things Green leaves in *Nothing* and *Doting:* the living talk which creates the characters, and the humor which dogs them in their sorry state. Both the talk and the levity provoke the commonest sort of human response from the readers Green never disdains. These are the qualities that make the artifact potentially communicable, instead of something the craftsman is building for himself.

If, as I think, we may take Green at his word, we can assert quite baldly that situation and character, the requisites of the traditional novel, are never supplanted by form. Form is a medium for Green, not an end. In the first place, when he imposes from without a form controlling a whole novel, he establishes boundaries within which to operate. And second, the dialogue scenarios economize expertly on space. Both of these strategies have the purpose of supplying contexts with dispatch, and contexts alone give clues to the meanings of Green's novels.

CONTEXT AS COMMUNICATOR

Green began his second B.B.C. broadcast by describing a bit of communication that he had observed on a bus ride. His double-decker was stopped at a red light, opposite a hospital. A woman passenger had waved in the general direction of the hospital, and a handkerchief had appeared at a window in answer; but the bus was delayed overlong at the light, and the lady gave over waving. "A trivial thing, you say?" Green asks his listeners. "Perhaps," he goes on, "but I maintain, first, that this thing seen holds in it the essence of all communication between a writer and his readers, and second, that his possible treatment of it . . . is, in itself, what may be the whole essence of how a reader can be brought . . . to a deeper realisation of what is being described." [13]

Reader and writer may share the "thing seen," the reader may respond to the visual image, if the writer prepares him adequately for response. The writer's appeal is to the reader's memory, to the subconscious reservoir of things seen, really, and not to particular memories. Hence, as Green says, the woman herself is not described —her looks, her age. But what is universal about the situation—embarrassment, hypocrisy, the fact that for mankind empathy is impossible—the artist must grasp and attempt to evoke; and what he leaves in (the unexpected and fracturing delay, for example) forms the context which transmits the meaning. Meanwhile none of the meanings I have suggested is forced upon the reader—they may be only *my* meanings.

The imagery Green employs in his novels is constantly of this detached, visual sort, involving color, planes, figures, and linear movements which, with the modulation of contexts, often reach the intensity of symbols. His formal constructions work toward the same end. The outward forms he imposes are first of all symmetrical, and second, enclose the dynamic situations so effectively that Green might be said to be cheating time and space of their debilitating effect upon experience.

Least symmetrical of all is the structure of *Living,* for here the subject matter has compelled Green to range over a large cross section; in form this book is really strengthened from within, by a style as sharp as clanging on anvils, and by symbolic combinations— juxtapositions and motifs. Yet Melchiori has called attention to the "choral" effect of *Living*'s "fairly elaborate construction," through which the story line is deliberately delayed until a series of vignettes have established the setting.[14]

Blindness, whose three sections are entitled "Caterpillar," "Chrysalis," and "Butterfly," is organized like *Party Going* and *Loving.* The blindness is a trap, which for the greater part of the novel arrests all growth; the hero is isolated in a rudimentary situation, and this is exactly what happens on a social instead of physical level in the other two books. Fog stays the party-goers at a hotel; war and an enchanted castle imprison the servants on Ireland. The space limitations are virtually absolute (and *Party Going* covers only four hours).

Concluding is also limited spatially, to the grounds of a boarding school, but its structural control is primarily temporal; like *Ulysses* and *Mrs. Dalloway,* the book runs the course of a day. *Caught* is laced with time confusions, as its two important figures, Pye and Roe, fly back to their pasts.* *Back* breaks in the middle, and a corollary episode from the elegant eighteenth century is introduced by way of memoirs that come to Charley Summers's hand. Each story, the little and the big, serves to universalize the other and to offer wry comment at the same time on the disparity of settings. *Doting* and *Nothing* are limited by a specific direction of action. The action of one is bounded by two parties; the other locates a great party in the center and builds up to and down from it.

These structural schemes really operate like that drop cannon shot of which Green is so fond: they channel the "ordered revolutions" each book "must roll softly through." Static and complete envelopes around dynamic action, they supply the contexts within which the characters express themselves, that is, the peripheral or general situations that confront them. From the structural schemes it can be seen that these people are most often either insulated or isolated; yet their talk remains on the garden plane, and the enormity or puniness of situation does not seem radically to affect them.

The two chief devices within the novels that create judging con-

---

* *Caught* is also built on a scheme of night-and-day episodes; London is shown by night, Roe's country estate by day. Perhaps the most structurally complex of Green's novels, *Caught* is the only one in which two characters become almost doubles of one another, by occult suggestion, while on the surface remaining long odds apart.

texts are those of leitmotiv and montage. The repetition of material with variation and expansion, a technique of echoing, is the symbolic process to which William York Tindall, in *The Literary Symbol,* gives the term leitmotiv.[15] In Green's work motifs are threaded into the novels in different ways. An entire novel, for example, may be based on a single motif (as happens in *Back,* when Rose, as the name of a girl, of a flower, even as the past tense of a verb, carries a complex theme of carnality-and-purity to conclusion). More often, sporadically recurrent images generate motifs, as homing pigeons do in *Living,* or images of fire in *Caught.* But stark figures of rose, bird, and fire vie in Green's work with very subtly modulated motifs; these may involve slight, sometimes arcane echoes of sound, or color, or reflection (reminding one of Mann's technique, say, in *Death in Venice*), or may present in new forms the elements that compose entire settings. (For example, *Living* and *Loving* contain many crucial scenes in which different static and dynamic elements are counterpoised.) At one mundane extreme, talk itself may acquire symbolic proportions through leitmotiv, as when, facetiously, Raunce and his subordinates in *Loving* twit each other about being members of one family, although their later actions signify just that kind of bond to have grown among them. At an opposite, grotesque extreme, fearful intimations slip into *Concluding* when, apparently at random, metaphors drawn from an undersea world work a sea change over organic nature.

Within the novels we also encounter heavy use of the device of montage, the juxtaposition of scenes to record simultaneity of either similar or disparate actions. Green likens such treatment to the painter's establishment of tonal contexts, and says that "the superimposing of one scene on another, or the telescoping of two scenes into one, are methods which the novelist is bound to adopt in order to obtain substance and depth."[16]

The Russian movie director, Sergei Eisenstein, has discussed two special qualities of montage which make it indispensable to a symbolic novelist like Green. Insisting upon a new or third quality which arises from the conjunction of carefully selected material, Eisenstein writes that "each montage piece exists no longer as something unrelated, but as a given *particular representation* of the general theme that in equal measure penetrates *all* the shot-pieces." [17]

Green's most sustained use of montage occurs in *Party Going* when he cuts from scenes in which old Miss Fellowes may be dying to scenes next door in which party-goers continue seeking enjoyment. But all of his books employ montage to epitomize their themes. Its indefiniteness enables it to realize the function of symbol, and Eisenstein's remarks on the effect of montage on the viewer exactly express Green's hopes for his novels:

> And we can now say that it is precisely the *montage* principle, as distinguished from that of *representation,* which obliges spectators themselves to *create* and the montage principle, by this means, achieves that great power of inner creative excitement in the *spectator* which distinguishes an emotionally exciting work from one that stops without going further than giving information or recording events.[18]

Eisenstein's explanation of montage can be applied to the methods of such poets as Pound, Eliot, and Stevens, who consistently arrive at meaning through juxtaposition. In fiction, too, the technique is not uncommon, but is perhaps most frequently employed, as in Proust, in superimposing past upon present sensations. (The familiar flashback technique of modern novels is a form of montage.) Green utilizes the technique to effect transitions in stories confined usually to the present—hence my emphasis on the remarks of a movie director, whose purposes are similar.

Scenes juxtaposed enable the reader to judge and "create" at moments when the characters remain unenlightened. The symbolic occasions when characters "share" cannot be accomplished by montage, but spring out of accruing context. We assent to John Haye's mystical illumination at the finish of *Blindness* as we do (if we do) to Lily Briscoe's completion of her picture in *To the Lighthouse.* We need the whole novel back of us to do so.

But not every juxtaposition of Green's tends toward symbol, certainly; and the nuclear incidents that trigger many of the novels, the images which lead Green away from characters through passages of intense description, the sharings of the characters themselves, are by necessity few and far between. Yet the novels must be made to engage their readers, and what keeps them going for Green is dialogue, with its attendant humor.

Although the conversation pieces *Nothing* and *Doting* may seem new departures by Green, written to accord to his theory of 1950 that description should be reduced to stage directions, as far back as *Blindness* he gave dialogue a commanding position in his work. In fact all of his novels can be judged in the light of his later critical pronouncements. His aim has always been to relume the reader's conscious imagination. "For a long time," he says, "I thought this was best lit by very carefully arranged passages of description." [19] Even though his later theory subordinates description to dialogue, his darkest antagonist has remained the printed word too easily passed over, too unmystifying.

Aware that words accrue multiple meanings as language continues in use, Green has relied on dialogue to discharge two opposite functions in his books. The first would seem to *unmystify* language, but the deeper function is symbolical.

First, dialogue gets past a semantic hurdle, so to speak, to make for economy at the starting point. Says Green, "if the materials of narrative . . . are a series of sound symbols which create words of no precise meaning outside their context, surely the means of communication between writer and reader . . . should be dialogue, the reason being that we do not have time to define what we mean in conversation and that we thereby arrive easier at a general conventional understanding of what is being said." [20]

This "conventional understanding" furthers both verisimilitude and disguise. But those readers who, chagrined at the cloudy action and at the talk which gets nowhere, put Green down and do not pick

him up again, miss the point. For, he goes on, "At the same time
there can be no precise meaning in a work of art. . . . Life itself is
capable of several meanings. Therefore the future function of narrative prose is not to be clear. . . . Narrative prose in future must be
as diffuse and variously interpretable as life itself." [21]

And here is where dialogue does its heaviest work. Enclosed in
their solipsistic worlds, Green's people do not give answers to questions, but pose other questions; what they know is not what they
have seen and heard, but what they tell themselves they have seen
and heard. And all the time they are talking the author does not have
to give away *his* meaning. Dialogue has a built-in means of disguising
or getting over awkward ground in theme presentation. Let us illustrate with some exchanges that occur near the end of *Nothing*.

The most inscrutable character in *Nothing* is middle-aged John
Pomfret, a reflective person, a man who glowed with enthusiasm at
the announcement of his daughter's engagement to the son of his
old flame—yet a drifter unerringly taken in tow by that woman,
Jane Weatherby, during the visits set ostensibly for making wedding
arrangements. A loyalty to his daughter Mary is fairly solidly established in John's character even up until the end, when he contracts
diabetes. He has again become used to Jane, but has persuaded himself that it is in Mary's interests that he continues to see the woman.
Then one evening Jane mentions "how bad all this working life is
for these girls," and lets into the air a small idea she has been
saving:

> ". . . But John don't you think she should get right away
> before she settles down?"
> He turned rather white.
> "Rid ourselves of her for a bit?" he inquired. (pp. 196–197)

At this candid response Jane is forced to smooth over the waters
a little, and when the conversation turns to the subject of sickness,
she commiserates with John over his diabetes, brings him a drink,
and then for the first time in many years places her cheek against
his. At this point Green cuts immediately to the next scene:

A few evenings later Mr Pomfret said to his girl Mary "Monkey I've been thinking things over and I should like you to go to Italy for a bit."

"Italy Daddy? Whatever for?" . . .

"Wouldn't you care to travel then?"

"Daddy, did Mrs Weatherby also think of this?"

"Good Lord no Mary. Whoever put it in your head?" (p. 199)

John Pomfret seems inexcusably to have forgotten who put it in *his* head. But it is by no means as clear that he has consented to give over the plans for his daughter's marriage. It is rather as if with two halves of his mind he is contemplating Mary's happiness and Mrs. Weatherby's charms. For he goes on to tease Mary about the forthcoming wedding (something he would not do vindictively), until she remonstrates.

"Now you of all people are not to laugh at me! . . ."

"All right poppet." He laughed. "So anyway you don't say no to your Italian trip."

"I haven't said yes have I?"

"I don't want you hanging about while there's still so much to be decided Mary" he declared and was serious. (pp. 201–202)

Knowing no more than the dialogue tells us, we can make no single interpretation of these passages. The endearing terms, "poppet," "monkey," are the same John has used lovingly all along. The last sentence, declaring John's seriousness, seems best received as typical of Green's cosmic irony. To be sure there is "much to be decided," and Mary has to be got out of the way—so that Mrs. Weatherby can step in and lead John to an altar—but this is not what John is telling himself will be the upshot of things. The example suits Green perfectly. He does not reveal John's conscious motive, and John's words indicate it may be one of two.

While we are being confused and delighted, the writer's sentiment need not be bared. Humor is the bridge as theme remains obscure. (Is John rationalizing, or has the combination of diabetes and a soothing cheek driven him to plot-making?) Between writer and reader, says Green, "it is the presentation of the theme which creates the communication . . . and as dialogue in life consists largely of humour, to create life between writer and reader humour should in future be the bridge." [22]

Where the symbolic combinings arrest or intensify action, and where the novels' structures make their inroads on time and space, humor operates kinetically. More than anything, certainly more than symbol, it fosters the illusion of life. Humor is at the bottom, for example, of the communication to us of Raunce the butler's ability to serve his beloved Edith by nailing up a peacock's carcass in the cook's larder. While Edith is dallying with Raunce instead of tending her mistress's children, a dog drops the bird, killed by the cook's nephew, in Raunce's bedroom. This Raunce sees immediately as a stroke of luck, for it puts him in position to browbeat the cook, to whom he gleefully refers as "the old cow":

> "Now then," Edith interrupted. "That's all right," he went on. "I'm thinkin' of you, ducks. See?"
>
> "No I don't."
>
> "Well she's got it in for you about that waterglass, an' now we've something on her. Get me?"
>
> A noise of high shrieks and the clapping of hands announced Miss Evelyn and Miss Moira, tearing along towards them down passages. . . .
>
> Meantime Raunce had dashed out into the pantry, snapping his fingers at the dog. It picked up the dead peacock and followed. . . . For a moment Edith was alone as those children raced towards her the other way. Then they had arrived. She was holding her breasts.
>
> "Mercy," Miss Evelyn exclaimed . . . "why Edith you do look thrilled at something." (*Loving,* p. 119)

Such is Edith's first evidence that she is loved. And if humor brings along such blazing evidence as this, spaced between *Loving*'s symbols of vitality-amid-decay, humor can also act as a check, or countering force, in such a book steeped in pessimism as *Concluding*. The schoolgirls who have formed a cabalistic society in that book, for instance, and who seem utterly depraved as they intimidate old Mr. Rock, may only be harmless gossipmongers after all. Their secret cult abounds with humorous examples of children feeling very grown up and important. At one meeting of theirs that he attends, Mr. Rock's fears are quelled momentarily when the girls grow rapt over an old-fashioned polka—he had expected anything but that from their secret-sourced radio in a cellar, and for once he is able to chuckle over their mysterious doings. Humor, then, a spacer of symbols for Henry Green, is also a balancer of mysteries.

STYLE AS AWAKENER

In the article in *Contact* in which he explained his theory of the conspiratorial value of the dialogue novel, Green warned that a writer should beware of self-imitation in fashioning a prose style. He was referring to the non-dialogue portions of a book. Dialogue poses a different problem of alertness, the alertness of the ear to speech. Green's ever-surprising record of what human beings say has shown an unfailing alertness of ear, that has made dialogue the stable element of his prose style, as well as the chief vehicle of his humor.

Artistic selectivity can of course not be neglected by the writer of dialogue—written speech is not the same as spoken speech. Green's dialogue operates on a plan by which common words and phrases are just barely misplaced, and redundancies and ellipses chosen just off the norm. The result is that his people talk, not with phonographic realism, but just far enough from it to freshen the idiom as inflection freshens speech.*

* The following examples come from a fifty-page span in *Nothing*: "The moment those two children tried to get engaged Jane has had the man living in her pocket" (ellipsis, p. 204); "Always have often swallowed the wrong way all my life" (redundancy, p. 247); "What Liz might dig up to say could hardly be disinterested, would it?" (grammar, p. 211).

From *Blindness* to *Doting,* Green's dialogue remains his least modified method of presentation; he could get conversation as right at twenty as he could at forty-five. A single illustration from *Blindness* will I hope bear out this assertion. Late in the book Green records a meeting between beleaguered Mrs. Haye, mother of John who is blinded, and a neighbor who tries to persuade her to remain at Barwood (the Hayes' estate: it has oppressed John with its rural inactivity and he feels he must be off to London to begin his career as a writer). Mabel, the neighbor, has been appealing to Mrs. Haye that she remain to keep the affairs of Barwood's village in order.

> . . . "Why, [urges Mabel] it would all be indecent and disgraceful if you went so that there was no one left to look after it. You know how it is, illegitimate babies immediately, my dear. Oh no, Emily, you cannot go. Besides, what does the boy want to do in London?"
>
> "Yes, but you see he is artistic."
>
> "But Emily, painters always go to the country for inspiration. I have never heard of a painting of a town that was any good. And there is nothing to write about in a town. Don't let him ruin your life, Emily." (p. 249)

A typical dodge for Green's people is to incorporate others' arguments into their own. So Mabel, intent to push further her own argument, rapidly associates "artistic" with painting and thrusts home a dubious point, that has little bearing on John, the writer. Similarly, Mrs. Haye is so intent on her own interests that she does not reply to the direct question (Green's people rarely do), and rallying against Mabel dismisses the appeal to save the village with a "Yes, but . . ." Finer still than this exchange are Mabel's words, "look after it" (referring to the village), and "illegitimate babies immediately, my dear." Spokesman for all harried estate owners, Mabel reveals her patronage by words exquisitely chosen for her. Can we measure what would have been lost had not Green's ear decided upon "illegitimate babies immediately, my dear," and had Mabel been made to say "illegitimate children"? Her word is all mothering—and is probably just the word affected women of the landholding class would use in their demonstrative speech.

The non-dialogue prose of *Blindness,* though, is not the prose of a "terrorist" of language. There are few syntactical and grammatical variants to be found in the sentences. If it could be demonstrated that Green's style underwent many transformations, the most patent difference could be found between the prose of *Blindness* and that of any later book. Here are comparative treatments of roses from *Blindness* and *Back:*

> Then there had been father's roses. They bordered the path from the drawing-room French window to the door in the wall. Just over it climbing roses scrambled up and hung down in clusters. And little rose trees stood out on each side of the path, and red and white roses peeped out from the green leaves that hid the thorns. (*Blindness,* p. 146)

> For, climbing around and up these trees of mourning, was rose after rose after rose, while, here and there, the spray overburdened by the mass of flowers, a live wreath lay fallen on a wreath of stone, or on a box in marble colder than this day, or onto frosted paper blooms which, under glass, marked each bed above in the green grass, the cypresses and in those roses gay and bright which, as still as this dark afternoon, stared at whosoever looked, or hung their heads to droop, to grow stained, to die when their turn came. (*Back,* p. 3)

Different as *Blindness* may be from other Green prose, the truth is that Green never does develop a recognizable prose style. In any book, his sentences may be tight or loose, his diction clipped or lush, his syntax pure or convoluted, depending upon the job he is trying to make the individual sentence perform.

Green is an experimenter with language, and at times an experiment will appear in one book and be dropped in the next—as happened when he eliminated most expletives and articles from *Living,* and modified many verbs in *Loving* with adjectives. But such changes apart, and *Blindness* excepted perhaps, the development of his style is not easily traced.

Critics disagree even upon the prose of individual books, and documentation bears out their respective claims, because examples of Green's flattest and of his most redolent prose can be quoted from any of them. Thus Mark Schorer can say that "the early style was clipped and spare," and quote the opening sentence of *Party Going* for illustration: "Fog was so dense, bird that had been disturbed went flat into a balustrade and slowly fell, dead, at her feet." [23] Similarly, Martin Greenberg can find the "flat, abbreviated statements" of *Caught* acquiring a "pregnant poetic quality" by "their very prosiness, their restrictedness and renunciation of all effect." [24] He sees the spareness of William Carlos Williams in a passage from *Caught* beginning, "The staircarpet was white, and the walls. The banisters pink. He saw yellow curtains" (p. 79).

Both Schorer and Greenberg contrast to these examples the sensuous and pulsating language of *Concluding*. Giorgio Melchiori, on the other hand, traces a growing preciosity in Green's style through *Party Going* and *Caught* to *Back,* after which "the prose of *Concluding* . . . seems restrained." Melchiori quotes from *Party Going* to illustrate "precious ornamentation . . . light and elegant like rococo scroll-work"; he perceives in *Caught* "the farthest point Green reached in contriving elaborate adjectival expressions." [25] (*Party Going*'s scroll-work: "Aromatic steam as well from her bath salts so that if her maid had been a negress then Amabel's eyes might have shone like two humming birds in the tropic airs she glistened in" [p. 154]. *Caught*'s adjectives: "this soft evening aching room" [p. 107]; "this hyacinthine, grape dark fellowship of longing" [p. 112].)

These opposing opinions suggest that an analysis of Green's style will necessarily lead to subjective conclusions. The sparest and most elliptical renderings of stark images will be found, and so will mazes almost as intricate as the description of roses from *Back*. Both extremes have served poets, and Green is of no school. There is as much of Keats in him as there is of Eliot; the flatness of William Carlos Williams is counterposed in his writing by syntactical permutations worthy of Faulkner.* And saying this much, by the way, is telling only half the story. The emphases so far have been on different ways that Green gains poetic effects. But in the most thorough study of Green's style, one that works in part through statistical count, Edward Stokes shows that "its basis is the short, syntactically simple sentence," and that the great bulk of Green's "precise and economical prose [is] colloquially unobtrusive. . . ." [26]

Because Green's writing is so flexible, I feel that judgments of his style are apt to be unrewarding, unless it is granted right off that his restraint and his ability to pull out stops are ever waiting on his vision. Quantity—the prevalence of, say, Green's "sinuous" over his "stark" descriptions—is not necessarily telling. That opening sentence from *Party Going* ("Fog was so dense, bird etc.") marks one of the very few times in the novel that Green eliminated articles as he had done regularly in the preceding book, *Living*. Yet the instance is significant. It is a way of seeing which is not forgotten when the prose takes on later lushness—it is a bony, unaccoutred token of what is in store for the impersonal "her," Miss Fellowes, who at that moment makes an instinctive compact with death. Perhaps such a way of seeing permeated the whole of *Living*, reflecting Green's impression of people in an industrial environment, which is to say that Green may not have been posturing or experimenting so much as he was recording. But even in *Living* we find a style which emotion takes past understatement, a syntactically wrenched writing more frequent in later books. Here is one passage:

> Now first that feeling which had soaked all through about Mr. Jones, how everything, everything was wonderful, she was the sweetest girl in the world and wouldn't the old people be glad to see her, now first that feeling ebbed and died in him. (p. 230)

And here is another, just as rhetorical, though periodic in a different way:

* For analyses of Green's Faulknerian prose in context, see below, pages 106 and 211.

Is nothing wonderful in migrating birds but when we see them we become muddled in our feeling, we think it so romantic they should go so far, far. Is nothing wonderful in a woman carrying but Mrs. Eames was muddled in her feeling by it. As these birds would go where so where would this child go? (p. 246)

Anaphora—repetition of the first phrase in successive sentences—is used here. "Is nothing wonderful," we read, and also twice, "muddled in . . . feeling." But because the second sentence is shorter, at its end we are awaiting a natural completion of thought, and of sentence pattern as well. By interrupting the rhetorical momentum, Green creates a pause in which we feel the need for balance; a pause which he fills with the magnificent geometric sentence, "As these birds would go where so where would this child go?"

These passages, and others like them in Green's "prosaic" second book, I feel substantiate my assertion that from first to last he evolved no series of styles, but that he was equipped early to cope with what challenged him.

"Style as awakener," after this, does not seem a just phrase to apply to Green; but turning to his remarks in 1950, we perceive that his consciousness of audience, and his belief that standard English is dormant, account partially for his treatment of language. That part of the novel not written in dialogue, he says, must be written in a very personal prose, not in impersonal journalese or in the "good English" of leading articles, because the plethora of impersonal prose in the modern day tends to retard the awakening of the reader's conscious imagination.

At this point in "The English Novel of the Future," Green mentions the one writer whom he believes to have accomplished an artistic transmutation of the language. This was Charles M. Doughty, on whom Green had written his one critical article,[27] and whose Arabic English in *Arabia Deserta* probably comes closest to influencing Green's own style. Doughty's reasons for creating his pure form of English are the same as Green's for his more modest aims. "The *Arabia Deserta* volumes," Doughty wrote to D. G. Hogarth, "had necessarily a personal tone. A principal cause of writing them was besides the interest of the Semitic life in tents, my dislike of the Victorian English; and I wished to show, and thought I might be able to show, that there was something else." [28]

It would not do to force a connection between Doughty's wanderings among Bedouins and Green's among laborers and servants and office workers. Yet we are back with things and people when we compare the two writers; their sources of inspiration are the spoken languages of people (people most distinguishing in manners, but engagingly unsophisticated in speech).*

A passage from Doughty on the nomads strikes exactly the same note as Green's praise of the workingmen-humanists:

> Well could he speak (with a certain erudite utterance) to his purpose, in many or in few words. These Orientals study little else, as they sit all day idle at the coffee in their male societies: they learn in this school of infinite human observation to speak to the heart of one another.[29]

Their affinity of feeling seems to be brought out by Green's prose. In no other writer except Doughty have I seen so many of Green's special tamperings with English. A London reviewer cites a description of a mare from Doughty which might almost have been written by Green:

> Never combed by her rude master, but all shining beautiful and gentle of herself, she seemed a darling life upon that savage soil not worthy of her gracious pasterns.[30]

Note the epithet "darling life," then place against this a short sentence from *Loving*: "She looked for a second time full at him seriously with her raving beauty" (p. 157). Both passages illustrate a technique which Theodore Kalem ascribes to Green as follows:

---

* Walt Taylor writes that Doughty "felt intuitively, what the philologists now confirm, that a primitive language is more concrete than a more civilized language; that a civilized language is addressed more to the reason, and is therefore more abstract." (*Doughty's English* [London, 1939], p. 4.)

"He alters the context of a devaluated word or phrase and restores its purchasing power in the mart of meaning. . . ." [31]

Physical associations with nonphysical entities also help make the styles of Green and Doughty concrete. Doughty will mention "these fat weeks of the spring pasture"; [32] in *Caught,* Green concludes a metaphor with a similar association, speaking of "the fat white winter of her body" (p. 117). For another kind of concreteness, compare this sentence from *Loving,* "He licked a palm of his hand, then smarmed his yellow hair" (p. 156), to this one by Doughty: ". . . he fetched him a clean back-stroke upon the neck-bone, and swapt off at once . . . the miserable man's head." [33] Note the expressive coinages "smarmed" and "swapt"; mark also the almost cumbersome effect of forcing things, already concrete, onto the page more concretely. Green does not say "licked his palm" but "a palm of his hand"; Doughty does not see the stroke of a sword upon a neck, but a "back-stroke upon the neck-bone."

Though Doughty punctuates his writing more heavily than Green, there are times when in sentence structure and punctuation the two writers come again into accord. At times they will run subordinate clauses and phrases into the mainstream of the sentence with no punctuation, and frequently they use commas instead of semicolons to yoke independent clauses. Both the omissions and the commas serve for torturing phrases and clauses into closer articulation, in hopes of investing them with feeling, of striking out against abstract logic.

In Doughty we often come across sentences punctuated like these:

> No sweet chittering of birds greets the coming of the desert light, besides man there is no voice in this waste drought.

> The Akaba is not very deep, in the end I found, where the pilgrims remounted, that we were come down hardly 250 feet. [34]

The idea in each second clause is tightly related to that of the first. The second clauses re-describe what the first propose. Green's splicings work the same way:

She wondered whether she had been wise to choose spirits, she really did not feel well, they did not seem to have done her any good. (*Party Going,* p. 25)

A curious thing is that those who belonged to the exclusive club were privileged to use a bamboo rod, ordinary prefects could beat only with a cane. (*Pack My Bag,* p. 114)

But he was not so blind, he said under his breath, spectacles or no, he could see Birt coveted the cottage. . . . (*Concluding,* p. 175)

Just as Green's conversations are often written elliptically, so is his prose often elliptical, seemingly when it is written close to speech patterns. Many expletives, and "that's" which introduce noun clauses, are eliminated by both Doughty and Green. The comma splices themselves often point to ellipses. In the second of the three examples just given, either formal "whereas" or informal "while" could have linked the clauses. Note also, in the third example, the curious use of the word "no." The usual construction here, one would expect, would be "spectacles or no spectacles"—but Green cuts the second noun. Doughty is similarly elliptical. He will write,

The stiff neck of any reluctant brute is gently stricken down . . . then without more he will fall groaning to his knees.[35]

The word "more" is serving Doughty as a substantive; he has cut a word from speech while giving us the pattern of speech.

Curiously, the styles of these writers show similar idiosyncrasies even when their writing is not informed by speech patterns. For example, Edward Stokes has noted a peculiar redundancy in Green, which he calls "his unusual trick of introducing a relative clause with a redundant conjunction." [36] The examples he gives seem to run quite contrary to speech patterns. Here are some, the conjunctions italicized:

Immediately the mucus reappeared, almost Eton blue in this brilliant light, *and* which trembled, weaving with each breath he took. . . . (*Caught,* p. 168)

. . . Paddy [lay] snoring between these windows, a web strung from one lock of hair back onto the sill above *and* which rose and fell as he breathed. (*Loving,* p. 54)

. . . the girl began, raising limpid, spaniel's eyes to Miss Edge, *and* that were filling with easy tears. . . . (*Concluding,* p. 175)

I was agreeably surprised, after reading Stokes, to return to Doughty and find the very same queer redundancy. Here are two within five pages of each other:

Now seeing themselves evenly matched, they said to him of the ass, *and* who was their tribesman, "Turn thou and let us kill him!"

Near the sûk's end is their corn market, *and* where are sold camel-loads of fire-wood, and wild hay from the wilderness.[37]

Such expressions would be infrequent in speech, surely.

Some further idea as to the range of Green and Doughty may be gained from a final illustration, in which their employment of the relative pronoun "who" seems derived from some ancient source (perhaps the Bible), and is used far more formally than speech generally permits. Doughty writes,

The dying derwish gave a weak cry much like a child, and hastily they raised the camel under him and gathered his bag of scattered victuals and reached it to him, who sat all feeble murmuring thankfulness, and trembling yet for fear.[38]

From *Back* we take similar constructions:

He might have been watching for a trap, who had lost his leg in
France for not noticing the gun beneath the rose. (p. 3)

She said this with an easy mind, who had a ton and a half
stowed safe in the other cellar. (p. 35)

These mannerisms seem self-conscious and literary; everyday speech
is remote from such expressions.

The purpose of this section on style has been to illustrate the elas-
ticity of Green's prose, which he can use in innumerable ways to
foster his purpose—that of forcing the reader to waken to the po-
tentials of language. Neither Green nor Doughty, it seems to me,
could be parodied effectively: both are too close to their sources. I
would not say that Green has written a new language in quite the
same sense that Doughty has, for Doughty's source, Arabic, is too
special a thing. But Green is explicit in his praise of Doughty's ac-
complishment: it was an overthrowing of a mother tongue grown
dormant by leveling. Green's effort has been in the same direction as
Doughty's. I have tried to make their affinities of spirit explicit by
showing relationships in their styles, though it would be dangerous
to insist upon direct and conscious linguistic influence. For Green is
ultimately nonderivative. As Diana Trilling has said, "His syntax
is his own wild and brilliant secret." [39]

ASPECTS OF THE FIRST NOVEL

In 1950, Henry Green told Harvey Breit that he had come to believe that "the true life has nothing to do with sudden death and
great tragedy," [1] and he told a B.B.C. audience that life impinged
upon man obliquely, except when disaster struck him. Green's first
novel, though, composed a quarter-century before he made those
remarks, deals with sudden blindness. And this is no symbolic blindness being explored, but an actual physical blindness in all its fear-
some reality. John Haye, a student at Noat School, is blinded on a
vacation trip home; before that point John has been established as
a character sundered from his schoolfellows by his arrogance, and

the novel goes on to trace the effect of blindness on the victim and his people—family and servants and neighbors at Barwood, his stepmother's country estate.

Granted its cathartic relationship with at least two of Green's later books (*Caught* and *Back*), *Blindness* is all the same uncharacteristic of his work. Both *Caught* and *Back,* for example, display the rapidly shifting surface texture of Green's other books, a texture compounded of fantasy and humor. *Blindness* has little of either. And it lacks the fast juxtapositions, the hallucinatory angles of vision, the mythological plot situations, that come to be favorite devices of Green. All this is a way of saying that this first book, despite its imaginative subject, is too *real,* too closely oriented with physical reality, to bear much resemblance to Green's later work. Only *Living* matches it in realism, perhaps because the workers' lives he observed so captivated Green.

Oddly enough, as Green's characters in later novels collide with and withdraw from one another, or establish instinctive, fragile, often occult relationships, we get to see less and less of the insides of their minds, and come to learn their private obsessions by watching their behavior. But in *Blindness,* and to a lesser degree in *Living,* we eavesdrop on thoughts and reveries, so that we perceive fairly definite parallels between thought and resultant action. I believe our being able to perceive these parallels takes much of the mystery from the characters of *Blindness*—which is to say that I think a direct ratio exists between the amount of interior monologue we are allowed to hear and the degree of realism Green achieves. And *Blindness* is his least characteristic book because we see so much of the workings of his characters' minds. The question is mainly one of relative space allowed for different methods of presentation. On this matter Beekman Cottrell has observed that "*Blindness* falls into almost equal parts of straightforward expository writing, interior monologue, and direct conversation." [2] The interior monologue, meanwhile, is not presented in an undiluted stream-of-consciousness but rather in third person and past tense, the conventional method by which an author translates a character's thoughts rather than renders them directly.

There are other conventionalities in *Blindness* that differentiate it from Green's later work. There is, for instance, his organization of the book into three parts, "Caterpillar," "Chrysalis," "Butterfly" —sections which correspond to John Haye's lively adolescence, his beshrouded physical and mental state after his blinding, and a slow, but urgent, process of bursting forth for which the butterfly's emergence makes so appropriate a metaphor. Green's use of such overt divisions as titled sections and chapters is also worth notice, for never again does he resort to these conventional devices. In *Living* (in many ways a transitional book), he employs Arabic numerals to separate twenty-one different sections, but even these signposts disappear later on, and the succeeding novels are made to announce their more abstract structures from within. (*Concluding* and *Nothing* happen to be arranged in three parts like *Blindness,* but blank pages constitute Green's only formal notice of the divisions.)

Green's unwillingness to label broad divisions, after *Blindness,* is related to his tendency to present brief scenes in uninterrupted sequence. Beginning with *Living,* this tendency seems to foster a certain discontinuity with which Green's work is shot through. Each scene is significant in itself, and can exist on its own because life itself, Green comes to hold, does not consist of chains of causation but rather of coincidences which precipitate unpredictable behavior. This development in his thinking is quite different, we perceive, from the implication of "Caterpillar," "Chrysalis," "Butterfly." The deepest difference between *Blindness* and the rest of Green's work lies in an attitude of the author toward his material which the structure of *Blindness* bears out. For all the success of its multiple characterization, *Blindness* remains introspective. As a schoolboy-writer, Green's experience was limited; to supplement his native talent for observing he drew upon himself—which caused him to describe a boy's character in logical development, the boy a product of his past.

THE DIARY

Blindness begins with another device not again used by Green: a public schoolboy's diary, covering some fifteen months of John Haye's last two years at Noat School. The only similar document in all of Green's work is the memoir of an eighteenth century Frenchwoman of fashion, which he uses in *Back*—but not, as with the diary, for purposes of character development.

There is an excellent reason for Green's having chosen the diary convention in *Blindness*. Had he limited himself to dialogue, his characterization of John Haye at Noat could have been impaired; for conversation among those of Haye's dilettante set might have sounded *superficially* disdainful—as if the speakers were only living up to the criteria of their group (the Noat Art Society). Occasionally the diary records the kind of language this set resorted to. For example, John observes that "it is 'the thing to do' now to throw stones at me as I sit at my window. However, I have just called E. N. a 'milch cow,' and shall on the first opportunity call D. J. B. a 'bovine goat,' which generally relieves matters. These epithets have the real authentic Noat Art Society touch, haven't they?" (pp. 7–8).

The incident is typical of a pattern of self-incurred ostracism and "intellectual" retort, by which means John can "relieve matters." But he is exulting over these epithets *to himself;* he sees in them real sources of retaliation. Had we evidence of such exchanges only in dialogue, we should run the risk of misreading John's character. We might tend to look below the surface of dialogue and conclude that John's snobbery is a defense mechanism. (We have only to think of the effect of language in *The Catcher in the Rye* to realize how outwardly sophisticated talk can engage the sympathy of readers.) The diary, on the other hand, enables Green to show how *inwardly* supercilious is this boy, most of whose public school life is spent endeavoring to cut antagonists, to shock everybody, and to avoid football. Green is bringing an indictment against John Haye, and a diary serves as a more credible witness than potentially ambiguous conversation.

The diary presses the indictment in another way, too: it prevents any of John's contemporaries from coming alive. B. G. and Seymour, his dearest friends and rivals, are as anonymous in spirit as in name. (We do not know whether Seymour is a given or a surname.) They exist only as carbons of John. Fellow-feelers and accomplices they may be, but each is walled from the other by unbridgeable self-interest.

The diary, out of which no person springs to life but the diarist, is an adequate vehicle for presenting John Haye's self-centeredness and its contingent loneliness. His sense of superiority makes him the nonparticipant, and while, still having his sight, he can retain his superiority, loneliness is a comfort to him. Blindness is soon to tap the self-sufficiency dry. But before the blinding episode, we discover in the diary a wealth of ingenuousness alloyed with the smugness. "What an odious superior fellow I am now!" John writes on one occasion. "It is my mood tonight. Sometimes I think it is better to be just what one is, and not to be everlastingly apologising for oneself in so many words" (p. 31).

The diarist is candid, and in his candor lies potential salvation. John's declaring himself "odious" somehow forces us to take back the very word that has been forming on our lips. A reviewer once wrote of the young people of *Party Going,* "We see how close their extreme sophistication is to extreme innocence. . . ." [3] The equation seems to hold for John Haye.

Best indicators of John's "sophisticated innocence" are his frequent bald pronouncements on art and literature. He can conclude an entry which has dealt with British steaks, beer, and a marionette show with such unsupported dogma as, "The only modern Germans who could paint are Lembach and Boechel" (p. 30). Or he can end another quite as positively: "The most beautiful letter ever written is undoubtedly that of Charlotte Brontë's on her sister Emily's death" (p. 9). But blended with their self-assurance his remarks have a genuine enthusiasm; they reveal an emotional response to beauty that eclipses self-awareness.

There is one entry in this diary which, significantly, does not record anything of the self-conscious rovings of John's mind, and, written under the spell of literature, consists entirely of the following:

But surely this is most beautiful:

The thrills of a lark fall drop by drop down an unseen aery ladder, and the calls of the cranes, floating by in a long string, like the ringing notes of silver bugles, resound in the void of melodiously vibrating ether.

He is a poet: and his book is in very truth a poem. It is Gogol. (p. 28)

It is no accident that Green has had John Haye unconsciously reduce himself to a sounding board by allowing his reaction to Gogol to stand for an entire day's thoughts. The passage foreshadows John's capacity for spiritual union with outside things, which is to be realized in the final pages of the book. Nor is the description of birds singing accidental. Very early in *Blindness,* imagery derived from sound appears, and as it is repeated this sound imagery suggests concord between individual and environment. The blind boy learns to detect nuances of sound and reaches depths of perception he had not reached previously; the sound images displace those visual ones that had expressed John's shallow self-concern. Even before he was blinded, in fact, he had been charmed by the sound of a moving brook: "What is it that is so attractive in the sound of disturbed water? The contrast of sound to appearance, perhaps. Water looks so like a varnished surface that to see it break up, move and sound in moving is infinitely pleasing" (p. 36).

That "contrast of sound to appearance" amounts to an early symbolic statement of a theme *Blindness* proposes. In possession of his sight, John is continually attracted to flamboyant visible objects. In one place, neckties in a shop window beguile him, and in another, a cigarette case draws this comment in the diary: "Fell in love with a transparent tortoiseshell cigarette case for three guineas, very cheap I thought" (p. 4). Both the preciousness of the tortoiseshell and the transparency are qualities that betray the "varnished surface" of the kind of achievement to which John aspires.

Taken alone, his remarks about the neckties and the cigarette case could not be forced to bear such interpretation, but in other places in the diary, John reveals his delight in superficial aspects of things, and especially takes into account the visual effect of his own actions on observers. "With an eye to theatrical effect," he records, he had once leashed a bulldog and investigated traces of a reported prowler at Barwood (p. 14). But whereas sight increases self-awareness, promotes self-sufficiency, and even favors posturing, the wonders of sound John perceives after he is blind permit the same escape from self which Gogol's writing had permitted. Late in the novel, for example, he is glad to apprehend the signals birds make to each other, whereas earlier he had tried to visualize birds and other things around him, and just after he was blinded such attempts had brought him to despair. As he ceases to try to visualize he begins to extend his feelings beyond himself. The outwardly directed feelings that sound can induce come to replace the superficial designs of the schoolboy. A thought the diarist would have been incapable of occurs to the invalid as he listens to birds signaling: "The deaf might dream of a soundless world, and how cold that would be" (p. 180).

Of course the book is not so cut-and-dried as this. These outgoings of spirit occur only sporadically. Still, Green's ability to handle so delicately two antithetical patterns of imagery, neither of which obtrudes, shows in this first book his power of investing theme with symbolic overtones through carefully controlled imagery. If *Blindness,* as I shall suggest, is a book dealing with crime and punishment, then sight itself has been criminally used by John, and the development of a new and unifying sensitivity—to sound—parallels symbolically John's mental resurgence after his blinding.

The diary concludes with two entries in praise of *Crime and Punishment,* the first puzzled, the second ecstatic:

What a book! I do not understand it yet. It is so weird and so big that it appals me. What an amazing man he was, with his epileptic fits which were much the same as visions really.

. . . It is a terrible book, and has had a profound effect. Technically speaking, it is badly put together, but it cuts one open, tragedy after tragedy, like a chariot with knives on the wheels. The whole thing is so ghastly that one resents D. harrowing one so. And then it ends, in two pages. But what a *finale*! . . .

What a force books are! This is like dynamite. (pp. 37–38)

With these closing passages we have, in little, the structure of *Blindness*. It is a book of crime and punishment, to be resolved in two pages by a fit that is much the same as a vision, really. The resolution involves a shift on John's part from an intellectual to an emotional response to life—the same kind of shift Raskolnikov was to make.

Before his loss of sight, John Haye's had been at worst a predatory, at best a vicarious life. We have noticed his vicarious attachment to art; the satisfactions of his active life meanwhile were gained at the expense of others. Often elderly people of the lower classes gave him good sport. Baiting laborers or haranguing Socialists on polling day offered one choice kind of amusement; he could also rejoice that a friend of his named Brown hit a storekeeper in the stomach "so that he crumpled up behind the counter: the best thing that has happened for years" (p. 17).

His attitude toward schoolmates was no better. This may be the same Brown who at summer camp foolishly soaped tentcloth which was leaking in a rainstorm, "and now soapsuds drip down on to his face. We have also told him that his grousing is intolerable, and will be dealt with unless he suppresses it, so that he lies in a misery too deep for words, and is the only thing that keeps us happy" (p. 12).

It would be absurd to magnify the content of these offenses-against-fellow-man that titillate John and his set. They are typical, of course. John, though, is not typical. He is endowed, as one reviewer put it, with a nature "naturally hyper-sensitive to beauty in

all its forms, material and moral." [4] Yet he has exploited intellect
and sensitivity to snub contemporaries or to capitalize on their misfortunes, and that is about all. His diary indicts him, then, and in
doing so serves two structural purposes. It gives glimpses of ingenuousness in the snob (foreshadowing the resolution), and also makes
the reader assent, so to speak, to the "punishment." That throwing
of stones against his window signifies the protest of John's schoolfellows, who hate his arrogance. One understands that *was* "the
thing to do." What the students attempted—to break in upon John's
self-sufficiency—is carried out by a sort of *deus ex machina,* for it is
a stone, thrown by a little boy, that shatters a train window when
John is traveling home, and blinds him.

GROPINGS INTO THE PAST

Green dedicated only three books: *Living,* to his fiancée, *Caught,* to
his son, and *Blindness,* to his mother. In these books the figures we
associate with Green—Dick Dupret, Richard Roe, John Haye—are
involved respectively with a girl, a son, and a mother. (Mrs. Haye
of *Blindness* is, however, John's stepmother; in this first book Green
shows his proclivity for creating family situations with individuals
not related by blood, of which more will be said later.)

Mrs. Haye is a hunting woman in tweeds, a member of com-
mittees, a matriarch. Husbandless, she has devoted her energies to
supervising Barwood's house and grounds and the affairs of its
village. Her characteristics seem chosen especially to make for a
lack of rapport between her and John. Her life is energetic and
directed outward, his is contemplative; she is a lover of horses and
guns, he likes scenery and fishing. When blindness strikes, the
chasm between mother and son immediately widens, and in the
"Chrysalis" section she is just as much a victim as John. Their characters are not altered, but both their lives are arrested and held in
the suspensory state of the cocoon.

No matter what personal experience Green drew on for this book, its success depends upon the portrayal of actual blindness. Green succeeds, I think, in evoking the stunning initial effect of the blindness by making the effect identical for mother and son. To Mrs. Haye in the midst of her planning, and to John while he weighs the effect he is having upon others, the physical fact of the new blindness strikes intermittently as a lighthouse stroke. As Green rivets our attention on the daily musings of woman and boy, we, as well as they, tend to forget that John is blind and then see it in total flashes that are harrowing, that threaten to sap all their ability for carrying on. John may be intent, for example, on the effect he is having on the nurse dressing his lacerations, and may despise himself for moaning, only to have his thoughts take a sudden turn: "And he was blind, was he?" (p. 64). Mrs. Haye is dogged by the same kind of reminders. If she sets out to attend to committee duties in Norbury, she will soon be wondering if there are any blind boys in Norbury; if she rings for her correspondence, her mind, in the interval before the butler's arrival, will turn full on the blindness, so that she cannot remember why or when she rang.

Not only does the blight descend upon Mrs. Haye but also it affects the long-established routine of Barwood, and so announces a motif of change and dissolution. In the beginning, the hired nurse causes dissension in the servant ranks by refusing to eat below stairs. Eventually, the entire household is to be set adrift by this ruinous blindness, after Mrs. Haye makes her last move and sells Barwood to bring John to London. But before Barwood is dissolved, its connection with the past is put to some scrutiny by Green.

A sub-theme in the novel, the apparently invidious comparison between enriched past and blasted present, is introduced in the "Chrysalis" section with the appearance of John's old nanny, for whom his blindness affords unexpected solace in her waning years. This woman is a sort of professional sentimentalist (the first of a long series of nannies in Green's work), who now is able to repossess her nursling. Their sickroom conversations are reminiscences of an easy past, in which the nanny lives. But old Miss Jennings is to die in *Blindness,* her death a kind of pronouncement on the fatuity of her pursuit.

For John, under her influence, the past has the lure of comfort; but in very short space his hauteur checks him from "being sentimental, and talking about memories," and he will not submit to her cooing. "No. Prehensile, that is all a baby is, and the nurse a ministrant at the knees of Moloch, the supreme sentimentalist" (p. 58).

In the beginning Mrs. Haye, too, daydreams of the past, and of her dead husband, but she is essentially a woman of action: "work and forget, till some plan emerged" becomes her rallying cry (p. 69). Marriage for John is her woman's solution, the next-to-last one that occurs to her, but one that will not materialize. In her early musings the sub-theme of dissolution is sounded again: taxes are high, money low; the landed classes of England are stiff up against it; it was not so in the old days. There is no money left for the dual life of town and country, and the stepmother's final sacrifice for John will be the sale of her beloved Barwood, which she has kept up in hopes of passing the estate on to him.

As the effect of the only son's blindness settles like a pall upon Barwood—the blindness as foreboding to the continuity of landed families as was the loss of fertility in *Lady Chatterley's Lover*—a new character is introduced into the stasis of *Blindness*. She is Joan, daughter of a deposed and drunken former vicar of Barwood, and a girl out of D. H. Lawrence—sexually forsaken, stupidly longing, earthy and domestic. Like many of Lawrence's women, she fearfully cherishes masculine violence. Her face is scarred as a result of her father's throwing a shard of glass at her, an incident she recalls with mixed fear and wonder. The girl is rooted by circumstance to the ruined cottage in which, surrounded by sardine tins and gin bottles, she cares for her ruined father.

JOAN'S FUNCTION IN THE NOVEL

For at least three reasons, Green's portrait of Joan has structural significance which unifies and expands the thematic proposals of this first novel. His achievement with Joan marks a precocious ability to realize a character in full round who has probably been conceived for technical purposes. Green's stature as a novelist may well rest on this ability, for it enables him to answer two demands made on a work of art: one, that art have universality (roughly, theme answers this demand), and two, that art create life convincingly (character and situation traditionally satisfy this requisite).

When Green positions a chapter about Joan at the end of his "Chrysalis" section, the three structural purposes may be analyzed as follows:

First, Joan's excursions into the past both re-present the theme of sustaining past and blighted present, and implicitly but decisively modify that theme.

Second, the novel's basic situation, of women caring for men, is reintroduced with the generations inverted: where a mother had cared for her son, a daughter now cares for her father. Both men are ruined intellectuals, and both women act instinctively to support them—in which action lies the resolution of conflict in the book.

Third, Joan is to serve as chief illusion for John, in his attempt to grope out of his confinement. But as he *uses* her he fails; only after illusions fail him will he make a readjustment that is signaled by a compassion for her.

Joan carries forward the theme of past richness versus present waste. In fact Green uses diurnal imagery to parallel this theme. The rich and promising morning of a day we share with Joan is soon to be ravaged by a masculine sun. "All are one community," girl, bird, shrub, in her morning garden, "but it will not be for long" (p. 112). When the prophecy of the morning is fulfilled, and life in Joan's garden is quenched, Green writes, "No bird sang, no breath of air stirred, nothing moved under the sun who was drawing the life out of everything except Joan" (p. 132). On the next page a "tortured dead pear tree" is mentioned, and the broken glass of a hothouse—the garden presents a full catalogue of Eliot's

. . . heap of broken images, where the sun beats,
And the dead tree gives no shelter. . . .[5]

It is significant, though, that the sun draws life out of everything "except Joan," for feminine capacities for managing life are signified in her, and will supervene. Precisely here, where he propounds a native resilience in women, Green departs from Eliot in the direction of Lawrence.

Caught as she is in oppressive circumstances, Joan in her bed at night flies to that past to which Nanny returned, and Mrs. Haye returned, when blindness struck. Joan's girlhood is connected with her father's roses at Barwood vicarage. Her father had "planted more and more, till the vegetable garden was invaded and in the end was a jungle of roses. His duties had to wait while they were being sprayed, or pruned, or manured" (p. 146).

For Joan that efflorescent past recalls a girlhood unblemished in vitality—but Green's muted voice makes the roses of the past ominous as well as beneficent (and roses will carry these two meanings in *Caught* and *Back*). The roses and their expense caused a rift between the vicar and his wife—brought on the gin, brought on the wife's scandal with the postman. These in turn forced Mrs. Haye to dispossess the reverend. But Mrs. Haye had only paid lip service to religion while the vicar was in good standing. By referring obliquely, through Joan's memory, to the hypocrisy of having vicar and church simply as installations at Barwood, Green discloses multiple responsibility for the eviction that has brought a small waste land to cottage and garden. No *one* was to blame; but more relevant to *Blindness,* that past which appears to Joan to have been bountiful has itself been corrupt. Roses, appealing and sensuous as they are to author and character, are material traps—they riot into "jungle" if too much doted upon.

Therefore, when Joan thinks about the past, the theme of dissolution is modified. And therefore the chapter dealing with Joan and her father bears the title, "Picture Postcardism." Those roses had been wonderful in their blossoming days. "Just like those beautiful picture postcards Mrs. Donner had in the window sometimes," Joan thinks. "They had been lovely, those days" (p. 148). But there is no escaping the implication of "picture postcardism": the scene on the postcard is never a true rendition. Like any postcard, Green implies, the past is a convenient fiction. When we recognize this view that permeates all his work, we must beware ascribing to him too seriously a theme of dissolution. I mean that Green does not contend that a stable order is dissolving, or that things of the present are continuing corroding processes which began only in the recent past. He may watch the estates of the landed class dissolve, but at the same time he looks on them ambiguously: the past has not necessarily been sound at any time.

Putting Joan into daydreams, Green modifies the past-present theme; having her care for her father, he reproduces the central situation of the novel. Both women, Joan and Mrs. Haye, absorb the predicaments of their charges, so that a stasis results that throttles as effectively the non-sufferers as it does the sufferers. Deluded into thinking himself a genius, Joan's imperious father sheds his vexations on her, and similarly John chooses courses of action that are really directed against his stepmother, who becomes his subconscious antagonist.

Joan and Mrs. Haye are able to bear up because of their passing chores. They are stimulated repeatedly into physical action; in contrast their charges are dormant, or at best baffled into inaction. This contrast between the dynamic and the static, always on a very domestic level, is a recurrent one in Green's novels. It may occur between sexes (as here or in *Living*), between generations (in *Nothing*), between social classes (in *Party Going* and *Loving*), or even between schoolmistresses (in *Concluding*). Always, Green suggests that those powerless to act, for whatever reason, are thereby self-defeated; for those capable of action, meanwhile, possibilities of solution remain, however limited these may be.

After Joan's brief tryst with John comes to nothing, a change in the weather finds her refreshed and "sauntering," strangely happy about her unimproved prospects. We last see her and her father enjoying a rare quiet moment; as she muses preparing breakfast, we are presented with a combination of squalid detail and inner serenity that suggests Green's belief in the reality of the state of mind as a force superior to objective reality of any sort. Having disposed of greasy dishes, Joan discovers that a mouse has been at the butter;

but she is infected with lassitude, and contentedly lays the table for her father.*

Mrs. Haye's adaptability is quite like Joan's, and resolution for Mrs. Haye comes in the form of the same minor-key happiness in the face of dismal prospects: her home and servants gone, the bare chance meeting with a friend in London whets her appetite for chit-chat. The change that comes over his stepmother is given us through John's consciousness. "Mamma's voice was quite different, as if it had suddenly leapt into youth again, it was so happy and excited. So London was a success with her, she was really enjoying herself for the first time!" (p. 278).

These women lay up vague hopes for the future, to be sure (the father will get some job, the son will marry). But it is the present that excites them—when the weather changes, or an old friend turns up. To the immediate situation they characteristically address themselves, so that, though they are trapped as much as their charges are, their dynamic responses preclude despondency. "Work and forget," Mrs. Haye wills herself when John is first stricken—but it is not a question of will. She cannot help but work and forget.

The third structural purpose Joan's appearance serves brings us back to John Haye. Cut by a sardine tin, Joan is treated at Barwood and comes into contact with John. The boy lunges after her, stupid

* For a radically different interpretation of *Blindness,* see Kingsley Weatherhead's dissertation, "A Critical Study of the Novels of Henry Green" (University of Washington, 1958). Weatherhead believes that Joan and John are faced with choices of achieving "selfhood" (by breaking the restraining holds of their parents), or of being arrested in development (by yielding to the known security offered by these parents). Hence he contrasts John's later "victory" over his stepmother to Joan's "stasis and acquiescence" (p. 19). "And [Joan's] sacrifice of selfhood to her father," continues Weatherhead, "is only heroic in the sentimental appraisal which would make Dedalus and Meursault villains" (p. 23). Without intending to denigrate Meursault and Dedalus, I feel I should restate my conviction that Green, unlike Camus and Joyce, finds no efficacy in rebellion. Therefore I acknowledge the triumph of Joan's inner serenity. Her ability to transcend circumstance is matched by several of Green's later heroines. And this chapter goes on to contend that when John rebels against his stepmother, he embraces a series of illusions, and that it is through her resilience that he is rescued.

and earthbound though she is, in the first hard attempt to salvage something from his blindness.

Their relationship is doomed; Joan cannot respond to John's aesthetic raptures on their walks together, in the first pages of "Butterfly." "How slow, how slow this was," John thinks, when her answers fail to gratify him (p. 215). Because his feelings are reserved for himself, John achieves nothing, the affair soon ends, and he remains emotionally blighted. "He was not sufficient in himself," he had judged right after his blinding, and had then estimated his predicament as follows: "He must live on himself, and on his own reserves of mental fat, which would be increased a trifle perhaps when Mamma or Nan read to him, as steam rollers go over roads, levelling all sense, razing all imagery to the ground with their stupidity" (p. 62). One hundred and fifty-five pages later, when he announces to Joan that he intends to be a writer—and gets no reaction at all—he tells himself in a rage: "She was lamentably stupid" (p. 217). And we perceive that his contempt for others is as inflexible as ever. He has not made an inch of progress.

PUNISHMENT

When John is blinded, he is subjected not only to the affliction but to himself. What essentially waylays him is his respect for his own intellect—an intellect that virtually dictates the feelings its owner will permit himself. Even as he rigorously finds fault with himself, his self-esteem increases. And here we come upon a certain blind spot that Green will exploit ultimately to John's advantage.

For example, we find him one time mocking himself, as he remembers a day he had knelt before a daffodil, "with Herrick at the back of his mind"; then he genuinely hates himself for having mocked; at which point his thoughts take a characteristic turn: "How unlucky he was to have been born like that, so infinitely superior to the common ruck. The herd did not feel all that he did, all his private tortures, and he was unfit to die like this, shut up in the traditional living tomb. A priest ought to have said offices over him as the glass entered his head and caused the white-hot pains there" (pp. 61–62). What is remarkable is his shifting to self-dramatization again, after having ridiculed this propensity. We get the feeling that he revels in mental pictures, that priestly offices are indispensable, in his mind's eye, to the figure of importance he feels himself to be.

But we notice also that he does not detect a discrepancy, that his intellect is slightly flawed as he gives way to theatricalized self-pity. Green's crowning achievement in this book has been to exploit the slight flaw; for he lets John be helped to a reconciliation by the misfortunes of another—a process John never sees unfolding. Had he seen what was happening, he would not have permitted it to happen since it was not of his ordering.

The process involves John's unwitting choices of illusions. After he has recovered from the initial shock of the blindness, he inculcates and cherishes two illusions. In the past is his real mother (whom he had not known), in the present, Joan, whom he persists in calling "June," thinking the word prettier. John idealizes both, early in the "Butterfly" section. The real mother ("Mummy") becomes a sort of accomplice, posed against Mrs. Haye in John's imagination: "What talks they would have, telling Mummy what June was like, Nanny how inferior June was, and Mamma how sorry he was for June, though she would see through that" (p. 182).

Although he is not conscious of it, clearly John is pitting against his actual stepmother a figment presence. And in attaching himself to Joan, he again unconsciously goes against the stepmother (he had not been able to get along with a Miss Blandair, a "nice young thing" Mrs. Haye had brought to Barwood). But with his parting from Joan, these illusions must be replaced. For John now, there is but one salvation—town. Deftly, he convinces Mrs. Haye that they must remove to London.

Although John has grasped yet another straw that is to prove illusory, we should realize that again he has chosen a refuge opposed to the heart-interest of his stepmother. With her sacrificing of Barwood, in fact, the burden of John's blindness has almost been transferred to Mrs. Haye. That is to say, John has attempted escapes that virtually yoke the stepmother and her way of life with the affliction itself as his antagonists. He has successfully victimized *her,* because of the overwhelming blight of *it*—struggled against her baffled and ineffectual helpfulness, and been sustained by the gradual transference of the burden to her. This does not mean that John's suffering ceases, but rather that unconsciously he makes his stepmother the butt against which his grief breaks; and upon her, in his psychological resentment, he inflicts equivalent suffering. It is imperative to the outcome of the novel that John not *know* he is doing this, just as it is imperative that Green develop the character of Mrs. Haye so that she will have the strength to assume the burden. Most important of all, perhaps, for our purposes of relating *Blindness* to Green's later work, is the hint of a symbolical transference of burdens which is to reappear in those other books of calamity, *Caught* and *Back,* and which will figure in the struggle-and-resolution patterns of those novels.

SPEED

Toward the end of *Blindness,* events succeed events in a crescendo as the move from Barwood to London is prepared for and accomplished. The train that will carry off John and Mrs. Haye becomes for him a symbol of escape. "Everything would give way to it, it was his train" (p. 263). But things do not give way—not even a laborer's cart that impedes their way to the station. While Mrs. Haye bridles within herself at the laborer, the symbol of the train is augmented by another—that of a motorbike that comes by them, racing pell-mell to nowhere. "What was that?" Mrs. Haye wonders. "No. Yes, it was the Vincent boy on his motorbike. Mabel had been right, it was mad the pace he drove. Look at him—no, he was gone" (pp. 263–264).

We have in this motorbike what William York Tindall would call an epitomizing symbol—the entire psychological dilemma of John Haye, his mind rushing here and there at senseless speeds, is summed up in the picture of a juvenile tearing along a road to no destination, because youth will not abide slowness. And fitting it is that from the poky auto John will board a poky train: that illusory express, "tearing across the country," materializes as a local, and another bubble bursts. Green has merely accelerated the sequences of a pattern he has developed all through *Blindness*.

At the house in London another woman appears—one Margaret, the married housekeeper, with whom John engages in a pathetic love attempt, in a room dominated by the presence of a gift lily the two have been attempting to move. Alternately finding and losing her arm, John keeps coming up against the lily, and grows sick with despair at the whole awkward game, "when all at once her arm mysteriously came up over his mouth, glowing and cool at the same time, and the scent was immediately stronger, tangible almost, so that he wanted to bite it" (p. 272).

Whatever the potted lily may represent, it surely does not betoken fruition, as lilies will do in *Living;* it seems rather to be intrusive here, another barrier posted by blindness. Perhaps its transplantation and confinement suggest the illusion of the city, to which John is transplanted and where he is confined. Yet although his attempt after Margaret fizzles in the end, there is in the magical resuscitation at the verge of despair, when her arm comes up over his mouth, a foreshadowing of the epiphany John will finally be permitted.

As these illusions come one upon the other with such speed, then shatter, John is thrust in upon himself repeatedly, and finally real self-pity floods from him; it is as if Green has been proposing all along that a release from a state of alienation is bound up only in such giving way—in a flooding of the intellectualized dikes the boy has thrown up, to allow real grief to run out unchecked by theatricalism.

A final symbolic episode, charged with zest and promise, occurs as soon as a last defense is down. John has acknowledged that moving from country to town has been but a ruse. He goes to open a window, and an incident occurs such as could only have happened in a town:

He got up and groping toward the window opened it. As he did so there was a sudden lull in all the noise, he could only hear the clop-clop of a horse receding into the distance, and then mysteriously from below there floated up a chuckle; it was a woman and someone must have been making love to her, so low, so deep it was. He was on fire at once. Love in the street, he would write of it, love shouting over the traffic, sweeping over the park, wave upon wave of it, inciting the baboons to mutiny in the Zoo, clearing the streets. . . . He was on the crest of a petulant wave, surging along, when his wave broke on the sound of a motor horn. There were his scars, and the sun pricked at him through them. He drew back into the room, his face wet with the heat. Oh, he was tired. (pp. 274–275)

The culminating force of this vision and its fracturing calls to mind an almost identical summarizing symbol used by Joyce at the end of "A Little Cloud." In that story Little Chandler, another would-be writer, is moved by a poem of Byron, only to have the child he is rocking burst out in a fit of crying.[6]

Noises, crass and insistent and real, take moments of release from John Haye and Little Chandler. But their reactions are opposite. Chandler is then and there defeated, but John has still a resilient faith in himself. The passage that reveals this faith begins with typical resentment. "Why did Mamma leave him alone, a prey to all his thoughts?" But something new enters his train of thought. "And was she happy here, away from Barwood and all the worries that she had lived for? As for him, it was only that he was dazed by all these new sensations, he would rise above them soon, when he knew how to interpret them, and then he would have some peace" (p. 275).

There is no arrogance in this tone, and for the first time John has wondered about his mother's feelings. Now is when Mrs. Haye enters with her new-found friend, and John perceives that she *is* happy. His reaction is instantaneous: "This happiness of theirs was exasperating. . . . There was no air now that they had shut the window, they had muffled the room so that they might muffle him the better with this talk of theirs" (p. 275).

His stepmother's suffering has been John's support through tribulation. Reciprocal suffering, for the first time, now ceases. She is happy. In John's mind stepmother and friend have combined to throttle him; he feels this way, I think, because she is no longer the victim he has unknowingly made her. Mrs. Haye does perceive that their chatter has crushed John. Her friend departs, and she sits down to knit, knowing him inconsolable.

It is then that church bells ring, near, and the novel begins to end. No sooner has John's last and least conscious selfish goal been denied him, than

> . . . suddenly, and for no reason, like a gust of wind through the room, purifying it, came the sound of bells from the church along the street, tearing through the room, bells catching each other up, tripping, tumbling and then starting off again in cascades. . . . He loved bells, and, inexpressibly happy, he was swept back to Barwood and June—"Listen, June, how the sound of them comes over the country," and her father being hunted by them through the mazes that gin had created in his brain, and their walks stretched in a gesture to the sky, they had been so unfortunate in their lives. (p. 281)

Pure images of sound, so different from the crass motor horns that had truncated his joy, the peals of the bells permit that extension of himself signaling John's completed purgation. Green has enhanced the effect of this release by having had those windows just closed; yet the sounds come "like a gust of wind through the room, purifying it"; the imagery is religious. It is impossible to paraphrase the ending of *Blindness* (I have given it only in part); at the very end, "A ladder, bring a ladder," John calls, over alarmed protests from his mother. (Green has John call for a ladder at this climax; the Greek word for ladder is *klimax*.) We are not given his actions, and are told only, "In his ears his own voice cried loudly, and a deeper blindness closed in upon him" (p. 285). He has had a fit, much the same as a vision, such as he sensed must have visited Dostoyevsky. We know his vision will have enduring results, for the last thing we read is a letter from John to an ex-Noat comrade, announcing the clarity with which he sees his way as a newly fledged writer, in a tone charged with humility.

When the peals of bells sweep John's mind back to Joan, we sense the new feeling that makes him envision "their walks stretched in a gesture to the sky." It is compassion, not come by through the reasoning and bullying mind. In the last pages of the book John is ruled only by feeling. So, too, was Raskolnikov, of whom Dostoyevsky wrote at the conclusion of *Crime and Punishment,* "But he could not think for long together of anything that evening, and he could not have analysed anything consciously; he was simply feeling. Life had stepped into the place of theory and something quite different would work itself out in his mind." [7]

Neither John nor Raskolnikov is an intellectual when we leave him.

POSTSCRIPT

The adverse criticism one might reserve for *Blindness* would probably be colored by one's familiarity with Green's later work. Earlier I said that the chief difference between *Blindness* and the later books was that *Blindness* was too real. To transform this remark into a criticism, I might say that the book seems to indicate that the young author knew a little too well just where he was going. The cause-effect relationships are labeled so well that the book lends itself readily to such a critique as I have given it. (This is not to detract from the praise I have given to the inner mechanisms of the book, such as structure and imagery and acceleration of pace.) It is true that Green knows just as well where he is going in other books. But later books never reveal his direction so well, never show a reliance on pat cause-effect relationships, because his sense of the many possible motivations for action increases to an extraordinary degree. By the third novel, *Party Going,* he has announced this conviction: "People, in their relations with one another, are continually doing

similar things but never for similar reasons" (p. 114). If we apply
this logic to *Blindness,* which gives clear reasons for most consequences, we may be apt to find its realism suspect. Congruous personalities are not, in Green's later view, what the close observer of
real life will describe.

Joan and Mrs. Haye, who resolve their situations with such surprising ease in *Blindness,* have really closer affinities with later
Green characters than has John Haye—which is to say that these
women are unpredictable. As for John, Green has masterfully lo-
cated his potentialities in the diary, and then brought them to fulfillment. He has made him convincingly blind, for a convincing reason.
But he has spitted John too cleanly, because he knows him too well,
and in a way forces his readers to take the view of John that his
creator takes: that such hauteur both deserves and needs punishment. In *Pack My Bag,* detached from himself, Green was able to
take a sympathetic view of the snob he had once been. But in *Blindness,* I think, the young writer felt he must blind the arrogant and
predatory young man—blind him to make him feel. Such an attitude
is rigorous, more uniformly serious than the attitudes later books
reveal. Green was still "dressing to shock" and still living "in a
contradiction" when he composed *Blindness,* and guilt seems to have
weighed on him.

A passage from *Pack My Bag* both corroborates this statement
and shows the difference between his early and later attitudes. He
is writing of Oxford:

> . . . as the best of two worlds [intellectual and convivial] will
> always be meeting so we wined and dined each other. Inasmuch
> as we did so we lived necessarily in a contradiction. The two
> circles should not have met but they do always everywhere and
> the life I led I felt then I should not lead although I am not of
> that opinion now. (p. 217)

". . . they do always everywhere" is a crucial phrase, offered by a
mature writer after he has assimilated a good deal of experience. A
critic says of *Blindness,* "An English schoolboy of seventeen, on the

verge of living, is totally blinded in a railway accident." [8] Green, too, I think we may say, was on "the verge of living" when he wrote his first book. In it he observed himself more carefully than on any future fictional occasion—and shaped a character by drawing consecutive and uncontradictory pictures of him. This was an ambitious book, as its title implies, but not so ambitious as the second, whose title promises wider scope: *Living*. For Green, living means being absorbed in the lives of others. They come to be seen more from the outside; and as Green observes more of them, they tend to get more enigmatic.

A DEPLOYMENT OF SOCIAL CLASSES

It is probable that Ruth Chapin had not read *Living,* when, in 1951,
she said of Green's third book, "Written in the nineteen-thirties,
Party Going may mark the closest approximation to a 'proletarian'
novel Henry Green's . . . talent could devise. . . ." [1] Yet she was
right. However directly *Living* focuses upon the Dupret foundries
at Birmingham, its impressions of working classes are no more intense than those *Party Going* recreates at Victoria Station during
four hours of fog.

Party Going, published ten years after *Living,* makes a counterpart for that book. It stands as does the negative to the printed

photograph—in a very strange way, to be sure. *Living* centered upon working people's lives, and, broad-flung in scope, gave breadth to its picture by admitting vignettes of the people at the top, the Duprets and their set. These were the party-goers of *Living*. *Party Going,* in turn, put the rich folk to scrutiny for the duration of a novel, while they waited for their Calais train. Below them (for the party-goers were privileged to wait out the fog in the terminus hotel) it packed workers homeward bound into Victoria Station, and in terms of space gave these about as short shrift as *Living* had given their employers.

These unequal space divisions may make the metaphor of print-and-negative appear unfit; yet it is appropriate insofar as it epito-mizes the tone of each book. All in the foreground of the print that is *Living* is black as a foundry floor, or gray as outside, yet things can be seen for what they are: the sharply defined activity is vital. So the prose of the book, the "bald, clipped, angular, often deliber-ately clumsy style," as Edward Stokes has described it, ". . . effec-tively captures the din and blackness and the geometrical shapes of the foundry. . . ." [2] But what *Party Going* shows is best captured on its negative. The kind of blackness that there appears in fore-ground conceals a dead thing. Whereas *Living* is ambitious in scope and accurate in title, *Party Going* misleads; just as ambitious, it aims at viewing a segment of life scummed over with torpor. Hints at physical death throughout *Party Going* are grimaces made in the direction of emotional death, which has already visited the char-acters. Where *Living* presents movement and noise and a conflux of symbols expressive of escape and return, of fatigue and support, *Party Going* "appropriately," says one writer, "sounds a muffled note throughout"; [3] all of its early symbolism is deadly, and its later lushness seems to be infectious, through the help of tone estab-lished before the midway point is reached.

Different from one another as Green proves his idle rich to be, they are the same in one essential: ". . . these people avoided any sort of trouble over what might bother them . . . and by so doing they proclaimed their service to the kind of way they lived or rather to the kind of way they passed their time" (*Party Going,* p. 134).

With "or rather," we perceive the gap between the subject of *Party Going* and that of *Living*.

Perhaps because Green was younger when he composed *Living,* the festivities Dick Dupret attended were house parties and hunt balls of the younger set, rather than junkets to the South of France. At the house parties boys and girls in their twenties played games in the dark, and Dick, jilted by his beloved, is revolted at everyone's "spurious emotion": "For in their games they sublimated all passions, all beliefs. . . . And so he saw these games they were always playing to be charades of the passions. So was there no other way to her heart?" (*Living,* p. 138).

In *Living* these charaders are set against the equally fumbling but truly passionate Birmingham citizens; in *Party Going* the hard-pressed Londoners on the station platform are again vitally emotional commoners, juxtaposed to the party-goers. Deadliest to the rich people is their having the means to avoid trouble: they cannot help, first, becoming comfort-seekers and then, satiated, are forced to induce agitations in themselves to conquer their satiety. The two processes Green shows clearly in *Party Going* because his ten rich people are stratified: only two, Max Adey, who is host to the entire party and cannot tolerate anyone else's paying, and his paramour Amabel, are extremely wealthy; the others are hopeful of trapping Max or parasitically seeking comfort. All, necessarily, are forced into the relationships Dick Dupret had called "charades of the passions": in drawing rooms the rich form conversational alliances; in bedrooms the alliances, just as attenuated and often as unproductive, are sexual. Such pastimes make the terminus hotel, with adjoining sitting and bedrooms, the logical place for Green to probe the emotionally defunct.

For those who would compete with each other to be in the good graces of Max Adey, the motivations for forming such alliances are understandable. The Max Adeys are forced to go further, however; for having everything, they must inflict themselves with want—so that Max, a sexual pawn for Amabel, must engineer this party to France as an escape from her—then feel guilt, hire a suite at the station hotel just to telephone her, immediately lie that he is at the airport, and then in a frenzy cancel the rooms because he senses she will trace the call.

Max, living up to an image of himself he has had too much time to construct, founders in the most complex charade-life of all. But all of his company are charaders, and *Party Going* shows them up at every turn—fearful, agitated, each thinking all the others selfish— as virtually *not living*. But let us leave them for the time being, and turn to the living.

SYMMETRY AT THE FACTORY

What has been said of *Party Going* and *Living,* that each gives short shrift to one class, using it to deepen our understanding of the society sharply in focus, is valid only when these books are taken in the aggregate. It is dangerous, in fact, to speak of "such and such a class," when one is dealing with so ubiquitous an observer as Green. In *Pack My Bag* he said, "There are not two or three social classes but hundreds well defined throughout Britain . . ." (p. 193). In *Living,* within that laboring class at Birmingham, there is as rigid a hierarchical system as in any military force. When Mr. Gates, molder's mate, begins to associate in pubs with laborer Tupe and his cronies, we are told, "This was loss of caste for Gates to be perpetually with them, as he was step above a labourer" (p. 155). Keeping in mind the variations, then, we can say of *Living*'s surface texture that it is at least four-ply. A series of vignettes fills in the many foregrounds that center about the works; in these are presented the owners, their London staff of deputies, the works manager and his staff, and the laborers. There is contention between the two middle echelons: Walters and Archer, making policy in London, are at odds with works manager Bridges and his draughtsman Tarver, getting the work out in Birmingham. Archer and Tarver are young, and are collaterally pitted against their older superiors (that is, they suck on to Dick Dupret when he comes into command) for a theme in *Living* deals with the ousting of old incumbents, and in their subfunctions these four play out one segment of that theme.

It is characteristic for Green to employ such balanced inner structures, even while he manipulates minor characters. We have seen him use such methods in *Blindness*. When we look closely at the major structural pattern in *Living,* a book anything but abstract, we find a symmetrical arrangement that rivals the mathematical designs of the last novels, *Nothing* and *Doting*.

The plot development of *Living* is kept moving by two love stories, each a tri-cornered affair totally disrupted at the finish. A girl of the upper class (Hannah Glossop) and one from the lower (Lily Gates) choose badly; the boys who have real feeling for them are tongue-tied, and everyone comes off a loser. These are the bare bones of it, at any rate, and this plot enables Green to manipulate into contrasted positions the people at his two extremes—the owner Duprets, with their power over people's sustenance, and the workers, with their variously diluted powers of affection. In Joycean manner, Green fuses his two plots on the physical plane when Lily Gates and Dick Dupret pass each other on the same street in Bridesley town.

By this time, Mr. Dupret is undone, and we are to see him but once more in the novel, for he has by now performed his largely catalytic function. This was to reorganize the firm (he had become head of it after his father's death), in a fit of work and self-assertion after his miserable love affair. "But Mr. Dupret said constantly in his mind, 'I must work, work.' After Miss Glossop it was most necessary for him to do something tangible violently, and in this Mr. Archer, and Tarver also, egged him on" (p. 197). Apart from sad consequences, this reaction is funny enough, quite pat and according to Freud. Work for Dick means causing a major turnover at the factory, and giving the oldest men their cards—this done, Green straightway dumps Dick from the novel.

Green is concerned with results of Dick's action, as these impinge upon the central character of the book, Craigan, against whom the two parallel plots have mounted tandem threats. Chief molder at the foundry and head of a household of boarders that includes Mr.

Gates, Jim Dale, and Gates's daughter Lily, Craigan is threatened with loss of his job and his beloved Lily, whose allegiance has long since been transferred from her father to him. On the one hand, Dupret means to cut Craigan loose, and on the other, Lily, in love with Bert Jones, aims to fly Birmingham and be off with Bert to Canada.

The duplicate structural pattern of *Living* is furthered by yet another parallel, the opposition of Craigan and old Mr. Dupret, two patriarchs camped in socially opposite quarters of the one field. Their fearfully hard work has produced different effects in them. Old Dupret, broken down and hospitalized, sinks into abject lassitude, for bonds have grown between him and the business, but extend no further; but Craigan, so sick for a time he can barely move, feels he must act and does, for "Home was sacred thing to him. Everything, his self-respect was built on home" (p. 153).

Both men are old, but only one is apathetic. Powerful commentary this juxtaposition makes; for Craigan, unmarried, is bound by love to Lily and to that household, whereas the Dupret blood runs cold in the father and in the son courses hot with expectations of becoming head of the firm. The irony with which Green invests their situations provokes the wryest judgments: Craigan in the foundry narrowly escapes a wrench falling from a crane, while the most ludicrous of accidents spells Dupret's undoing. "Mr. Dupret 'pater' indeed had fallen on his shoulder after slipping on dog's mess and was in bed now . . ." (p. 56).

That theme of the conflict between generations is brought to two conclusions when by structural implication one patriarch is pitted against the other. Where mutual love exists, conflict is resolved—and this happens when Lily returns to Craigan's house. Just as the servants in *Loving* are governed by familistic ties though no family exists, so does Lily's and Craigan's affection surmount blood ties. But much has to be weathered before this resolution. Lily is bent on escaping the grooves the workers' lives run in. She wants to expend herself for a husband and children of her own, not for Craigan and his molders:

I am I, why do I do work of this house, unloved work, why but they cannot find other woman to do this work.

Why may I not have children, feed them with my milk. Why may I not kiss their eyes, lick their skin, softness to softness, why not I? I have no man, my work is for others, not for mine. Why may I not work for mine? (p. 109)

Against this scene, in which Lily's yearning is only for self-fulfillment, Green places a scene presenting Dick Dupret alone with his thoughts:

Young Mr. Dupret sat in their country house picking nose.

Why, he said in mind, why could not the old man die? Of course was gratitude and all that of sons to fathers but, old mummy, why couldn't he die. (p. 110)

The juxtaposition is more heavy-handed than most of its kind, and is untypical of Green in this respect, but his aim at least is clear. Lily is presented with capacities for love which will not later be revoked when her love affair comes to nothing; but Dick Dupret is confessedly lured by prospects that will work for his interests alone.

MRS. EAMES AND MR. CRAIGAN

While the sub-themes in *Living*, which oppose old and young, or leisure class and working class, are carried forward by structural arrangement, the strongest of all relationships in the novel is a very personal one, established between Craigan and Lily. To it is oriented most of the symbolic imagery of *Living*, along with the prevailing textural pattern of the novel (a series of vignettes that evokes the milieu of the factory people). Among the diverse scenes that comprise this textural pattern are a number of passages that deal with Craigan's neighbors, a couple named Eames, who are seen only at home, never at the factory. Kept out of focus and uninvolved in the plot line, the Eameses nevertheless lend this novel its qualified note of fruition. It is to their baby that Lily Gates extends her heart on the last page of the book, in an action equivalent to John Haye's affirmation in *Blindness*.

Eames is a turner at the factory, a gardener where we see him, at home. His house contains Blakean joy. It is Mrs. Eames who, late in the novel, thinks the most beautiful sentence, one which Green placed as a headnote to the book: "As these birds would go where so where would this child go?" (p. 246). But she had answered her question two ways, early in the book musing over her first child:

> "When you grow to be a man, a man." She put her face up against his. "Maybe like your dad you'll be a turner when you're a man. Beauty! . . ."
> His father said: "a turner like his dad?" and she answered for him saying: "Yes and so long as 'is lathe goes round he'll be there, earning 'is money like 'is dad." (p. 24)

Her words signify her allegiance to the continuum, that promises fruition—a continuum Lily Gates will be unable to contribute to physically, but to which she commits herself spiritually on the last page of *Living*. Mrs. Eames's other answer to her question ("where would this child go?") foreshadows Mr. Craigan's enduring state of mind:

> "And when you're grown you'll marry and we shall lose you and you'll 'ave kiddies of your own and a 'ouse of your own, love, we'll be out in the cold. . . . Why do we bring kids into the world, they leave you so soon as they're grown, eh? But you don't know one of these things yet. But sure as anything you'll leave us when you're a man, and who'll we 'ave then, eh cruel? Sons and daughters why do we bring them into the world?" She was laughing. "Because, because" she said laughing and then lay smiling and then yawned. (pp. 24–25)

Mrs. Eames's laughter, which may be an opiate but is also a victory, recurs in the book's last sentence. Craigan cannot laugh so, for he is too dogged and too perplexed. His question always has two answers, as Mrs. Eames's had: Lily will stay; Lily will leave. But he cannot assent to that second answer, and is therefore incapable of Mrs. Eames's joy. Even when Craigan has Lily back, he assesses his situation despondently: "He thought when she wasn't many days older, strong hearty wench as her would soon find another man and they would be married this time. . . . And then what would he do, would they have him? Where would he live?" (p. 250).

The relationship between Craigan and Lily ultimately transcends personal status, and as far as larger applications of *Living* are concerned, may best be described as a symbolic contest between forces of stasis and flux. (*Living* reaffirms what *Blindness* had first announced, Green's tendency to associate males with stasis, females with flux.) Bereft of aspiration, Craigan exerts all effort toward maintaining nothing more than a *status quo*. He commands with his money (he has a bit laid by). Plotting to reunite Lily and Jim Dale, he forbids the embarrassed Jim to find other lodgings when Lily takes up with Bert Jones; in hopes of persuading Lily to stay, he recounts to her the story of her aunt whom he presumably had loved. The aunt had run off as Lily intends to, and Craigan had gone off then to make his way in the world—much as Dick Dupret turned his energies to running the firm. "But I'd've been better where I was," Craigan tells Lily. "I wouldn't 'ave got the money but I broke the old people's hearts and where am I now, with no one of my own about me?" (p. 95).

Jim Dale is a copy of what Craigan once was, and in making him this, Green accentuates the fixity of Craigan's predicament. To Jim, embittered enough finally to break from the household, are passed on Craigan's vulnerability and the dismal prospects that result from it. Thus it is with males, Green seems to be saying. So when the Welshman Arthur Jones, gifted of voice, charms all the laborers with his singing the morning after a son is born to him, Jim grieves. "Every one looked forward to Arthur's singing, each one was glad when he sang, only, this morning, Jim Dale had bitterness inside him like girders and when Arthur began singing his music was like acid to that man and it was like that girder was being melted and bitterness and anger decrystallized, up rising in him till he was full and would have broken out—when he put on coat and walked off and went into town and drank" (p. 90).

The girder image, and that of a vessel filled full yet not relieved, suggest the unrelieved pressures Jim and Craigan wrestle under. Craigan is kept going by a bleak sort of fortitude, which serves him while Lily is gone but is insufficient after she returns. His hopes are all bound up with keeping things as they are, whereas his intelligence shows this to be impossible—so that he is left intransigent. Yet, brought into confluence with Lily's aspiring heart, with her resiliency, that bleakness of Craigan's is tempered for a time. He is both strengthened and weakened by her support—strengthened in a strange way, because he mildly takes to dreaming (as she instinctively does, her spirit drenched with corrosive experience but remaining unaltered). Mr. Craigan "grew remote in the memory of his young days," we read, just after Lily's return, and for a brief space deludes himself into happiness: "And Mr. Craigan's youth, where he had to go looking through the lanes to find Lily in her aunt Ellie as they both of them had once been, enchanted him like noise of bells" (pp. 255–256). The duality of Green's own vision of life is here perhaps for the first time expressed. Craigan, one of his strongest and least self-deceived characters, and capable of action in the face of any threat, is happy only this once when he deludes himself.

But because of Lily, Craigan's authority is broken. Mr. Gates, irrepressible and a parasite, fathoms this when he finds Lily has returned. He understands he will be safe under Craigan's roof because of Craigan's attachment to his daughter, and thus speaks out in the face of one of Craigan's orders. "Indeed, he was all right," Green says of Joe Gates. "Craigan was imprisoned by his love for Lily, he was tied down by it. Miss Gates chained him to her father and this he had never seen. So when Mr. Gates spoke out Craigan seemed to shrink and now for ever, except for one time later, his old authority was gone" (p. 249).

The one time later epitomizes Craigan's character. All the fired old hands are in a pub when the works manager, Bridges, a pathetic figure now that he too is fired, walks in, ministered to by the sycophant Tupe. Craigan "hated Tupe so, it made him feel younger"; then Gates, in trying to get at Tupe, reviles Mr. Bridges. "And Joe was about to draw attention of all the world to Mr. Bridges, and bar tender was already saying with appeal Joe, Joe when Craigan got up and butted him in the stomach with his head. Both being so old this looked very silly, Mr. Gates more so where he lay trying to get back his wind" (p. 259).

This last significant action of Mr. Craigan, if not his most heroic, is the most humane of all the episodes in the book—and is both funny and poignant. After it Craigan takes to his bed, gives himself over to Lily's care, and sees as the payment for a life of work, nothing. Yet in that living gesture, made to save one more defeated man from embarrassment, shines the quality of Craigan's humanism.

Out of the barrenness and negation of such hard positions as Craigan's, and those of the other workers at Bridesley, springs life which is beautiful and which, as E. M. Forster would say, "connects." Like Forster and Mrs. Woolf, Green pays tribute to the capacities some women have for composing and fostering life by being in intuitive accord with the processes of nature. (In *Party Going,* it is the incapacity of women to make such responses that he exposes.) An image very early in *Living,* of a tile pattern on a wall, retroactively suggests both physical and spiritual fecundity which are seen to be part of women like Mrs. Eames and Lily, who overcome Bridesley's oppressive environment: "pattern on the tiles was like beetles with backs open and three white lilies in each of these" (p. 21). Doubtless the name Lily is connected with this flourishing symbol.

And Mrs. Eames, again early, comes on a scene in which a sparrow is caught between upper and lower window frames. Craigan and Gates and Jim Dale cannot extricate the bird, and then Mrs. Eames wordlessly lifts it out and frees it. "Mr. Dale said it looked easy the way she done it, and Mr. Craigan, dignified and courtly, said they had to thank Mrs. Eames for what three men could not do" (p. 20). Outward-going, "full of purposes," those women can free other creatures, can conquer where men stand muddled and inept.

Parallels exist between Craigan and Mrs. Eames here and Mr.

and Mrs. Ramsay in *To the Lighthouse*. There is Craigan's ponder-
ous dignity, for instance. Ramsay too, for all his dissatisfaction and
incapacity, is imperious toward his family. Lily Gates, we might
add, responds emotionally to life she has not herself fostered (signified by Mrs. Eames's baby) much in the same way that Lily Briscoe
in one moment of vision completes her picture, having been brought
to the brink of her achievement through watching the Ramsays on
a quest from which she is excluded. Yet Green's solution does not
wholly parallel Mrs. Woolf's. Mr. Ramsay himself achieved his goal,
by completing that journey of fulfillment to the lighthouse; not so
Craigan. He is left more like Mr. Wilcox of *Howards End;* both
men are incapacitated and managed by young women, when the
novels conclude. Yet the incarceration of the imperialist Wilcox was
necessary to the resurgent hopefulness of Forster's conclusion.

What we can infer, I think, from the brief three-way comparison,
is that the sustenance offered by the women of *Living* is more temporary and limited—and that individuals are inevitably thrown back
upon themselves. The approximation of mutually sustaining relationships becomes the highest achievement Green's later novels
strike toward, but as early as *Living* he seems convinced that man is
mostly alone.

SYMBOLS — AND LAWRENCE AND ELIOT

That entrapment, that fixity of beetles which is the lot of the inhabitants, provokes escape yearnings in every heart at Bridesley.
For a young man there may be Canada or "Orstrylia"; for Craigan
there is the wireless and Dickens. For unattached men, drink; for
lovers, the movies. These various escapes may all be illusory, but
some illusions are more sustaining than others. By means of the
dominant image of birds—mainly of homing pigeons—Green is able
to approximate the welter of emotions that pull his people two ways:
toward the new life of other places, then back to the known life of
home. A very early image contains the seeds of the escape impulse

and the situation that engenders it: "A man next door to them kept racing pigeon and these were in slow air" (p. 13). The trap which factory and town make is rendered almost surrealistically in Lily's desolate dream, as she lies on a hillside above town with Jones, and a bird figures harrowingly in this: "All was black with smoke, here even, by her, cows went soot-covered and the sheep grey. She saw milk taken out from them, grey the surface of it. Yes, and blackbird fled across that town flying crying and made noise like noise made by ratchet. Yes and in every house was mother with her child and that was grey and that fluttered hands and then that died, in every house died those children to women. Was low wailing low in her ears" (p. 108).

But this scene forms a constituent image, a partial image of the whole, and its deadly greys stand only as negatives to the finale. Then pigeons with fierce red eyes swirl around the Eames baby, whom Lily and Mrs. Eames have out in the clear afternoon, Mrs. Eames in her plum-colored coat. (These are pulsing, promising colors in Green's work.) We see no more blackbirds in *Living;* moreover, that blackbird escaping was balanced by the first bird image in the book, that of sparrows feeding at the works. "And you can't stop it," says works manager Bridges to young Mr. Dupret. "You can't keep the sparrows out" (p. 3).

Homing pigeons replace these sparrows and blackbirds, almost neatly; for late in the novel when Lily has fled and cannot keep her thoughts from Craigan, Green explains his symbolism: * "For as racing pigeon fly in the sky, always they go round above house which provides for them or, if loosed at a distance from that house then they fly straight there, so her thoughts would not point away long from house which had provided for her" (p. 217).

Immediately after Green describes her homing thoughts, Lily sees from her train window a couple walking along a path which had been made on a slag heap. They arrest her attention. "She could not

* This is rare for Green; in fact, his explanation transforms the passage from symbol into analogy. Still the explanation here does not detract from the suggestiveness of the homing pigeons as they come before us in other contexts, full-fledged symbols.

take eyes away from looking at those two, O it was so safe and comfortable to be walking on this slag heap. For where was she going
herself? . . . Miss Gates felt she didn't want to walk any place
where she hadn't walked before" (p. 219).

The slag heap makes conventional daydreaming productive in
terms of continuing image patterns in *Living*. It is both waste material and solid substance—permanent bedrock built up from slag,
and fostering a bleak but flourishing civilization (a path is cut into
the slag heap, young lovers dally upon it). We think once more of
lilies sprouting from the backs of beetles. And Lily's thoughts turn
homeward when she is in the very act of escape, her lover at her side.

The predicament of unattached Craigan, who had once made good
an escape, but was forced to create and preside over a synthetic
family, argues the homing instinct of the birds and of Lily. The
illusions of the hearth are truly sustaining; escape wishes, keeping
the heart in flux, sustain as long as they remain in the wishful (or
potential) stage. So in the movies Lily and whole audiences are
transported: "battalions were in cinemas over all the country . . .
over above up into the sky their feeling panted up supported by each
other's feeling, away away, Europe and America, mass on mass their
feeling united supporting, renewed their sky" (p. 59).

Such feelings form grounds for more illusions. Lily is at another
movie. "This film was of the tropics and again . . . all her muscles
softened under the influence of dreams and imagination of that
warmth. She felt in her heart it must be a soft thing, not the cruel
beating heat it is" (p. 160).

Soon after, Lily is nagging Bert to change plans and be off to one
of the tea plantations the Empire has to offer. Says Bert,

> "Well and if we did go out, what about the 'eat. It's the
> tropics where tea grows you know."
> "Oh yes I could stand it, yes I like it where it's warm."
> "Oh, but it's hot out there. How'd you know you could?"
> "H.O.T.—warm," she said and rubbed arm between palms
> of her hand. "I know I could dear," she said and he kissed her
> while she laughed at him. (p. 167)

Here is the same old round, the male with his perennial facts and doubts (Mr. Ramsay had them, and Mr. Craigan); but we must not underestimate the power of that laughter, nor the purposiveness of that girl. The mind makes its own state, Green may be saying. Precisely here is where he grows most complex, and where the reader must draw his own conclusions. Can the mind make over those tropics? Green intensifies the question in this instance because he has employed leitmotiv. In a movie house with Jim Dale, Lily had long before enacted an equivalent scene. Jim was trapped by his inability to speak out his heart, and so self-conscious and wooden that he could not respond to music which exalted Lily and the theatregoers.

> "Why not take a bit of fun Jim when it comes your way?" she softly said. He said "I can't enjoy the music when I'm not in the mood. . . ."
> She hummed tune band was now playing whey widdle o.
> "It's 'ot in 'ere" he said.
> "H.O.T. warm" she said. (p. 27)

If the mind does determine reality (and we cannot say one way or the other), it does so because of a certain obliviousness, Green seems to suggest. Yet there comes, inevitably, fatigue. Witness Lily at still another movie: "Sweetness of agitation in her, both her and he sitting bolt upright." They decide to see the re-play. "So still upright. But she tired" (p. 59). And when she suggests that they go, she is trembling.

And because of fatigue, Green allows another image, more muted than that of the birds, to develop to symbol through repetition. In the first of the cinema scenes, he had written, "Later her head was leaning on his shoulder again, like hanging clouds against hills every head in this theatre tumbled without hats against another, leaning everywhere" (p. 16). Much further on, another shoulder cushions the same head. Lily and Bert are aboard their train for Liverpool. "He rested his head on hers where it rested on his shoulder. So their heads inclined one to the other, so their breathing fell in one with the other, so they took breath together in one breath as they had been, once before in night" (p. 221).

This mutual support is compensatory, to serve when fatigue encroaches. The first symbolic pattern of the book, that of hungering after escape and then return, necessitates the second, that of fatigue and mutual support. Both patterns, of leaning and of wheeling, are fused in one place; they form an epitomizing symbol of the whole of *Living*. The image occurs just before Lily is about to set off with Bert. From her kitchen she watches a man,

> . . . in garden next theirs digging in his garden. Behind him was line of chimney pots. . . . This man, then, leant on his spade and was like another chimney pot, dark against dark low clouds in the sky. Here pigeon quickly turned rising in spirals, grey, when clock in the church tower struck the quarter and away, away the pigeon fell from this noise in a diagonal from where church was built and that man who leant on his spade. Like hatchets they came towards Lily, down at her till when they were close to window they stopped, each clapped his wings then flew away slowly all of them, to the left. . . . Then again she looked at that man and he also had been watching the pigeon. He began again to dig. . . . (p. 199)

That element of time which dooms the pigeons down, their leaning symbolizing plight, escape, but certain return, the man and permanent church and chimney pots and more permanent, supporting, desolate land—all are visualized simultaneously, kernel the novel, and defy definition. This symbolic epitome both arrests time, and yet hints that time's only significance resides in the moving moment. Man and girl are both eased (perhaps as movies and pubs and wirelesses ease people all through the book) by focusing on the pigeons. But against the background of time arrested, the pigeons are enacting the systole and diastole of life. Lily, certainly, reflects only an instant on this scene, then continues her preparations for elopement. All of her responses, in fact, suggest Green's latent kinship with D. H. Lawrence, and Lawrence's commitment to the tempo-

rariness of time strikes closer to Green's response than does Mrs.
Woolf's attempt to compose flux and arrest time's progress.

Green's kinship with Lawrence can best be brought out, I think,
by turning to Lawrence's preface to the American edition of his
New Poems (1920). Lawrence champions the immediate present in
images of rose and lotus (water lily) ; Green will exploit the rose in
Caught and *Back,* but now we are concerned with the meaning of his
Lily. Says Lawrence,

> A water-lily heaves herself from the flood, looks round, gleams,
> and is gone. . . . We have seen, we have touched, we have par-
> taken of the very substance of creative change, creative muta-
> tion. If you tell me about the lotus, tell me of nothing change-
> less or eternal. . . . Tell me of the incarnate disclosure of the
> flux . . . laughter and decay perfectly open in their transit,
> nude in their movement before us.[4]

This is certainly part, though not all, of what Green also en-
visions. His symbol of lilies growing from beetles' backs celebrates
that surging force of organic life, and so does Lily when she rejoices
over the Eames baby. More astonishing is the connection between
Lawrence's "laughter and decay perfectly open in their transit," and
Mrs. Eames's laughter coming one breath after she has envisioned
her own decay (when her children will leave her foundering). She
laughs in the end too, at Lily's rapture, hiding her small son's eyes
even while laughing.

Though Lily and Mrs. Eames react positively to the fact of
change, Green is concerned with fixity as well, as this is perceived
in life by recurrent patterns (and in *Living,* particularly, by the
negating, unfruitful pattern which passes on from Craigan to be
embodied in Jim Dale). Lawrence denigrates pattern. The poetry
he favors, like Whitman's, "is never finished. There is no rhythm
which returns upon itself, no serpent of eternity with its tail in its
own mouth." [5] Similarly, in *The Rainbow,* "How rich and splendid
his own life was," reflects aging Tom Brangwen. ". . . Always it
was so unfinished and unformed!" [6] But for Green, pattern, signi-

fying completion, vies with the transient instant as containing life's secret. How his total response differs from Lawrence's may best be gathered by citing from Lawrence's preface his praise of the "supreme mutability" of a bird on the wing: "Whence such a bird came: whither it goes: from what solid earth it rose up, and upon what solid earth it will close its wings and settle, this is not the question. This is a question of before and after. Now, *now,* the bird is on the wing in the winds." [7]

But for all Green's birds on the wing, slag heap and solid earth are also his concerns. The motto of *Living* asks the question Lawrence will not entertain: "As these birds would go where so where would this child go?" Even Mrs. Eames had two answers to this question. Green cannot make Lawrence's unswerving commitment to the moment, and his own answer to the question seems implicit in the structure of the novel, with its overall symmetry and promise of patterned renewal.

Three images, each involving the play of light over surfaces—they might be called images of fixity-and-flux—may help show us Green's simultaneous wish for "static perfection" and his distrust of the possibilities of attaining it in life. The images mark intense experiences that occur to three young men who are lovers in this novel. Dick Dupret, first, mounting stairs to a ballroom with Hannah Glossop on his arm, thrills to light that tumbles down a chandelier. "So, as they went upstairs, and she had put her arm on his (she did not know it), so happiness tumbled down his spine" (p. 123). Dick here is deluded. When Hannah is lost to him, he recollects this scene and convicts himself of spurious emotion for having been moved by a thing so artificial.

Soon after, Jim Dale is entranced by Lily as she washes dishes. "She swilled water over the plates and electric light caught in shining waves of water which rushed off plates as she held them, and then light caught on wet plates in moons. She dried these. One by one then she put them up into the rack on wall above her, and as she stretched up so her movements pulled all ways at his heart, so beautiful she seemed to him" (p. 160).

But transfixed as he is, caught at an emotional peak just as the light is caught momentarily, Jim cannot express his feelings. And though under the impulse of sudden confidence he does ask Lily to a movie, she is still Bert's girl when she accepts: "Bert and she were saying, Jim would pay for her into movie, why yes why not . . ." (p. 160).

Green's own deepest longing, perhaps, involves a shift from individuals to things, something like that of Yeats in "Sailing to Byzantium." At least Bert Jones's epiphany betrays neither the artificiality that dupes Dupret nor the transfixion that ruins tongue-tied Jim Dale. Jones is addressing himself to a difficult job on a lathe. "Now the job, revolving so many turns each second, now it had a stillness more beautiful than when actually it had been still. On the smallest surface of it was sheen of light still and quiet, for noise of his lathe could not be heard above noise of other lathes working about him. And pace of events bearing on his life quickened so that for two moments their speed had appearance of stillness" (p. 196).

What Green seems to illuminate here is the satisfying beauty of pattern, and of the tendency of recurrent pattern to approximate static perfection. His method and vision seem akin to those of T. S. Eliot; the following lines from "Burnt Norton" state the proposition Green has just dramatized:

> . . . Only by the form, the pattern,
> Can words or music reach
> The stillness, as a Chinese jar still
> Moves perpetually in its stillness.
>
>   *   *   *
>
> The detail of the pattern is movement. . . .[8]

The concept of repetition approaching stasis, well illustrated by the turning lathe, may perhaps be applied to the slower patterns which evolve in *Living;* though what the pattern repeats may be tawdry enough (there may be dealt out a procession of Jim Dales replacing Craigans), the pattern itself is perceived by the artist as beautiful. But Green realizes that order and stillness are approachable only in art, and are outside the realm of human intercourse.

The young author has pointed old Craigan in a single direction after all. ". . . but that which is only living / Can only die," wrote Eliot just before the lines just quoted. It is no accident that Bert Jones's sensation of stillness and peace occurred, not as a result of his relationship with Lily, but because of a lathe on which he was fashioning a product.

Whether the patterns the artist perceives are not also illusions, as Lawrence challenges, is another question, and may be approached indirectly by referring to the illusions Green's people harbor in *Living*. I have reserved the most conclusive till now—those involving the convictions of people that they are sharing mutual experience. Although his theory of art is built on the premise that people can mysteriously share, as early as this second novel Green reveals an awareness that this rapport is uncertain. Just as Gabriel Conroy mistook his wife's feelings in Joyce's "The Dead," so are the characters of *Living* misled by their own feelings. When Dick has Hannah on his arm, she is transported by dance music—but she is thinking of a different boy. " 'Oh,' she whispered, 'oh' and he felt quite transported." The song the band is playing goes like this:

> Your eyes are my eyes
> My heart looks through. (p. 124)

Now when Lily and Bert are on their train, their heads together, Lily feels a secret communion, but Bert is wondering whether his parents will be in Liverpool, and is hardly aware of Lily's presence. Their situations are very soon reversed, for Bert confesses he isn't sure where his parents live, and Lily begins to worry over this piece of news. Just then nine musicians board their car. Lily sees the green muffler one of them wears. "That was bad luck about, seeing green like that" (p. 225). But Bert, conscience clear, is now expansive; and one of the musicians now suggests they play a tune. "As he took saxophone out of case this turned red in sunset light (p. 225).

The color green signifies anxiety; opposed to it, red here implies need's fulfillment; and Lily is alienated when Bert in his turn feels at one with all things. "As he listened beat of that music, so together, made everything in the world brother to him" (p. 226). Lily is meanwhile growing distraught, and now a tenor sings:

> "Your eyes are my eyes
> My heart looks through." (p. 227)

Lily is horror struck, for the dingy outskirts of Liverpool have appeared in her window.

The motif which the words of that song form in *Living* affords perhaps the most ironic and deepest insight of the novel. Times come when one thinks he is seeing truly and wholly through another's eyes, times when he feels himself brother to the world. But this belief has no effect on that world or on that other. Individuals rarely, perhaps never, understand what state their closest fellows are in; however sure they are of mutual feelings, their deepest joys and sorrows are apt to be lonely ones. So earlier, when Dick Dupret had succumbed to that same illusory song, Green had immediately juxtaposed a scene consisting of a single line: "Just then Mr. Dupret in sleep, died, in sleep" (p. 124). Such a sentence presents the nadir of aloneness, and the simultaneity of the two actions makes comment on the fatuity of the younger Dupret.

We may pause on the repetition of the word "sleep," for it reevokes a very recent scene. Dick Dupret had been sitting in a garden fronting on the Thames,

> . . . and soon he thought no more but as river Thames slipped away to the sea so drifted into sleeping.
> Sunshine was pale. So drifted into sleep. Yet came party from Maidenhead in launch up the river, men and women, a silver launch. Laughter came like birds from women in it. It came on slowly and he opened eyes and it went by. . . . Laughter from it fluttered back to him and then in wide circle launch turned leisurely and came back past him and he thought why did they turn it there. Why did they turn it there he thought and then man on launch played dance tune from the wireless they had on it and it went on down with stream. . . .

> . . . They would be back at Maidenhead for tea, he thought.
> . . . Still flowed river Thames and still the leaves were dis-
> turbed, then were loosed, and came down on to water and went
> by London . . . and out into the sea. (pp. 114–115)

In this passage is a galaxy of images recurrent in *Living*—of
homing, of birds, of laughter, of dance music. But what is predomi-
nant is the question "why did they turn it there," and the single
direction of the autumnal river. They turned it, perhaps, because tea
awaited them at Maidenhead. Such, Green may be saying, are the
reasons we perceive pattern in the lives of men and in their world:
what goes out must turn round, and this seems graceful and soothing. But the pattern is also illusory—the real direction, like that of
the Thames and like that of sleep in which a man dies, is one way
ever. I should not try to insist upon these meanings, but in this passage I feel Green is aware of what Lawrence insisted upon: the
straight-line direction of flux, upon which it is deceiving to impose
pattern, in hopes of approximating stasis.

To me, Green seems to oscillate between the extreme positions of
Lawrence and Eliot.[9] Where the one demands dynamic and affirmative participation in the flux, the other enjoins the abstract contemplation that leads to the disclosure of form, which in turn approximates the absolute. Lily illustrates Lawrence's dictum, yet Lily is a
virgin, and so is another of Green's heroines, Edith, of *Loving*.
(The same is true in a sense of Nancy in *Back*.) They are celebrated
in their unrealized potential; yet their appeal is the sensuous appeal
to which Lawrence subscribes. Green's art, highly formal, captures
people in situations or in relationships to one another that are abstract. Characters further the symmetrical structures of his novels.
But his best people are invariably dynamic.

That all affirmative response to life is illusory is a possibility
Green may have implicitly confirmed when he said, in one place,
"We must not expect too much of life," [10] and in another, "You've
got to close your heart to something in this world, now don't
you?" [11] One thing is certain, however. Green is receptive to man's
emotional needs, so much so that he virtually champions illusions;

the people who achieve a measure of happiness in his novels are those who take positive steps toward fulfilling their needs, and who are blessed by being thwarted from entirely attaining what they desire. His characters who get by are always resilient, and often oblivious. Lily recovers from her fearful night in Liverpool streets, when Bert in panic deserts her. R. M. Linscott makes Lily's recovery grounds for a perceptive remark about Green's appraisal of characters like her: ". . . his working girl suffers no evil effects from her elopement and desertion, thus flying in the face of one of the most sacred traditions in fiction." [12]

Mr. Gates, a man who "could never be sad," is seen in the next-to-last scene of the book, cheering among thirty thousand other workers at a soccer stadium. The field Green describes as "green, green pitch. Everything but the grass is black with smoke, only thin blue waves of smoke coming up from the dark crowds . . . gives any colour, and the pink brick" (p. 266). The contrast in colors is startling, and it is toward that bright green turf, a substitute for their needs and hopes, that the faces, "lozenges," of the massed crowd are turned—and here lies the grandest illusion of all—in order to shriek and clamor "at 11 men who play the best football in the world. These took no notice of the crowd, no notice" (p. 266).

Both Lily's extension of herself toward Mrs. Eames's baby, when she takes the child ecstatically into her arms, and her father's extension of himself toward the players, might be called illustrations of sporadic illusions by which people are sustained; in each instance there is a sense of union with something (a baby, a team) thoroughly insensitive to the surge of feeling. Lily's triumph, it may be argued, is a selfless commitment that has no close relation to the vicarious attachment her father has with the team. True enough, yet we must allow for some ambiguity in the final scene, for Green has stressed Lily's youth as having helped her respond so fervently. And that man is alone in spite of all is suggested by the single paragraph Green inserts between father's and daughter's activity, showing Mr. Craigan on his bed. "He thought what was there now for him? Nothing, nothing, He lay" (p. 267).

Yet on the whole, *Living* strikes a qualified note of hopefulness.

Though its setting is like that of *Hard Times,* its people have in abundance the "Fancy" that Dickens found stifled in Coketown's inhabitants. Most of the workers in *Living* are blessed with their slag-heap-and-soot environment, which enables that "green, green pitch," that other world, to exist for them as actuality—a treasure untainted because it is remote. The party-goers of *Party Going,* with their money and leisure, have had the deadly opportunity of finding out for themselves that life gets no better when the means for making it better seem everywhere at hand. This is perhaps the sharpest point of contrast between *Living* and *Party Going,* and Green's knowledge of the difficult position the wealthy are in perhaps accounts for the sympathy, well hidden, he reserves for the Mayfair set, who in their hotel are so paralyzed to act and so fretted by spurious emotion.

A DEAD PIGEON

It would be an injustice to Green to suggest that he deals categorically with the working classes and the rich, placing one in a promising and the other in a chilling light. Some of his working-class people exhibit the same basic fault as their wealthier counterparts. They try too hard to get too much. In *Living,* Tupe's way of getting ahead is that of the sycophant, a way open to the meanest-born, as Green indicates again by creating an identical informer and flatterer, the old fireman Piper, in *Caught.* And if the frustrated rich of *Party Going* are bent on exploiting others, at least one of their number has come to the station only to see a niece off. This is Miss Fellowes, all of whose actions are instinctive and mysterious, but part of whose character is shaped by a heritage the same as that of the party-goers she has come to see off.

Miss Fellowes is a delicately conceived character, but she serves Green chiefly as a device. Sick from unknown causes (or drunk from known), she remains in a hotel room which is one of a group Max Adey has taken for his party because their train is delayed. The young people go through the motions of inquiring after her, but she is strictly an inconvenience, and is left in the care of two old nannies, "dressed in granite," who have scented out death and have come to attend it.

But Miss Fellowes's function goes deeper than that of exposing others' apathy. Her instinctive actions can be associated with her exposure to something from which she had always been insulated. This could be called life unaccommodated; whatever adjective we use, it is certainly organic life to which the woman, late in years, is exposed, as Mrs. Eames and Lily had been from their childhood; and Miss Fellowes reacts, when her turn comes, as instinctively as the women of *Living* had reacted from the beginning. The full bearing her instincts have upon *Party Going* may be measured when we realize that she may be a prototype of the young people, who remain insulated for the duration of the book.

Party Going takes on its deadly hue when Miss Fellowes accidentally encounters a thing that has just been vital, but is no longer. A dead pigeon falls at her feet, as the book opens. "She bent down and took a wing then entered a tunnel in front of her, and this had DEPARTURES lit up over it, carrying her dead pigeon" (p. 7).

Many images that reappear throughout the first half of *Party Going* are introduced at this point: a bird, a "pall of fog," tunnels and Departures, all carrying connotations of death. Miss Fellowes takes the pigeon to the ladies' room and washes it, then wraps it in brown paper and carries it with her for the remainder of the book. In doing so she has made an instinctive pact with death, and has been surprised into doing so. She never analyzes her own actions.

No sooner does Miss Fellowes return to the platform with her wrapped pigeon than she begins to feel ill, and meets two of the young people, Angela Crevy and her boy friend Robin Adams (who has come to see his girl off with Max's party). Miss Fellowes draws on her reserves to keep up appearances, smiles "over clenched teeth," and then in desperation gives the parcel to the young man, not wanting to faint before him. When he goes off with the wrapped pigeon, she feels better at once.

Her actions here are of formidable significance. Only in response to the demands of a life she has always known—a life of appearances—does she rally, when she relinquishes the bird. But afterward she intuits her rightful relationship, symbolized by the pigeon, with the world of realities and decay, and retrieves the parcel as soon as Angela and Robin leave. Perhaps the brown paper itself stands as a disguise, hiding the meaning of her compact from her, so that she never achieves self-knowledge. Later, when she fights for breath in the hotel room, Green again appraises her motives: "As for Miss Fellowes, she was fighting. Lying inanimate where they had laid her she waged war with storms of darkness which rolled up over her in a series, like tides summoned by a moon. What made her fight was the one thought that she must not be ill in front of these young people" (p. 72).

If, as this passage implies, Miss Fellowes's experience has come too late to induce a reassessment of values, we may ask how in the first place is she prompted to conduct private obsequies over the pigeon. It is because fog twenty feet in the air has altered the atmosphere of London, and the envelope of routine, which means being tended by servants and sheltered from rough contacts, has been pierced. "And there was that poor bird," Miss Fellowes thinks, wondering why she has ordered whisky in a tea room. "One had seen so many killed out shooting, but any dead animal shocked one in London, even birds, though of course they had easy living in towns. . . . One did not seem to expect it when one was cooped up in London and then to fall like that dead at her feet" (pp. 24–25).

While Miss Fellowes muses, various members of the party, making their way beneath fog to the station, are haunted by phantoms. In all, seven make up the party. Besides Max there are Miss Fellowes's niece, Claire Hignam, and her errand-boy husband, Robert; then there are Alex Alexander, virtually a eunuch, beautiful young Angela, and two other young ladies, Evelyn Henderson (least well off of these rich) and Julia Wray. Julia is the most important. Childish and worried, calmed by a word from anyone, Julia's mind revolves around her indispensable charms (an egg, a top, and a pistol) and around her plans for this party—for in the South of France she hopes to gain the party's prize, Max. In past and future lie Julia's treasures, and the present is her eternal menace. Her walk to the station, when trees and lovers are picked out by reflected headlights and then vanish, is eerie and disquieting. She sees "leaves brilliantly green veined like marble with wet dirt" (p. 17); under the trees the lovers' faces and clothing reflect only white.

Images reminiscent of marble and wet dirt accrue when Green traces Alex Alexander's journey, not through a park this time, but along city blocks, through "ravines of cold sweating granite with cave-dwellers' windows and entrances" (p. 37). The only reflective member of the party, Alex translates the fog in terms of death, but does this smugly. "Humming, he likened what he saw to being dead and thought of himself as a ghost driving through streets of the living, this darkness or that veil between him and what he saw a difference between being alive and death" (p. 37).

To be accurate in reconstructing atmosphere, we should say that the fog in *Party Going* suspends the characters between life and death, for they go on living of course, yet are separated from others as from the dead, as Alex notices. Nobody dies in *Party Going;* rather division and death are *foreseen,* the one to continue till the other interrupts, even though trains have resumed running when the book ends.

This atmosphere of living death circumscribes what slight action there is in the novel, and, along with symbolism not yet discussed, forms the most substantial commentary upon the characters' collective state of life that the novel provides. Meanwhile, each character taken separately is so acutely differentiated that a remarkable living semblance seems struck in every instance, and unanimated as these people may seem, no *one* of them could be judged lifeless. (For one thing, they crave comfort and other men's services too perseveringly for "dead" people.) In such characterization lies the only conventional appeal of *Party Going,* and a rather thin appeal this is; yet perhaps it checks us from labeling the book a *tour de force.*

Green's establishment of a funereal atmosphere is done, in fact, surreptitiously. When Julia flits through the park, thinking "It was so strange and dreadful to be walking here in darkness when it was only half-past four" (p. 18), one does not grasp right off that the fragment approximates the benighted emotional states of the party-goers, eclipsed in the mid-afternoons of their lives. Rather, one follows the action and laughs at silly Julia's impulse to return for her charms, or at Max when he lies into the telephone because he is so bored with wealth he must subsist on charades and impersonations. When David Garnett reviewed *Party Going,* he confessed reactions which tell a good deal about the novel's initial effect. "As I read the book aloud," wrote Garnett, "we were continually held up because it was so funny: almost every page sent us into fits of laughter. Yet an hour afterwards none of us remembered the book as comic. . . ." [13]

The reason the humor does not carry over may be that it does not serve as relief, but, arising from sterile conversation, only underlines an already static physical situation. Conversation begins in earnest once the station master has ushered the party into the terminus hotel. Having provided for everyone's comfort there, Max takes no part in the talk. Robert Hignam is absent most of the time on interminable errands. The females congregate around the last male, Alex, whose mind operates as theirs do anyway. One Embassy Richard, an absentee member of their set, is the yeast for their talk.

Richard is Green's funniest invention in *Party Going.* It seems someone used Mr. Richard Cumberland's note paper to advertise in the newspapers that he could not accept an invitation to an Ambassador's party. When the notice appeared, "the Ambassador, thinking to strike out for a host's right to have what guests he chose, had written to the Press pointing out that he had never invited Mr. Cumberland and that this gentleman was unknown to him" (p. 21).

The party-goers fasten onto this topic, which provides grounds for argument because they know Richard to be flattered by the publicity; some suspect he sent the original notice himself. And while his name commands the foreground, the central conflict in the story, equally superficial, is slowly phrasing itself into this question: will Julia succeed in winning Max? When the book is half finished, Julia has faced only the very remote challenge of Angela's beauty, a potential mantrap. Once the reader apprehends this challenge, though, he has come upon the abstract structural principle of *Party Going.*

which makes the novel divide equally into two halves. Miss Angela Crevy's function has been fulfilled when, in the exact middle of the novel, she takes her tamed boy friend Robin "by one finger of his sweating hand" (p. 132). With no warning to the reader, part two begins with the very next word, "Amabel."

TWO KINDS OF WOMEN

More than anything else, I think—and the book is about many things—*Party Going* is about women. And if the women of *Living* were a unifying force, the women of *Party Going* are a divisive force. Miss Fellowes excepted, the women of the upper set fall into two categories: the anxious and the calm. The anxious fall under Julia Wray's banner, for Claire Hignam and Evelyn Henderson are hoping that Julia will conquer Max, so that they may benefit from the likes of this party in future. Right at the start Green distinguishes these three from Angela. They are all irrational victims of train fever, and their anxieties are ill concealed. But Angela is described quite differently. In the most elaborate metaphor of the first half of the book, Green takes pains to mark Angela out from the crowd on the station: "Like two lilies in a pond, romantically part of it but infinitely remote, surrounded, supported, floating in it if you will, but projected by being different on to another plane . . . stood Miss Crevy and her young man, apparently serene, envied for their obviously easy circumstances and Angela coveted for her looks by all those water beetles if you like, by those people standing round" (p. 27).*

This, a rare example from the first half of the book, reminds one of Faulkner's syntax; after Amabel's arrival, *Party Going* burgeons with such prose. The phrase "apparently serene" may indicate

---

* Green's use of lilies and beetles is not at all symbolic, as it was in *Living*, and their occurrence here illustrates that Green attaches no systematic significance to his imagery, but that it may serve purely for description.

that Angela, insecure as the newest member of the group, is acting; yet at the same time the phrase helps contrast beauteous Angela to the other young ladies of Max's entourage. The contrast serves structural purpose chiefly; through Angela we are being prepared for sharper contrasts when Amabel arrives, so that this lady will strike us as both a phenomenon and at the same time a somewhat familiar phenomenon, an Angela full blown.

None of the ladies in *Party Going* can make any contribution to the well-being of others. When nervous Claire harbors longings to catch the boat train, she chooses Evelyn to ease her conscience publicly. Claire knows that Evelyn, poorest of them all, is even more anxious not to miss the train when the fog lifts, so she gets Evelyn to suggest that Claire's old Auntie Fellowes is not very sick and can be left in the care of the nannies. But just because girls like Claire and Evelyn are *beset* by such anxieties, their kind of behavior is one cut less deadly than the cool depredations of the likes of Amabel. It is almost as if Green finds a sort of therapy in the relief Evelyn experiences when Claire holds out to her the cup of connivance—or in the relief Julia experiences when, jolted from a sullen revery, she hears Angela offer to see if her luggage is safe on the platform. Julia had been distracted by the way Amabel was laying siege to Max, but Angela's offer made her "better at once," says Green, "for, like delicate plants must be watered every so often so Julia must have sympathy every now and then . . . and once she had it was all right for another little while" (pp. 240–241).

The worrisome characters are more vulnerable, and therefore more human, than the self-assured. The latter are predators in repose, expectant. Here, for example, are Alex's reflections on Angela and Amabel, which seem to be Green's own: ". . . now that he was alone with Angela and [Amabel] again . . . he suddenly felt more strongly than ever before how these girls were a different species and were quite definitely hostile. As he looked at them both, exquisitely dressed, Angela smoking and watching her smoke rings, Amabel looking at her nails like you and I gaze into crystals . . . it struck him again how women always seemed to expect things, and for that matter, events even, to be brought to them for their pleasure, in white cotton gloves on plates" (p. 148).

Structurally, then, *Party Going* pits the anxious against the serene, and the whole action of the novel, opposing forces of flight and detainment, may be seen to be symbolic. Not only the jittery women but Max himself is desperate to escape—from Amabel, for whom he is a sexual pawn. As for her, "She knew well she could deal with Max but he was always escaping" (p. 147).

The rushes and delays of the first half of the novel have hinted at some ubiquitous trap, and with Amabel's arrival in the middle the trap is sprung. With its springing we seem to have an equation by Green between sex and death, which loom as concomitant traps for man. (Notice that Amabel and Miss Fellowes seem to bear out the correspondence between sex and death in that both exert detaining influences on the party-goers.) Green's later novels, notably *Caught, Back,* and *Concluding,* sometimes present man's vulnerability to sex in terms symbolically equivalent with death. It is really overmastering sexual autonomy that Green sees in this light, and lovers fretting and bent on self-aggrandizement. In *Living,* conversely, the forces *opposing* death are those of genuine love—symbolized in the fruitful marriage of Mrs. Eames, and in the response of Lily, who is inviolate but potentially fecund. And a dead wife and two wives-to-be sustain *Caught, Loving,* and *Back.* None of them is in the fearful category in which Green places Angela Crevy: ". . . Miss Crevy examined her face in a mirror out of her bag like any jeweller with a precious stone, and it was indeed without price, but it had its ticket and this had Marriage written on it" (p. 197).

Angela's actions at the end of the first half of the book serve as overture to Amabel's entrance. Younger than Amabel, Angela is a novitiate in sex play, but at this mid-point, her Robin having returned, Angela begins to feel she has not been properly attended by this boy whom she has driven away several times. To teach him a lesson, she entices Alex into a bedroom before the eyes of everyone; then, after shunting Alex out another door, she claps her hands loudly, twice. Robin is in the room in an instant, to find her calmly powdering her face before a mirror.

"What?" he said, "what?"

"What do you mean?" she said.

"Was that you slapping someone's face?" he said and he was panting hard.

"Who slapped whose face? I didn't hear anyone," she said.

"I heard it twice," he said and his knees were trembling.

She burst into tears, her face screwed up and got red and she held her handkerchief to her nose and sniffled as if that was where her tears were coming from. (p. 121)

The ugly (though funny) final image is fitting for this self-induced hysteria, capping a scene David Garnett has called "disgustingly cruel." The couple's ensuing conversation ends when Robin is remanded to the status of hopeful suitor, with Angela in complete and emotionless control. Up until this point in the novel the autonomy of sexual attraction has been muted. Julia had kept Max at his distance in the extra upstairs room he had engaged. Green's structural stroke of genius was having Angela serve as acolyte for Amabel, enabling him to pour into the novel at this point intimations of the female's sexual supremacy over the male.

BATHS, BIRDS, BAMBOO

When David Garnett called attention to Green's abstract structural design, comparing it to the ballet *Les Sylphides,* he said accurately that "Not till half-way through does the leading star, Amabel, appear, dazzling us by a technique and a beauty far exceeding all that has gone before." [14] How dazzling can she be? One illustration may serve to demonstrate the prose Green employs to do justice to Amabel. Here is how Alex sees her:

> In her silence and in seeming unapproachable . . . it seemed
> to him she was not unlike ground so high, so remote it had
> never been broken and that her outward beauty lay in that if

any man had marked her with intimacy as one treads on snow,
then that trace which would be left could not fail to invest him,
whoever he might be, with some part of those unvulgar heights
so covered, not so much of that last field of snow before any
summit as of a high memory unvisited, and kept. (p. 144)

The passage sounds remarkably like Faulkner. For example,
negative constructions strain beyond the reach of superlatives: "not
unlike ground so high," "unvulgar heights," "a high memory unvisited"; and there is Faulkner's common method of syntactical
climax, involving an arbitrary antithesis: *"not so much of* that last
field of snow . . . *as of* a high memory unvisited." Each device aims
to attest the woman's allure, partly due to her remoteness, which in
turn is due to her great wealth. The syntax suggests the compul-
siveness of the attraction—for Alex here, for Max in other places.

Because the language reputes Amabel to be so dazzling, Green's
early establishment of an atmosphere of torpor and deadliness is
justified. We must see Amabel as an illusion, a Lamia who mesmer-
izes men, just as the early fog mesmerized birds into thinking night
had fallen. So as the prose begins to unwind celebrating Amabel in
her bath, attended by Alex who is for all the world like Mardian,
quick juxtapositions or deliberate echoes of earlier passages en-
croach upon the scene. If Amabel is imagined "pink with warmth
and wrapped round with steam so comfortable," in the next room
Miss Fellowes speaks up "from mists which wrapped her round not
sweet and warm" (pp. 154, 156). This is a bald and obvious montage. More sinisterly does the bath scene evoke former doings. "She
kicked her legs and splashed and sent fountains of water up among
wreaths of sweet steam" (p. 155), we read; and we recall the
pigeon's bath: "on the now dirty water with a thin wreath or two of
blood, feathers puffed up and its head sideways, drowned along one
wing, lay her dead pigeon. Air just above it was dizzy with a little
steam . . ." (p. 9).

And we hear a remarkable echo when Amabel lovingly dries herself. "She was gradually changing colour, where she was dry was
going back to white; for instance, her face was dead white but her

neck was red. She was polishing her shoulders now and her neck was paling from red into pink and then suddenly it would go white" (p. 172).

Sudden changes to "dead white" are suggestive enough, but we perceive a sort of occult transposition of Miss Fellowes and Amabel, when we recall that Miss Fellowes's hands changed color in reverse order when she bathed the pigeon; "for she was doing what she felt must be done with hot water, turning her fingers to the colour of its legs and blood" (p. 9).

Of course such imagery can hardly be paraphrased; yet in one place a woman near death seems to be refurbished, her white hands changed to massaging red, while in another a woman in carnal prime fades to pallor with surprising speed. Certainly Amabel's bloom and coziness are affected by the presence in the same book of an old woman and a dead pigeon.

Green employs similar motifs and juxtapositions to generate other constituent symbols in *Party Going*. Two images, of birds and bamboo (or artichokes), present man's self-delusion and man's separateness, themes we have examined in *Living*. Juxtapositions in turn contrast real and false instances of "fellow feeling." And since Green at the end of the book just slightly eases the spring of his trap (Max escapes temporarily from Amabel), these symbolic patterns center about Julia, whose great anxieties are relieved at the conclusion.

Where Claire and Evelyn, more aware than others of Miss Fellowes's presence, fear that wrapped pigeon of hers, Julia is so self-absorbed that live birds of the recent past comfort her. Sea gulls had flown under a footbridge when Julia was hurrying to the station, and she had found these promising; for something similar had happened when she first met Max: "doves had flown under a bridge where she had been standing . . ." (p. 19). The gulls stand in Julia's mind for the channel she and Max are to cross, and later in the novel she thinks of the gulls again, her thoughts reaching into a snug future. But soon that mood is fractured; Julia is not sure they will be crossing that channel. No sooner do future prospects seem forbidding than Julia performs a remarkable feat of adaptation: she forgets the sea gulls that betoken future and remembers the doves that had been favorable signs in the past. "And now she remembered those two birds which had flown under the arch . . . and now she forgot they were sea-gulls and thought they had been doves and so was comforted" (p. 161).

The two movements of her mind epitomize Julia. The most anxious of the party-goers, she unfailingly reassures herself by inventing havens in the other worlds of future and past, freely choosing whichever is the more convenient.

That the birds symbolize yearning and self-delusion is fairly clear, but what the bamboo (or artichokes) mean is more recondite. The image appears first when Robert Hignam is elbowing through a crowded tea room. "Robert thrust on and on. When small he had found patches of bamboo in his parents' garden and it was his romance at that time to force through them; they grew so thick you could not see what temple might lie in the ruins just beyond. It was so now, these bodies so thick they might have been a store of tailors' dummies, water heated. They were so stiff they might as well have been soft, swollen bamboos in groves only because he had once pushed through these, damp and warm" (p. 47).

Both sexual and deathly undertones can be discovered here—the dummies, "water heated," and the equally fixed, bloated bamboos. But these suggestions do not seem prevalent when the image is repeated. Near the end of the book, a mystery man who shadows Miss Fellowes (and who makes himself useful to the party) is bent on an obscure errand. He drops lightly from a hotel window and, forgetting a group of idlers with whom he has just been arguing, begins to push through the crowd on the station. "To push through this crowd," says Green, "was like trying to get through bamboo or artichokes grown thick together or thousands of tailors' dummies stored warm on a warehouse floor" (p. 178).

What Green seems to be symbolizing is blind motivational force, which keeps the individual pressing past obstructions. Like Robert in the tea room, or this strange fellow here, man may scarcely know what goal he seeks; but more distressing than that, he cannot perceive what lies without him as anything other than fixed, insensate stuff. In the same way the thwarted party-goers cannot regard those travelers on the station as living people, for they are too occupied with themselves. Robert Hignam as a child had forced his way through bamboo, seeking "what temple might lie in the ruins just beyond." When Green deals most poignantly with the crowd on the graveyard platform, he refers to them again and again as "ruins" (p. 201). The symbol of the artichokes seems to be the symbol of a ruinous solipsism. The disparity of experience, and man's inability really to know himself or his motives, prevent any accurate penetration into the heart of one by another. If this idea is contained in the image of people standing in one man's way like bamboo, thwarting and misguiding him, then *Party Going* as a proletarian novel takes on a special cast of thought. Green may be exposing his invidious rich, but he forbears blaming them for something they constitutionally cannot help.

A MITE OF FELLOW FEELING

To recapitulate the three chief symbols that are expanded in *Party Going* by structure and motif, we could say that the central symbol is one of detention thwarting escape, and that the fogbound station and the sinister Amabel reflect two aspects of one symbol, the trap of sex and death. A subsidiary symbol, next, expresses relief. In *Party Going,* relief lies in comforting delusions, especially those which enable Julia to choose different ways of least pain (as when she mistakes gulls for doves). The difference between this relief and the relief which operates in *Living* is that Julia turns inward to keep her plans from disintegrating, whereas the people of *Living* turn essentially to one another (that image of leaning heads being the correspondent image in *Living* that copes with dismay and fatigue). But both books present the thesis that man's inner complexities leave him sundered from others—an albino. Artichokes seem to perform this function in *Party Going;* a simple ironic song, played twice, does the same for *Living:* "Your eyes are my eyes / My heart looks through." [15]

When we turn, lastly, to juxtapositions of "fellow feeling," we discover the one vital fund *Party Going* holds in reserve. Whereas in every other part the book stands as a photographic negative to *Living,* Green's treatment of the working classes on the platform recaptures some of the vitality of that book.

Significantly, the crowd on the station, as seen most often by Julia and Max from above, is described as if it were an organism, a living design. Commuters remind Julia of "those illustrations you saw in weekly papers, of corpuscles in blood, for here and there a narrow stream of people shoved and moved in lines three deep and where they did this they were like veins" (p. 109).

The crowd excites Julia in a strange way. The first few times she looks out, her mind flashes away from herself; she thinks of her servant Thomson out there when she first looks down, but the next instant she is back to herself. "It's like being a Queen," she tells Max (p. 87).

The baffled vitality of the crowd may truly reach Julia, but if "its thousands of troubles and its discomfort put new heart in her," that heart does not go out to the source; instead, pitifully, she gets "this feeling she must exchange and share" with Max (pp. 151, 152). When, some pages later, Julia and Max have by no means exchanged and shared, Julia is once again solicitous for her Thomson, a sure symptom of her returned anxiety. But her agitation, humorously enough, comes just after Thomson has received a gratuitous kiss.

Thomson and Edwards, Max's stuffy manservant, have been guarding luggage and longing for their tea, while porters stand around drooping over their barrows. Then, with no warning, a girl looks round an upended trunk. Thomson asks coolly for a kiss, over Edwards's protest.

> "I like your cheek," she said scornfully. "Here," she said, "if you want one," and crept round and kissed him on his mouth. Not believing his luck he put his arms round her and the porter said, "God bless me," when a voice over that barricade began calling: "Emily, where are you, Emily?" and he let her go, and off she went.

"God bless 'er little 'eart," the porter said, smacking his lips. He called out to his mate . . . "Come up out of the bloody ground, and gave him a great bloody kiss when he asked her."

"Poor Thomson," Julia said just then to Max, putting on her hat again, "d'you think he's all right, and what about his tea?" (pp. 160–161)

No other scene in the entire novel is so superbly handled. Green's ironic shift to Julia reveals again the discrepancy between supposition and fact he often exploits: one cannot know what benediction may have befallen another.

Though Thomson is blessed here, he too is a forlorn figure in the end. When sheer fatigue breaks the harmony of those on the station, and the crowd begins to surge about "in their blind search behind bowler hats and hats for trains" (p. 202), Thomson remains at the luggage cache, telling himself he cannot bear that Emily has been called away. The moment of support is clearly not enough, Green seems to be indicating; just as in *Living,* his awareness of man's needs will not permit him to make any wholehearted optimistic gesture. Yet dim as the outlook is, that single dramatized instance of fellow feeling buoys up *Party Going.* "No," says Thomson to Edwards, who has disparaged the incident,

"No, it's fellow feeling, that's what I like about it. Without so much as a by your leave when she sees someone hankering after a bit of comfort, God bless 'er, she gives it him. . . .

"Waiting about in basements, with no light and in the damp and dark," Mr. Thomson muttered to himself, and if he and that girl had been alone together, in between kisses he would have pitied both of them clinging together on dim whirling waters. (pp. 162–163)

This last image, and one other in the book's culminating soliloquy, give the measure of Green's compassion. Alex is examining the sterility of the hotel room and marks the "public house lace curtains to guard them in from fog and how many naked bodies on sentry go underneath adequately, inadequately dressed" (p. 195).

Waiting about in basements, whirling waters, naked sentry bodies —these images have no referents in *Party Going* nor in normal life observed beyond the book's confines. They are lyrical—"the simplest verbal vesture of emotions," as Stephen Dedalus would say. Alex's soliloquy continues, recalling past images and pronouncing judgment on the party:

> Here he pointed his moral. That is what it is to be rich . . . if you have to wait then you can do it after a bath in your dressing-gown and if you have to die then not as any bird tumbling dead from its branch down for the foxes, light and stiff, but here in bed, here inside, with doctors to tell you it is all right and with relations to ask if it hurts. Again no standing, no being pressed together . . . no fellow feeling, true, and once more sounds came up from outside to make him think they were singing, no community singing he said to himself, not that even if it did mean fellow feeling. . . . (p. 195)

Yet the party goes on. They are about to leave Miss Fellowes. Julia, ecstatic over the news that the trains will run, rushes into the room where Miss Fellowes is, and is shocked at seeing the transformation in the woman, "who had . . . seemed ageless to her in that her appearance had not altered much in all those years. And now she saw her all at once as very old and for the last time that day she heard the authentic knock of doom she listened for so much when things were not going right. But it was impossible for anything to upset her now they were really going" (p. 244).

Miss Fellowes's legacy to the party is embodied in the man who joins them on the last page—Embassy Richard. None other than Max himself, who is so stunned by the effects of his wealth that he seldom speaks a genuine thought, had let himself say two things about Richard, early in the story. "Poisonous chap," he had said once, and another time, unasked, had offered an appraisal: " 'If he was a bird,' he said, 'he would not last long.' Julia asked him what on earth he meant and got no answer" (pp. 66, 64–65). Alex was to give the answer in the soliloquy I have just quoted.

The tainted core of people and party is hidden by a rind decked out in affluence. For Miss Fellowes, perhaps about to perish like any pigeon, the rind has for an instant been removed and she looks in. But with brown paper she quickly places another wrapping around what she means instinctively to keep. Max, too, has had a peep at a poisonous center, but he means to play Richard off against Amabel, so that he may try out Julia unmolested.* And anyway, the party must inherit an Embassy Richard when they are about to leave their Miss Fellowes. Green may have eased the spring of his trap, but the party-goers cannot be permitted to leave without carrying their authentic doom with them.

* One time in the book Max was able to grin at Amabel, at which her spell was broken: "She gave way at once, half opened her jaws and sat down again. He could see her pink tongue" (p. 185). But she has her day with Max later, and will have more, we feel assured.

''LOVING'' AS A NOVEL OF MANNERS

Henry Green's three war novels make the second war tangential to the lives of his English people. *Caught* and *Back* keep the war at a temporal remove, whereas *Loving,* coming between them, divorces its people spatially from war. At first glance it seems as if *Loving* enabled Green to circumvent the war, which left London ablaze near the end of *Caught,* and which deposited Charley Summers at a country cemetery, repatriated, minus a leg, on the first page of *Back*. *Caught* and *Back* deal with time preceding and following direct physical involvement with war; but *Loving,* set in Ireland when war is at its peak, deals with indirect emotional involvement.

I have chosen to examine *Loving* out of chronological sequence because, in terms of direction and conflict, it has affinities with *Party Going* and *Living*. *Caught* and *Back*, like *Blindness*, postulate calamities, but grant full resolutions to their principal characters. *Living* and *Party Going* do not conclude so affirmatively. Both are ambiguous: Craigan's predicament modifies Lily's affirmation; the party-goers, apparently relieved, carry their doom along with them. Roughly, the same ambiguity is true of the conclusion of *Loving*.

Up until the end of this novel, a family of English landlords, the Tennants, have more or less succeeded in keeping their Irish castle staffed with English servants. Because these servants know they are at a premium, and sweat to make the most of a good thing, they are rather insidiously caught by their safe-and-snug castle, just as the party-goers were caught by their hotel. On the book's last page, though, the two leading figures among these servants—Raunce the butler and housemaid Edie—run off from the castle, we are told, to live happily ever after in England. They have apparently escaped a trap that would have decayed their spirits. Raunce seems to have made a remarkable, positive, patriotic decision. Yet there is room for much speculation as to motive and outcome. What the novel has insinuated by the time the lovers escape provides ambiguous comment upon their prospects: Raunce has been aggravatingly sick, and besides, he had replaced as butler a man who lay dying in the opening lines of this book. That butler, Eldon, had called then a name, "Ellen"; our last look at Raunce finds him doing the same, when he awakes from drowsiness to find his Edie radiant among peacocks and doves.

> "Edie," he appealed soft, probably not daring to move or speak too sharp for fear he might disturb it all. Yet he used exactly the same tone Mr. Eldon had employed at the last when calling his Ellen. "Edie," he moaned. (p. 248)

There is no point in deciding whether Raunce is living on borrowed time or not. Here, as at the end of *Living* and *Party Going*, Green forces one to be equivocal. He left Craigan pining, and Miss

Fellowes exhausted; yet Craigan had shown his strength, and Miss Fellowes was perhaps only drunk—at least a physician pronounced her drunk, and, the party-goers ask, who is to say he was not right? Green himself turned consulting physician when he diagnosed Raunce's dyspepsia. "I myself have ended a novel," he wrote in *Contact*, "with the words 'Over in England they were married and lived happily ever after.' Since then I have often been asked how soon after they got to England the husband died. In this particular case, not unusually, the husband had been made ill—his stomach had been upset—by being in love. Of course, with the theories I hold, my answer invariably is, 'Whenever you think,' although when writing the book I had no idea but that they were to have anything but a long and happy life thereafter." [1]

Whenever or whatever you think—this is the liberty of judgment allowed by the *-ing* novels, whose patterns of continuing struggle rather than struggle-and-resolution make questions as to prognosis rather meaningless. In any of the three novels of catastrophe, a stricken character will be bewitched by his past, or try to assess what brought him to his impasse. But in the *-ing* novels, the stricter focus of both novelist and character is upon the immediate present. And the first level investigated in the *-ing* novels involves the social milieu. Not that society does not make up the enveloping medium of the other novels—it does—but their situations require that the author focus upon personal disasters, and their major figures only reattach themselves to society after having solved private dilemmas.

Remembering that Green once said, "except in disaster, life is oblique in its impact upon people," we might say that life impinges obliquely because, in integrated societies, manners intervene. Therefore, in order to give glimpses into the realities that underlie social relationships, Green puts manners to scrutiny, recording deviations from established norms, or distinctions between nominal conformity and patent disregard. *Loving,* his middle novel, is the last to focus upon the manners of two social classes at one time, and this is another reason why it is related to *Living* and *Party Going.*

When Lionel Trilling talked of "Manners, Morals, and the Novel," he spoke of the attitude of people toward manners as the chief index to their characters, and to their grasp of the differences between appearances and reality.[2] The fealty or faithlessness of characters to manners prescribed by tradition is a measure of both those characters and that tradition. Accordingly, when Mrs. Tennant of *Loving,* proprietress of Kinalty castle, admits to her daughter-in-law that she is keeping the place up for the sake of appearance, whatever is admirable in her tenacity must be tempered by our perception that she has substituted appearance for reality.

> "But in a way I regard this as my war work, maintaining the place I mean. Because we're practically in enemy country here you know, and I do consider it so important from the morale point of view to keep up appearances. . . . Because after all as I always say there are the children to consider. I look upon myself simply as a steward. We could shut Kinalty up tomorrow and go and live in one of the cottages. But if I once did that would your darlings ever be able to live here again?" (pp. 201–202)

Every reason Mrs. Tennant advances here can be traced to the lair of rationalization—the allusion to Ireland as "enemy country," for instance, which allows her to believe that castle-keeping is commensurate with war work. What is impossible for us to conceive is Mrs. Tennant *actually* living in a cottage, as she says she can. The symbol of aristocratic living is what she is trying to preserve—having mistaken it for reality—and not a truly aristocratic life with its attendant responsibilities.

THE WAR ACROSS THE IRISH SEA

The war is to blame for more than Mrs. Tennant's agitation, since, affecting privileged and servant classes alike, it partly accounts for the disruption of manners at Kinalty. For one thing, it has forced an ominous mingling of classes over in safe Ireland. (The cook's small nephew, evacuated from England, is brighter than the young Tennant ladies who are heirs to their grandmother's estate, and he lords it over these girls.) Then there is Raunce's ambiguous attitude toward the war, which affects in turn his responsibility to his position as butler at Kinalty. Pushing forty, Raunce still fears the British Labour Exchange and the Army, as he owns in letters to his mother in England. And since remaining in livery in Ireland means staying out of uniform in England, Raunce keeps the servants under him hopping with threats of the National Service Officer waiting to conscript them should they be discharged.

A casual reading of *Loving* seems to reveal that Raunce is self-interested and patriotic by turns, depending upon the immediate situation with which he must cope at Kinalty; however, I believe a fairly definite change of attitude underlies Raunce's return to England—an attitude involving a shift in loyalty from English mistress to English nation. Raunce resolves another conflict of loyalties, to Edith as a lover and to his mother as a son, by reversing a decision he made early in the story. Instead of having his mother come to Ireland, he decides to bring Edith to England. His mother's stubbornness about remaining in England does much to whet what might be called a quest for loyalty in Raunce. But his shift of allegiance from castle to country is provoked not so much by the war as it is by his involvement in activities at Kinalty that grow too complicated.

Ultimately, the war is a convenient catch-all for the principals in *Loving*. Mrs. Tennant can use the war as an excuse for keeping up appearances, and as an excuse also for the dilapidation of Kinalty; Raunce can use it as a threat, and by means of the threat help establish himself in the butler's position against concerted below-stairs opposition. To Miss Burch, head housekeeper and Raunce's chief antagonist, the war means the possibility of Germans overrunning Ireland and raping all women (a not too dismal prospect); to Albert, Raunce's pantry boy, the war is something to get off to as a tail gunner, in way of compensation for being unable to handle a pantry boy's chores and emotional problems. And the war enables every English subject at Kinalty to give vent to his dislike for the

Irish. As housemaid Kate puts it in one place, "The war's on now all right, and do these rotten Irish care? They make me sick" (p. 37).

But the cast of *Loving* care no more than the Irish—simply because the war is not real to them. Nor can it be, Green implies, for these servants are too avidly interested in themselves and their respective kingdoms—bedroom and nursery, kitchen and pantry, a stable for peacocks—kingdoms well defined within the bounds of "the most celebrated eighteenth-century folly in Eire that had still to be burned down" (p. 220).

Green liberally sprinkles guilt on these purveyors of their own sharply defined social niches; without a hint of censure, he makes it clear that they are guilty, not of selfish unpatriotism, but of contributing to the collapse of manners inside Kinalty castle. Key to this collapse is mutual mistrust on all sides. And source of the mistrust, a source remotely influenced by war, is the pursuit of self-interest at every echelon, resulting in an accumulation of transgressions. What makes *Loving* so funny is that every one transgressed upon is also a transgressor; yet although each character feels himself victimized, there is hardly a thought of self-reproach in the novel.

THE COMIC LEVEL

From this prevailing situation at Kinalty evolves a plot that keeps *Loving* going on its most consistent level—the comic level portraying the collapse of manners. The first and last actions in *Loving* involve transgressions: Raunce's establishment of himself as butler, and his abdication. By threatening to quit, Raunce virtually blackmails Mrs. Tennant into giving him the job; then by brazenly outfacing Miss Burch he is able to usurp old Eldon's chair at the servants' dinner table, and to complete the transition from footman to butler. And when Raunce and Edie finally flee, they do so, as one critic notices, "in defiance of one of the most prescriptive of master-servant relationships—without giving notice." [3]

Between the arbitrary beginning and end (Eldon's death, Raunce's flight) hangs the plot of *Loving*. Of the five chief incidents in the plot, only one does not involve a transgression. That is the loss of Mrs. Tennant's ring, which precipitates the symbolic central action of the story. As for the other four, various keepers of "kingdoms" are transgressed upon or scandalized by outsiders. Edie steals waterglass from the kitchen, intending to preserve peacocks' eggs for beauty treatment (thus a housemaid invades Mrs. Welch's realm); Mrs. Welch's nephew, little Albert, strangles one of Kinalty's peacocks (and now the cook has offended Paddy, the wild, inarticulate Irishman who is keeper of these birds); Edie finds Mrs. Jack Tennant abed with a house guest, Captain Davenport (whereby the housemaids are scandalized by their employers); and when Edie finds the lost ring, a sudden inclination to keep it results in its loss again (now the Tennants are offended by their employees), investigations ensue, and mistrust and guilt fill every scene in merry combinations.

Clearly these events can foster but a skinny plot. And it may seem impossible to relate these goings-on to a love story. Yet waterglass and peacock, the discovery of a ring and the discovery of adultery, are fashioned to fit the development of true love in *Loving*. This is true because the events are recapitulated many times over by the servants. In two scenes especially, the main episodes are recalled in extremely funny fashion. In the middle of the novel, Agatha Burch pays a sick call on old Nanny, custodian of Mrs. Jack's daughters, and drives home to this poor woman the juicy account of Mrs. Jack's adultery; and toward the end, when Mrs. Tennant has returned from a visit to England, Mrs. Welch accosts her with tales of the shambles the servants have made of the house. Burch's obsession is the Captain in the lady's bed, and Welch's the waterglass, but mingled in with their yarns to the nanny and mistress are accounts of the exasperating love affair of Raunce and Edie.

Under the eyes of everyone at the castle (where everyone is estranged from everyone else), squint-eyed Raunce and beauteous Edith have contrived to fall in love. All the evils that beset the castle are assigned by Burch and Welch to this pair. The love affair, in fact, so appals the older ladies that their sense of reality is impaired, and all hopes of genuine communication within the castle fail. When a mouse in the weathervane cogs causes Edie to faint, Miss Burch, arriving late, infers that Raunce has seduced the girl; and Mrs. Welch keeps furious vigil in her kitchen, expecting even pots and pans to be stolen, simply because she has translated the developing love affair into a Raunce-Edie compact to loot the premises. "Criminal?" cries Mrs. Welch to Mrs. Tennant.

> "That's just it Mum. For this is what those two are, that Raunce and his Edith. I don't say nothin' about their being lain all day in each other's arms, and the best part of the night too very likely, though I can't speak to the night time, I must take my rest on guard and watch as I am while it's light outside, lain right in each other's arms," she resumed, "the almighty lovers they make out they are, but no more than fornicators when all's said and done if you'll excuse the expression, where was I? Yes. 'Love' this an' 'dear' that, so they go on day and night, yet they're no better than a pair of thieves Mum, misappropriatin' your goods behind your back." (p. 193)

So we have accusations bred from obsessions, and directed at the lovers, whose condition only accentuates the isolation of the grim wards of the different kingdoms. These older women, as James Hall has pointed out, have been striving to prevent the younger women they stand guard over from being exposed to any biological temptations; but, as Hall says, "All the potential guardians of the moral law are happily ineffective. Mrs. Tennant is too unconcerned, Miss Burch is too horrified by events, and old Nanny Swift, sick, believes only good and sees no evil, hears no evil. The results are merrily anarchic." [4]

Like Craigan of *Living,* these matriarchs are trying to preserve a *status quo;* but they exert nowhere near the force he exerted (and even he was unsuccessful). And so their charges make alliances, and investigate phenomena as their instincts bid them. The cook's girls flirt with tradesmen. Housemaid Kate steals off to minister to Paddy, combs his beanfield hair in his saddleroom kingdom. While Nanny tells a euphemistic story, Mrs. Jack's girls watch doves at a dovecote "quarreling, murdering, and making love again" (p. 60). Edie is pursued by Raunce. And Mrs. Jack entertains the Irish Captain in bed.

In all of this Green is not doctrinaire; he does not side with the young automatically, or blur distinctions among the guardians of the moral law. Certainly the failing he lays bare most incisively is Mrs. Tennant's lack of real concern, which is the chief reason for anarchy below-stairs. Sacrificing everything for the sake of appearances, Mrs. Tennant has a lax grip on transactions at Kinalty, and is repaid by Mrs. Jack's infidelity—for the daughter-in-law has managed to keep up appearances, and has not therefore come under suspicion. But Mrs. Tennant finds, after returning from a sojourn in England, that even appearances have collapsed at Kinalty. The Irish Regina Assurance Company has investigated the lost ring, and appearances, impaired by the guilty consciences of the servants, indicate foul play where none exists. The servants act suspiciously because of *other* infractions they are trying to keep hidden.

With what we might call cosmic irony, Green contrives to have Mrs. Tennant shaken by the appearance of connivance that greets her return from a visit to her warrior son in England. Uncertainty drives her to evaluate the entire personal climate at Kinalty and to strike upon the word "distrust." Responding guiltily to that word, Mrs. Jack gives herself away to her mother-in-law, so that cosmic justice concludes its cycle, and near the end of the novel reality begins to make its first advance upon Mrs. Tennant's citadel of appearance. "I shall get to the bottom of it," she says, sending a grim look at her unsuspecting daughter-in-law's back (p. 224).

Green's treatment of Mrs. Jack's infidelity shows that he does not exploit the lost authority of Kinalty's matriarchs in doctrinaire fashion. For Mrs. Jack, who has let her passion for Captain Davenport get the better of her, is decidedly in no state of loving. Her guilt is overpowering, she shies at every word she hears—and what is more, she bickers with the Captain, wishing she could get him out of her system. Some critics of Green misinterpret *Loving* when they associate too freely the various incidents of "loving" as manifestations of sexuality not-to-be-denied. Of various possible citations, one of the most concisely expressed is this of reviewer John Farrelly: "The incidents [of loving] accumulate and reinforce one another, but there is scarcely any distinction between the servants, Mrs. Jack, or the doves. The 'loving' is impersonal passion. . . ." [5]

On the contrary, there are great distinctions among the three. Mrs. Jack's licentiousness, for one thing, causes her totally to disregard her own children. Those children in turn, at their ages displaying their accord with blind, greedy, often cruel processes of nature, are innocent and disinterested beings. While their nanny spins her euphemistic yarn, "facing that dovecote shut-eyed and deaf," Kate and Edie come upon the children watching the copulating, murdering doves. "All five," writes Green, "began soundlessly giggling in the face of beauty" (p. 58). But this scene is complemented later by another, after Edith has become more aware of her feelings for Raunce. The housemaids and Raunce's Albert have taken the children on a seashore picnic. Down by the water, a crab has fastened onto little Albert's toe, and the servants, with Peter the donkey, watch the proceedings from a hillock.

> The excited shrieks that came back from the children blanketed a screaming from gulls fighting over the waste food which they had thrown away, although Raunce's Albert still had some scraps in a paper bag.
> . . . Then just as Edith was about to get up to help that crab fell off. The children began to stone it, driving it blow upon blow into a grave its own shape in the sand. At which Peter put his ears back and snatched the scraps out of Albert's hand, swallowed them bag and all. (pp. 142–143)

Here we have cruelty and greed juxtaposed, tempered by a measure of the comic treatment. But if gulls, crab, donkey, and children are responding to instincts of self-preservation, Edith is not—she is careful, watchful; while Kate sleeps and Albert ogles, Edith sits "bolt upright to keep an eye on the children." Her matronliness, in fact, becomes accentuated after her affair with Raunce has begun to blossom, whereas beforehand she too had been essentially disinterested. It is important to recognize that Edith, who respects moral conventions, worries over Raunce's swollen glands, works hard in the castle, and dearly loves the Tennant girls, lives on a different plane from the children. Significantly, she herself regards them as "innocent." Although she consents to leave Kinalty without giving notice, she balks at leaving without saying goodbye to the little girls. "But it wouldn't be right," she tells Raunce. "Why they're innocent."

> " 'Ow d'you mean, innocent?" he inquired. "There's a lot we could lay to their door."
>
> "They're not grown up," she explained. "They've got their lives to live yet. They mightn't understand if I was to go off without a word." (p. 245)

Banal as they are, Edie's sentiments reveal her intuition of responsibilities accruing to adult experience. Those in a state of loving in this book may not be consciously aware of the alliances they have formed, but they actually do assume responsibilities—the process by which they become "loving" involves a shift from an innocent, self-centered fascination with the world about them to an attachment with and concern for others. This is illustrated during the course of the novel by Edie's gradual estrangement from lovelorn Kate. Where earlier their amorous small talk had made them thick as thieves, later Kate grows jealous and taunts Edie about her preoccupation with the butler. Edie, having begun to assert managing instincts, actually loses contact with Kate because she will not let a girlish complicity intrude upon her newly forming plans for herself and Raunce.

As Edith becomes purposive and competent she displays capacities that Green rather fearfully admires in those women in his novels who handily manage their men. But for Raunce, the change from free-lance butler to husband-to-be is radical and disturbing—and this is not only manifested by his swollen glands. Before his entanglement with Edie, Raunce had been swaggering and shrewd. He had ensconced himself as butler, set up a neat game of cheating on the books, and kept well oiled the machinery of the "smooth-running organization" (in James Hall's phrase) that he so admired. But complexities attend his new-found love. He must extend his purview and make schemes for Edie's welfare too. In one of the book's memorable scenes, he races off with the plucked carcass of a peacock, and nails it in the cook's larder; his motive is to defy Mrs. Welch, who suspects Edie of having stolen waterglass, by brandishing evidence that the cook herself is responsible for a greater transgression—her little Albert having wrung the peacock's neck.

Though we are charmed to find Raunce so spontaneously capable, the entangling responsibilities of butlerhood and love affair grow too complex for him in the end. One symptom of the new and protective role he assumes is his serious concern for the women at Kinalty— in view of the German invasion of Ireland which the servants dread so irrationally. Raunce reminds them that there are shotguns at Kinalty in the event of an emergency, and when they chide him about these inconsequential weapons, " 'What I had in mind was a cartridge each for you ladies,' he replied in a low voice. Utterly serious he was" (p. 104). And because he himself now has a vested interest, he continues off and on to succumb to the general hysteria. It is he who confuses the Irish Regina Assurance with the Irish Republican Army, which the servants groundlessly believe to be in league with the Germans. "Why spell me out those letters," he demands of his Albert, who has shown him the adjustor's card.

> ". . . Irish Regina Assurance. I.R.A., boy. So 'e was one of their scouts, must 'a' been."
> "I.R.A.?"
> "Where's my girl?" Raunce asked and dashed out. (p. 169)

Raunce's patriotism, too, bristles along with his sense of responsibility toward Edith and the household. Where earlier his conversation would grow threatening with allusions to "the Army for you my lad, old king and country and all the rest" (p. 63), later we find

less pungent expressions, indicating a gradual shift of attitude.*
And when Edie, having found and hidden Mrs. Tennant's ring, suggests that they keep this prize, Raunce runs for the first time against
a problem of moral responsibility, and blanches. (Custom may allow for slowly accumulating nest eggs, but it does not leave room
for capitalizing on lost rings and the like. Charley is explicit on this
point.)

Indeed, it is because Charley has had a taste of moral responsibility that the situation at Kinalty, changed wholly by the ring episode, becomes bewildering to him. He is forced to choose between
two loyalties; and in shielding Edie while she attempts to recover
the ring, he is derelict in his duties to Mrs. Tennant.

Not that Raunce realizes his dereliction. What is most excellent
in Green's characterization of both Raunce and Edith is the spontaneity of their self-defense—by which they seem to declare, and we
to accept, that they have been innocent all along. So at the inquisition, when the lisping adjustor Mike Mathewson seems to have cornered Edith, and Raunce's Albert blurts out that he has the ring,
Edie rushes to his defense in unfeigned self-righteousness:

> . . . she turned on the assessor, blushing dark.
> ". . . an' who may you be to come scarin' honest folk that
> earn a living?" She spoke loud. "You get off h'out, there's the
> best place for you. We don't want none of your sort here,
> frightenin' his wits out of the lad. . . . If I was a man I'd
> show him off the premises," she said panting to Raunce. (p.
> 163)

Raunce later reacts similarly to the stubborn investigation of
Mike Mathewson, who has of course smelled a rat. Raunce sets the
blame for the nerve-shaking ordeal on the absentee Mrs. Tennant,

---

* "Well it looks like we're out of it over in Eire as we are," he tells Edie
later. "I can't seem to express myself, but there you are" (p. 176). His
reasons seem clearer to him when the shift of attitude is complete. "It's too
bloody neutral, this country is," bursts from him near the end, and he has
even begun to worry whether he is a coward (p. 237).

even though Edith has pointed out that an investigation is a matter of course.

> "I'm not disputing that," Raunce countered, "but what I say is Mrs. T. should've been here to receive 'im. We're plain honest folk we are. This is not the first position of trust we've held down." (p. 229)

Because the lovers can so readily affix guilt in other guarters, they are in effect self-exculpated. Moreover, the guilt seems to stick in the other quarters; Mrs. Tennant seems in a way culpable when Raunce, feeling undervalued, decides to quit the place. If all the shielding Raunce must do makes life at the castle too complicated for him, Mrs. Tennant's inattention and willingness to deputize are the remote causes of the disorder. Raunce's laying the blame at her door is another instance of superb irony on Green's part. She has neither looked to her personal effects (and has therefore lost the ring) nor attended to any of the human problems which beset the wayward members of her feudal "family." The ring episode is structurally pivotal, because it brings to full development the two chief actions of the book: the disintegration of manners in a charade of feudal living, and the integration of the servants, who join forces under the stress of the investigation.

FAMILY LOVE

As James Hall has said, "Mrs. Tennant's loss of the ring implies loss of direction and loss of capacity for loving, while its passing to Edith, who has both in plenty, is the passing of a symbol of power." [6] The power is not Edith's alone, it turns out, but a power of alliance and mutual sacrifice, common for a time to all the servants, who have rallied to protect one another. Among these servants, temporarily, are established loving relationships which signify more fully than any sexual alliance the condition of life we might call "loving."

Perhaps William York Tindall comes closest of any critic to identifying the spirit of these loving relationships, when he says, "Surely wider than the affair of mistress and lover or the pursuit of servant by servant, 'loving,' responsible and adult, implies connection, giving, acceptance, all that is foreign to the house." [7]

Although Tindall believes it "foreign to the house," the kind of loving he talks about does occur just after the mid-point of the novel, and such loving should perhaps deserve the adjective "familial." The servants, in fact, act like a family, gathered round their table as we so often find them, airing their views and observing hierarchical distinctions. Green's view of loving relationships commonly includes the family structure, although it most often transcends bonds of blood-kinship (which Green often treats as detrimental to true loving).*

Without demanding point-by-point correspondences, we find that in the servant-family in *Loving* Miss Burch is cast in the role of mother, and Raunce as the aggressor who would split the old dominion (of Eldon) and acquire a partner in the process (Edith). But when an outside threat is posed—it might be war, it might be Mike Mathewson, I.R.A.—Raunce lapses into the father role and rules in fairly even accord with Miss Burch. (In this connection, note the possessives that are attached to many of the young servants' names: Raunce's Albert, Mrs. Welch's Albert, Miss Burch's girls.)

Now when Mike Mathewson interrogates Edith, lovesick Albert sacrifices himself most awkwardly for her by confessing he has the ring he has never seen. Amid the hilarity of the ensuing scene, a real union has been achieved among the servants present. Raunce responds to his girl's demand for manly action, and in a fit of agitation drives Mathewson from the castle. He is rescuing his Albert, not his Edie. As soon as the assessor has quitted the premises, Raunce wildly reviles palsied Albert, but later softens toward the

---

* Quick glances into past and future, in terms of this study, reveal Green's predilection for foster parents and pseudo-heads of families. Think of Mrs. Haye of *Blindness,* Craigan of *Living,* Pye's sister in *Caught,* old grandfather Rock of *Concluding,* and Mrs. Grant, who becomes Nancy's foster mother in *Back.*

boy. "It did your heart credit to speak up when you did, mind," he tells him later. "But you'll discover it don't pay to have a heart on most occasions" (p. 168).

Shortly after these incidents, a telegram announces that Mrs. Tennant will return from England, upon which Raunce decides to let the rest of the servants know about the unnerving visit of the I.R.A. man. He chooses to begin with a typically banal remark: "Well we're all one family in this place, there's how I see the situation," he tells them (p. 170).

Events prove the trivial sentiment significant, in Green's customary backhanded fashion, which again finds him punning on situations as Joyce does on words. Mention of the inquisitor only serves to work everyone up into the usual hysteria about invading Germans and traitorous Irishmen. At the peak of the commotion Albert speaks up from a face gone dead white, and announces that he intends to enlist forthwith as an air gunner.

The force of Albert's announcement is stunning, and all forget their individual phobias. Raunce blusters and chortles in turn, the girls sigh—then the sort of automatic cohesion that crisis can produce in the rattled little group shows itself once more, as Edith tends the bawling mother-of-them-all, Miss Burch, and Raunce finds himself, at the end of the disrupted meal, clearing away the dinner things "for his lad Albert. He surprised himself doing it" (p. 181). Later, still in consternation over the announcement, Raunce says to Edith, "Why it's almost as if 'e was me own son" (p. 179). (Raunce's tune changes whenever he happens to think of Albert as a rival lover. Then he may fume at Edie, "That damned kid's attitude was what got my goat. The highfalutin love he laid claim to, the suffering looks he darted, 'is faintin' snotty ways" [p. 234].)

From the time that Edie finds the ring, and simultaneously becomes engaged to Raunce, an atmosphere of gravity settles over the servant quarters. The gravity may be relieved by little flurries of merriment at the dinner table—as when at the last dinner the servants fall to mocking Mike Mathewson's lisp. Such capacity for merriment seems to be what Green admires most in his people, for it enables them unconsciously to debase totem threats, like that posed by the I.R.A. man, into objects of ridicule. In doing so, they reveal that they simply cannot take such threats seriously for very long. The trick is, of course, that the humor be spontaneous. Meanwhile, ambiguity is cast over the entire lisping scene because of its remarkable conclusion. Raunce, who has not been looking well, is "in his convulsions of laughter . . . noticeably paler"; all wear "a look of agony, or as though they were in a close finish to a race over a hundred yards" (p. 230). The entire scene, which appears to be terribly funny, becomes grim as well (in the manner of Céline). In spite of the pain, the servants cannot resist parting shots, which only double them further over in pain. (The same might be said for the elections people make in the regular courses of their lives—in their mating and their creation of families, for example.)

Loving, then, like most of Green's work, is both a funny and a grim book. Near the end we find Edith grave, obeying the generative instinct, not disposed to giggling, as she had been earlier. "It's a hard bloody world," she tells Kate, commiserating with her over her need for the uncouth Paddy (p. 210). And as Edie grows sober and possessive, the older ladies begin to disappear from the foreground. Miss Burch, Miss Swift, and Mrs. Welch are all ominously sick at the time of that final dinner gathering. Raunce now presides in full sway, with wifely Edith in Miss Burch's place next him. It would seem that, with his opponents remanded to their sickrooms, Raunce is in the ascendant—but he is grave, and moody. He comes out at last with some vulgarism about Mrs. Welch's kidney condition, as dinner commences, only to have Edith take offense.

> "Charley," Edith remonstrated.
> "Pardon," he said. He sent her a glance that seemed saturated with despair. (p. 225)

But for all the nagging and managing, for all the pitfalls of responsibility that accompany adult loving, it is within some semblance of family structure (the end product of such loving) that all gestures of "connection, giving, acceptance" are made in this book. The fact that Green loads the "family gatherings" with banalities does not diminish their temporary effect, which is to bind the servants to each other, even to the extent of their recognizing parental and filial duties. It is no accident that the servants possess the mansion and what joys and tribulations of the hearth it may entail. The most obvious structural divisions in *Loving* reinforce this notion. In the first and last divisions, covering approximately one half the novel, the Tennants are at Kinalty and manners and tempers are kept ruinous; but during the middle section, the Tennants are gone, and the bonds forged in the novel are forged then. The Tennants' folly in keeping the castle, for its testimonial to their way of life, is perhaps most ironically indicated through the name Green gives them. For they are no more than tenants. Even Kinalty's treasures, compounded of beauty and folly, are accessible only to the servants.

THE POETIC LEVEL

So far we have examined two levels at which *Loving* communicates. These might be called the social level, involving the collapse of manners, and the personal level, involving loving attachments formed between stress-ridden individuals. There remains a third level, the poetic or metaphorical, along which the novel moves. What Green communicates on this plane he does by images—sounds, colors, reflections, figures—and by scenes juxtaposing qualities dynamic and static. Although a pattern of symbols can be determined, one runs the risk of systematizing them and thereby reducing their force. Whatever meanings one fixes on, then, can be assigned only with the admission that other meanings may inhere.

We may begin by saying that besides the social "kingdoms" in *Loving,* there are also different worlds. The world of Raunce and Edie is most dynamic. (Once, after snipping a flower from a vase in the morning room, Raunce is seen to "shut that green door to open his kingdom," whereupon "he punted the daffodil ahead like a rugger ball" [p. 10].) Three scenes in *Loving* epitomize Raunce's kinetic world, by counterposing to it the worlds of English castle and Irish land, respectively dead and dormant.

To introduce these scenes better, we might note that Green mocks
whatever regality the castle or old Ireland may lay claim to. Kinalty's gold bedroom has harbored the adultery of Mrs. Jack and
Davenport; their affair began at nearby Clancarty bog, where the
Captain had been digging for the remains of old kings (and whence,
Edith knows, Mrs. Jack once returned minus her underpants). Most
of the kingly treasures the castle houses are locked away in disused
places, where furniture wears white sheets, and a ballroom lies
fallow with white blinds drawn. Into such places goes Edie, garbed
in her housemaid's royal purple, to hold temporary sway. And as for
Ireland, Paddy the lampman seems to have inherited its sceptre—
a dormant savage, as it were, made king of a regressive land. In
one of the three symbolic scenes, Kate and Edie spy on Paddy
asleep in his lamp room.

> It was a place from which light was almost excluded now
> by cobwebs across its two windows and into which, with the
> door ajar, the shafted sun lay in a lengthened arch of blazing
> sovereigns. Over a corn bin on which he had packed last
> autumn's ferns lay Paddy snoring between these windows, a
> web strung from one lock of hair back onto the sill above and
> which rose and fell as he breathed. Caught in the reflection of
> spring sunlight this cobweb looked to be made of gold as did
> those others which by working long minutes spiders had drawn
> from spar to spar of the fern bedding on which his head rested.
> It might have been almost that O'Conor's dreams were held by
> hairs of gold binding his head beneath a vaulted room on which
> the floor of cobbles reflected an old king's molten treasure from
> the bog.
>   . . . "If I make a crown out of them ferns in the corner,"
> Edith said, "will you fetch something he can hold?" (p. 54)

But Paddy already has his crown— a gold web spun on old fern.
From roof to floor the molten gold reflects (reflections and reverber-
ations are Green's favorite devices for robbing space of its limits).
Even Paddy's peacocks, behind their glass partition, are "hardly to

be recognized in this sovereign light. For their eyes had changed to rubies, their plumage to orange . . ." (p. 55). Metallic spiders' webs, ruby-eyed birds—what usually betokens organic force seems now converted to lifeless ornament, and the element of time is also distorted as the birds, as if "stuffed in a dusty case," show themselves from time to time "across the heavy days" as they come to look at Paddy.

Into this stasis Raunce intrudes, bent on examining the stores of corn for the peacocks. At his game of rigging the books for his profit, he frightens the birds off and startles the girls:

> Then again they were gone with a beat of wings, and in their room stood Charley Raunce, the skin of his pale face altered by refraction to red morocco leather.
>
> The girls stood transfixed as if by arrows between the Irishman dead motionless asleep and the other intent and quiet behind a division. Then, dropping everything, they turned, they also fled. (p. 55)

Intrusive, insensitive to any charm or beauty here, Raunce is nevertheless bold and dynamic; the "red morocco leather" of his face, usually pale, seems to signify a vigor that is keyed by his intentness. Green is the color prevailingly associated with Raunce, a color signifying his anxiety and physical need; * red, a vitalistic color, is associated rather with Edith; but at the time of this saddle-room episode Raunce has not yet fallen in love and hence has not yet felt physical and emotional urgencies later to beset him. His presence shatters the stasis.

This scene would not deserve such emphasis had not Green provided two more like it, which involve Edie, wrapt in the delights of the instant, her beauty highlighted by contrast to static and formal beauty disposed about her, of which she is unaware. Into these scenes Raunce again intrudes, uninnocent, bent now on finding his

---

* At the moment that Raunce proposes to Edie, for example, and she plays coquettishly with his question, we are told that when he glances her way at last, "His white face was shot with green from the lawn" (p. 153).

Edie, distressingly serious—and Raunce is the one who will dissolve her indifference. This is why, symbolically, Edie and Kate flee from the lamproom scene that had transfixed them—for their foreshadowed commitments to Raunce and Paddy signify their loss of pure detachment, the source of their pure delight.

On the second of these pivotal occasions, Raunce, having tracked Edith down to an unused ballroom by following the sound of a gramophone, enters grouchily upon one of the most resplendent scenes in *Loving*. Edith and Kate are waltzing.

> They were wheeling, wheeling in each other's arms heedless at the far end where they had drawn up the white blinds. Above from a rather low ceiling five great chandeliers swept one after the other almost to the waxed parquet floor, reflecting in their hundred thousand drops the single sparkle of distant day, again and again red velvet walls, and two girls, minute in purple, multiplied to eternity in these trembling pears of glass.
>
> "You're daft," he called out. They stopped with their arms about each other. Then as he walked up they disengaged to rearrange their hair, and still the waltz thundered. He switched it off. The needle grated. (p. 65)

Where Raunce in his approach to the ballroom has been furtive, has left sheeted furniture untouched and dipped fingers but once, tentatively, into a bowl of flower relics, the girls have flung up the white blinds and danced in a whirl of color. Raunce is too cautious and deliberate to be able to cope with new worlds, which Edith can transgress upon and make over as she pleases; here Green makes the same contrast he had made in *Living*, between Jim Dale and Lily, and in *Blindness*, between John Haye and Joan. Like Green's other males, Raunce is so burdened with immediate concerns that he cannot seize, as the girls can, upon the moment of joy. "You're daft," can only burst from him. He puts a stop to the waltz, makes the needle grate.

Green makes a final juxtaposition of static and dynamic elements when, on a rainy day, he has Edith, the Tennant girls, and Raunce's

Albert take part in a game of blind man's buff under oversize ancient statuary in Kinalty's Skullpier Gallery. The place is a replica of a Greek temple; the blindfold is Edie's sopping red scarf, on which are written the words "I love you I love you." The gods and heroes the statues represent—their immobility, their arrested attitudes hinting at the ideal-in-potential of the figures on Keats's urn—receive far from reverential treatment at Green's hands; his attitude to the fixed and the immutable can again be seen to approach Lawrence's.

Rain and damp have made the gallery sepulchral. We hear the children's giggles "ricocheting from stone-cold bosoms to damp streaming marble bellies . . ." (p. 123). The language itself tends to disparage the ideal. Here Green refers to "bellies"; a moment before, he had described one statue as "a half-dressed lady that held a wreath at the end of her two long arms." To those long arms Green contrasts the stubby arms of Miss Moira, when she catches Albert. Yet when Albert kisses her, "Her child's skin was electric hot under a film of water" (p. 122). Upon the child, water enhances vitality; but damp, streaming bellies only accentuate the lifelessness of stone-cold marble.

Statues and statue-like Albert are equally disdained by Edith and the girls, who circle about while Albert stands rooted, or shriek "disinterested" when he is caught. Their game goes on, until, during one blindfolding, "there was an interruption. As Edith knelt before the child a door in the wall opened with a grinding shriek of rusty hinge and Raunce entered upon a scene which this noise and perhaps also his presence had instantly turned to more stone" (p. 123).

Pursuing his Edie again, Raunce is announced by a grating noise which operates like that earlier grating victrola needle and stops all action. Raunce makes it clear he has no use for their game. Soon after, Edie asks a strange question. "How's your neck dear?" she says, and, her attitude shifting finally to one of matronly concern, she orders the butler back to dryer parts of the castle. Obeying Edith, he leaves.

Here, at the exact middle of *Loving,* Edie's power of remaining indifferent has been modified, and her power of taking joy indifferently from every environment modified as well. But the treasures of the other worlds she has entered—Paddy's lamp room, the ballroom, and the Skullpier Gallery—have been stagnant; their enchantment has lain solely in that they have furnished Edie with joy and wonder or served as backdrops to her flashing beauty. Eschewing such hideaways in the end, she becomes involved in Raunce's world—one of activity, efficiency, transience, need, and support. Still Edie remains life's high priestess in this novel, and though she has shifted allegiance from the many to the one—to Raunce, whom she will jealously manage—she retains sway over life and loving in flux.

PEACOCKS, DOVES, MICE

Toward the end of *Loving,* Edith has been laying out domestic plans so fervidly that she and Raunce have an altercation. She has had her eye on the unoccupied butler's cottage on the grounds, but Raunce wants to quit Ireland altogether, once he feels his efforts at Kinalty have gone unappreciated. Even though Raunce by this time has been fairly running in traces, he sticks with remarkable tenacity to his decision, and only accidentally wins Edie over, when she warms to the idea of being carried off in an elopement. No sooner does she assent than his usually gray-greenish face flushes "an alarming ugly purple," signifying in suffusion of blood the relief he feels at having got past this last crisis (p. 246).

It is here that the book ends with Raunce overwhelmed at the sight of his Edie, ministered to in her royal purple by "the peacocks bowing at her purple skirts, the white doves nodding on her shoulders round her brilliant cheeks . . ." (p. 252).

Screams of the peacocks punctuate many vignettes throughout *Loving* that are charged with currents of latent sexuality. When Kate teases Edie about having Charley in their room, before the love affair, Green juxtaposes to Edie's screech the scream of a peacock; and soon after, to attend our first glimpse of the Captain and Mrs. Jack, Green inserts the sentence, "Then there was a real outcry from the peacocks" (p. 41). All through the novel these birds make alarming, even fateful appearances. And their flamboyance, in their prime of life, is allayed by the continual intrusion of the two chief plot devices—the waterglass that preserves the eggs of unborn peacocks for beauty treatment, and the stinking carcass of the dead peacock, which cannot be distinguished from chicken, and which hangs in the larder, a fatal reminder.

Whatever optimism counterbalances such forebodings springs from the fact that the peacocks and all nature seem to be in an arcane conspiracy with Edith. At the first stirrings of sexual awareness in Edie, stirrings that lurk behind the shocked giggles she and Kate exchange, the peacocks parade; it is the onset of spring: "Both girls giggled. The sky was overcast so that the light was dark as though under water. The afternoon was warm. It was the first afternoon to be warm since autumn. Though they could not see them the peacocks below were beginning to parade" (p. 39).

And if this is a processional, then the recessional occurs near the end when Edie lets Raunce know, for the only time, what their marriage will hold in store for him:

> "I mean after we're married," she whispered, her voice gone husky. "After we're married I'll see to it that you don't have no imagination. I'll make everything you want of me now so much more than you ever dreamed that you'll be quit imaginin' for the rest of your life."
>
> "Oh honey," he said in a sort of cry and kissed her passionately. But a rustling noise interrupted them.
>
> "What's that?" he asked violent.
>
> "Hush dear," she said, "it'th only the peacockth."
>
> And indeed a line of these birds one after the other and hardly visible in this dusk was making tracks back to the stables. (p. 207)

Edie's trap for Raunce, body and soul, is wholly sprung here with the promise of a vice grip on his imagination. By such traps, Green may be saying, does nature provide her own continuum. Although in the contrasted splendor and decay of the scenes that celebrate Edie, in her hedonism and Raunce's unlovely desperation (that even makes him sick), there seem to be overtones of sterility that call to mind, say, Eliot's "A Game of Chess," Green still seems to perceive a kind of order and promise funded in natural processes of decomposition. Nature is in complicity with Edie, from the attendant doves and peacocks, to the sad dog Badger, who looks grief-stricken at her and Raunce on the last page. "He'd never catch a mouse that had lost all its legs," Raunce says of the dog in derision (p. 247). Raunce is just that kind of mouse, well-caught. Once, a hundred pages earlier, a real mouse had seemed in collusion with Edie—a mouse caught in a weathervane cog, behind a panel she had opened. After Edie had let out a shriek, a "silence of horror" had fallen: "Then even over the rustle of Kate hurrying up a paper-thin scream came as if in answer from between the wheels" (p. 48).

What can this mean? That nature's provision for a continuum leaves room only for an equal provision for horror? Perhaps. Perhaps again the mouse signifies the natural thwarted, trapped by the artificial—by the ludicrous machinery of a castle of folly, which the lovers must escape.

Whatever grimness inheres in the images of mice, and murdering doves, and murdered peacock, this grimness is softened by reverential images that abound in *Loving,* celebrating the instinctual responses of humans and animals. Paddy "worships" the birds, we hear, and Edie "worships" the little girls. Edie goes on her knees to Albert after his silly sacrifice for her, and in fact had been found kneeling by Mathewson when he had been admitted to the Red Library: "So it was Albert showed him in where Edith was still on her knees after a proposal of marriage, as if tidying" (p. 156). And when human beings honor nature, nature reciprocates by honoring them. Copying the doves bowing beak to beak at the dovecote, Moira and Evelyn nod deeply to one another across the lap of their shut-eyed nanny, and then spy Edith and Kate, who "bow swaying towards them in soft sunlight . . . fingers over lips" (pp. 57–58). The final image, of peacocks bowing and doves nodding to the housemaid, constitutes but a repayment in kind, from animal emissaries of na-

ture's thriving and destroying kingdom to its leading human emis-
sary in *Loving*, Edith.

What finally can we say of Green's vision in this his middle novel,
and how it may have changed? In the first place, *Loving* reveals that
Green's conviction of the reality of material needs has deepened,
and that because of this his optimism has declined. Kate, the most
forlorn figure in *Loving*, is incapable of making any such affirmation
in the face of disheartening prospects as Joan could make in *Blindness*, or Lily in *Living*. Kate's needs find succor only in her last-
ditch attachment to uncouth Paddy. Though she fosters this Irishman
(as Lily did Craigan, or Joan her father), it is on a more reciprocal
basis, for she means to marry the man.

Green seems now to feel that such intangible achievements as
those of John Haye and Lily Gates are not possible. *Party Going*,
meantime, has presented a formidable view of women (and *Caught*,
as we shall see, has involved a repudiation of them). Green's women
are henceforth seen to be aggressive and overpowering, whether
they are predatory (as in *Party Going*) or (as in *Loving*) maternal.
The sexual control wielded by Edith in *Loving* is as autonomous as
it was in the hands of Angela or Amabel. In *Loving* sexual control
is linked with the managing of spouses, whereas in *Party Going* it
was a means toward self-gratification.

It may be a dubious honor for males to be so managed (as Raunce
is), but marriage, Green seems now to think, is relatively speaking
the best of human lots, offering most happiness. One simply does
best to accept its unideal aspects, which range from the managing of
a man's table manners to control over his imagination. Insofar as
Edie will realize its promises, marriage seems most in harmony with
natural and humane designs—involving procreation and sacrifice.

James Hall has called Green the novelist of "a war generation
. . . that lives with so great a social and physical mobility as to
make ideals of continuity and traditional living like Forster's seem
impossible." [8] This assessment is sound; in the charade the Tennants
have made of traditional living Green does sense dissolution. Still,
Loving ends ambiguously; and when Raunce and Edie depart for
England, we have grounds for anticipating a productive union—for

we have seen their resilience as well as their crassness at Kinalty. Despite themselves, almost, they have acted unselfishly under stress, especially when Albert made his two eye-popping announcements— that he had the ring, and that he would enlist. Then the paternal surged upward in Raunce, and the maternal in Edith softened in solicitude. Remembering, as Hall says, that traditional English norms have become defunct in Green's view, we may still suggest that here he reaches back to the inception of civilized tradition— which tradition, arising from man's natural fecundity and his occasional ability to sacrifice, results in the configuration of the family structure. In short, Green falls back on loving.

INSULAR PASTS

In *Caught* and *Back,* the novels that flank *Loving,* Henry Green ex-
plores the phenomenon of interdependence—between individuals and
the state, and among individuals themselves. Dealing with England
in wartime, both books dramatize the ineffectuality of people and
government to discharge responsibilities to one another under the
stress of impending or actual war. Thus in one sense Green portrays
war as a disintegrating force, yet in doing so he keeps war largely
peripheral—at a temporal remove. We do not see much of the processes of war's physical destruction. In *Caught* there are two scenes
of London afire, but these in a way punctuate or offset the book's

crucial episodes, which have centered about the London Fire Brigade
waiting to go into action; in *Back* bombers intermittently pass over-
head, but they are incidental to the story of Charley Summers's re-
patriation. Moreover, his loss of a leg and his confinement in prison
camp are events of the past never faced frontally, because Charley
has wilfully barred them from his memory.

The settings of *Caught* and *Back* are more highly evocative of
London than are the settings of any of Green's other books. As is
usual with him, these settings go far toward accounting for his
people's behavior. In *Back,* the economic pressures on Londoners in
the late stages of the war charge the atmosphere powerfully and
give the book its "climate." By the time Charley Summers is sent
home by the Germans, the game among London civilians has become every-man-for-himself. In *Caught,* conversely—since the war
has not yet struck, much less abated—the main tension felt is the
need to consolidate; and in every possible way people force themselves to reach out to one another (though we know from *Pack My
Bag* that Green inclines to view such people as acting "with an eye
to self preservation").

It should be emphasized that war, as it pervades the lives of
Green's Londoners without quite touching them, intensifies their
phobias and incites their greed, and consequently, as in *Loving,* dis-
rupts free exchange between them. Because Mrs. Frazier, Charley
Summers's landlady, is fourth in a grocery line, and because the
grocer is serving up something special from under the counter, she
cannot respond to Charley's acute emotional need at one stage of
Back. He only wants to draw her aside to ask a question. "What?"
Mrs. Frazier retorts. "With me only four from the shop?" (p. 69).
And she finds a way to get rid of him, distracted in grief though he
is. *Caught* and *Back* teem with cupidity of this sort.

As for phobias, an example from *Caught* is typical of men who
throw up shaky organizations to bring concerted action against danger. Sub-officer Albert Pye, a regular fireman promoted when the
London Brigade absorbs civilian auxiliaries, is haunted in *Caught*
by the impersonal authority vested in higher echelons. Fire Station
Fifteen, the domain of Pye's immediate superior, Trant, contains all

that Pye dreads—and well might he dread officialdom, when it turns out that Trant is a snooping martinet, himself phobia-ridden. Once, for example, Pye describes Trant and a crony, about to hold a fire drill on Pye's substation, as having sneaked along a building, faces averted, like "cat burglars"—until they could dash into the watch-room and "put the bells down." "But the Job used to 'ave dignity," says Pye. ". . . The officers didn't go creepin' around" (p. 91).

Trant's craven action takes place within the frame of a Kafkaish hierarchy. When the London Brigade is placed under stress, every operative begins fearing the next higher echelon. All nerves stretch taut while the bombers are awaited, and detestable behavior like Trant's is no more than a form of psychological release, masquerad-ing as the official safeguard of a man in authority.

Trant's suspicion and Mrs. Frazier's cupidity may be said to have been caused by prevailing conditions in England, but we recall that mistrust and greed were the dominant symptoms of the characters in *Loving*, who were not in such a dangerous situation. The lesser characters in *Caught* and *Back* are of the same stamp as Trant and Mrs. Frazier; indeed, I have documented the behavior of these two in order to suggest their place in that great gallery of restive souls from which Green populates his comic novels. And once recognizing that many people in *Caught* and *Back* behave like people in the comic novels, we perceive that the peripheral threat of war is hardly a greater disruptive agency than was the fog of *Party Going*, or the lost ring in *Loving*. As long as war does not touch them, people living in its shadow are oblivious to its devastating import; no one's experience is transferable to another, and life continues to impinge obliquely. But when we meet the protagonists of *Caught* and *Back*, we discover that they differ from the minor characters in that the blighting force of war has driven into their lives; they have suffered acute physical loss, and what they have lost is indelibly connected with their pasts. It is as if war has announced its real self to these men, Richard Roe and Charley Summers, not only by catching them up in crises of violent action, but by bestowing on them legacies that cannot physically be attributed to war—a dead wife, and a dead lover.

Green employs coincidence to make these private losses symbolic of war's blight. Roe is freshly widowed when he volunteers for the Auxiliary Fire Service. In the early pages of *Caught,* he visits his son on the family estate near Wales, and there calls to mind his wife and their life together, "picking up the thread where the war had unravelled it" (p. 33). As for Summers, the very day he is committed to a German prison camp, his beloved Rose, wife to another man, dies in England. These bereavements are the bases on which the plots of *Caught* and *Back* are built.

Searching into their pasts as no other of Green's characters do, Richard and Charley remain unconscious of what marred their lives in those past attachments—two kinds of isolation from humanity—but they make a kind of oblivious atonement by their purgative experiences in the war. Quite simply, Richard's and Charley's pasts were insular, just as John Haye's past at Noat School had been insular.

No sooner do we differentiate Roe's kind of isolation from Charley's than we fix the relationship of *Caught* and *Back* to *Loving.* *Caught* deals with the problem of social class, and *Back* with the larger problem, as Green comes to see it, of society's obligation to the family structure.

Roe's past had been prosperous, his love genuine and rewarding, but his life insular all the same because of a snug and passive sort of snobbery. As the action unfolds in *Caught* we find that it is Roe's identification with the firemen that matters most, and that this identification is impaired by his class consciousness, by the fact that his companions revolt him. The terrible disintegration of poor Pye becomes the catalyst enabling Roe to identify with the firemen. Pye's death, and Roe's experience once the bombing begins and fires do break out, make him forget the past he cherishes jealously. It is effaced, and the book resolved.

Back, on the other hand, presents characters all on a single social plane, and focuses on Charley Summers's hallucinated grief when he discovers a girl whom he takes for his dead Rose. But what is imperative to the resolution of *Back* is that Charley deny Rose, for his love for her, we learn, had been possessive, adulterous, self-gratifying—and hers for him no less—to the disruption of the family to which Rose belongs. The final victim in *Back,* as we shall see, is Rose's son Ridley (just as Pye, the man of the lower class, is the final victim in *Caught*). Charley is healed of an obsessive love for Rose by an altogether different kind of girl, with whom he falls into an altogether different kind of love. The girl, Nancy Whitmore, is the illegitimate child of Rose's father (hence the resemblance of half-sisters), and even this old man must die in order for Charley to awaken to Nancy's love.

Richard's and Charley's direct contact with the destructive element of war saves them ultimately, by revitalizing them and quickening their humane instincts. In recounting some moments of extremity while fighting fires, Roe tells his sister-in-law Dy, "In some fantastic way I'm sure you only get in war, we were suddenly alone and forced to rely on one another entirely. And that after twelve months' bickering" (pp. 182–183). War, striking its utmost blow, despite itself exerts cohesive force. Green does not make much of Roe's new-found manliness—nor does he do more than allude to Charley's humane stirrings at the time of his imprisonment, after he had lost his leg. By an effort of will Charley had shut those times from his mind, but in one place near the end, when he was watching some kittens with Nancy,

> It had suddenly come to the tip of his tongue.
> "I had a mouse out there," he said.
> She had a quick inkling of this. "And the guards took it away from you?" she asked, as if to a child. But he did not notice.
> "No, I had it in a cage I made," he said. (p. 234)

This is absolutely all we hear of the mouse—yet it is enough. Springs of love come undammed. Fostering that mouse may have been Charley's initiation to the kind of love that comes to foster him in the end.

PI AND RHO

At the very end of *Caught,* Roe's sister-in-law, referring to the fighting of fires and death, asks him, "what's the meaning of it all?" At which he flares in sudden anger:

> "I know this," he announced in what, to him, was direct answer, "you've always been most unfair to Pye."
> She was astounded.
> "Pye?" she asked.
> "Yes, to Pye," he said. He stopped, turned away from her. "That's the tragedy." (p. 194)

Now Dy has had hardly any dealings with Pye in the novel; but she has secretly loathed him. In indicting her, Roe is indicting in effect the whole British social system for the suicide of the sub-officer. Roe's answer seems no less direct to the reader than to himself, yet the gap his mind leaps to arrive at this answer marks the achievement of identification with Pye that signals the resolution of *Caught.*

The original predicaments of Pye and Roe, conditioned by their different social standing, stem from their very peculiar personal relationship. Briefly, Roe is an auxiliary assigned to the substation of the newly elevated Pye. But earlier, when Roe was being trained, Pye's sister had abducted Roe's son, Christopher. The sister had been confined afterwards to a mental hospital, where throughout the novel she remains, haunting Pye as he grows to feel responsible for her condition. The confinement of the sister comes to merge with Pye's official problems at the substation, a process that marshals so many terrible coincidences that Pye is led to distrust his own good will, and drives himself into corners of fear and doubt, finally to a last corner, inside a gas oven. But before Pye is "caught in the determinism of crisis," [1] his star seems in the ascendant, except that he blames Roe for the consequences of the abduction, and the man is

always under his eye. Pye senses a connection between their different class backgrounds and the fact that his sister was shut in, and
himself given no chance to make amends to Roe. Still, Pye tries to
be magnanimous. As he says to Richard,

> "There's many in the Brigade would never allow a man beneath
> them, as you're beneath me now right enough, to forget a thing
> like that. Well, I'm not like that, I'm a man who has educated
> 'imself. Take education, what is education? I say it is a man's
> capability to see rightly for 'isself. I see my mother's daughter,
> in a manner of speaking, has wronged your wife, and has not
> been given leave, or I should say permitted, by the system we
> live under, to put it right." (p. 38)

One notices early that Pye, oversensitive to his inferior social
background (as his frequent assertions about education attest), will
whipsaw himself irreconcilably and magnify the issue; but as for
Roe, he can only withdraw from the sub-officer. No sooner does Pye
begin to speak, roundabout, of the abduction, than "An infinite sensation of tiredness . . . flowed over Richard" (p. 38); in fact, the
abduction means little to Roe, and the motive for his refusing to
speak of it to the men is this jealous one: ". . . that he must never
let them share, even though it was only in the telling, in the agony,
the death of his wife, not in the abduction, but in her death" (p. 154).

Roe is in fact jealously guarding his feelings from any admixture
with the feelings of the crowd. Like Mrs. Tennant, he has persuaded
himself that he cannot understand people of Pye's station.* He is
guilty, before the calamity of Pye's suicide strikes, of something
more vitiated than snobbery—like Mrs. Tennant, Roe simply does
not care. As late as his very last interview with Pye, Roe is still
dodging Pye's allusions to the injustice of the sister's confinement,
even though, at the last words they exchange, he becomes genuinely
alarmed at something Pye says. The sub-officer by then is so dis-

---

* Compare Mrs. Tennant's remark, "But my dear it's not for us to understand O'Conor" (*Loving*, p. 228), to Roe's "certainty that he could never
make this man [Pye] realise what had passed . . ." (*Caught*, p. 38).

traught that he speaks (as Raunce's Albert had) of becoming an air gunner in the R.A.F. "It came to Richard that Pye must be insane. At that date he was years over age" (p. 162).

While Pye is alive, Roe never commiserates. Only at the end, after there have been air raids, does he turn savagely on his sister-in-law, who had never forgiven Pye for his sister's act. It is in the logic of *Caught,* we infer, that Roe should come upon Pye dead, and that this experience coupled with his braving panic at the first great wharf fire should bring him to a full realization. As he tells Dy, concerning that wharf fire,

> "No, what I mean is, we were suddenly face to face with it, as I was with Pye two months before when I pulled him out of the gas oven."
>
> She wondered again, as she had often done, why someone else could not have found that hateful man. (p. 183)

Dy, fiercely dedicated to salvaging Richard and his son and their insular tradition, intuits the significance of Roe's discovering Pye. She makes one last defensive gesture, in form of a verdict, when she is walking with Richard, now convalescent, at the novel's end; but just before her "verdict" we learn that Pye himself had considered others in the act of suicide.

> "So Pye committed suicide?" she asked, although Richard had written to tell her weeks before.
>
> "In the gas oven," he said. "But he had the sense to turn off the automatic burners in the boiler first. Or we should all have been blown up."
>
> He waited, watching his anger. Then he heard the verdict.
>
> "I can't help it," she said, "I shall always hate him, and his beastly sister."
>
> This was too much for the state he was in. He let go.
>
> "God damn you," he shouted, releasing everything, "you get on my bloody nerves, all you bloody women with all your talk."

It was as though he had gone for her with a hatchet. She went off without a word, rigid.

He felt a fool at once and, in spite of it, that he had got away at last. (p. 196)

Of Roe's considerable achievement, here at the end of *Caught,* Mark Schorer makes a perceptive remark. "The novelist cannot at this point give him a more individuating name," says Schorer, "but he does in the last page give him his one physical characteristic: he has, we learn, red hair; he is the fireman." [2]

Truly, Roe is not granted an individuating name; but even in virtual anonymity his name seems to signal his relationship to Pye— as if these men are meant to stand together as indivisibly as the alphabet letters their names may be derived from, Pi and Rho. Indeed Pye may be considered Roe's double, in the sense that Septimus Smith, for instance, may be thought of as Mrs. Dalloway's double.* Says Frederich Wyatt, professor of psychology at Michigan, "Not without reason is Septimus Smith the counterpart or double of Clarissa Dalloway. Isolated and relegated to him are the morbid

---

* On Septimus and other doubles, see Tindall, *The Literary Symbol* (New York, 1955), pp. 204–205. After I had written this paragraph, I found that Kingsley Weatherhead had made a similar (and possibly more pointed) remark about the Pye-Roe relationship when he said that "they are linked by their names which put together phonically produce *pyro,* the Greek root for terms describing fire." ("A Critical Study of the Novels of Henry Green" [University of Washington, 1958], pp. 99–100.) But Weatherhead, believing *Caught* to be constructed in Freudian dream patterns and Pye to be a projected antagonist, "the creation of Roe's dream-work" (p. 102), emphasizes that Pye needs to be destroyed in order that Roe may be "self-created." Here as throughout his thesis Weatherhead disavows any concern Green may have for social defaults and commitments, since he is intent on describing the development of "free" personalities, self-created in the existentialist sense. Such persons must reject comforting ties and memories, become alienated, and begin their growth process by entering a period of darkness-and-dread; within this rationale, "Pye as the creation of Roe supplies the latter with the dread that accompanies his self-development" (p. 98). I can accept neither this relegation of Pye to the role of dream-antagonist nor Weatherhead's persuasion that Roe's fulfillment is signaled by his sexual success with Hilly, Pye's dispatch driver.

sensitivities and pathological liabilities which . . . a psychologist might infer [of Clarissa]." [3]

Roe indeed had once had a suicidal urge (to leap from a ledge at Tewkesbury Abbey), a sign of the vertigo that he wished to conquer by joining the auxiliaries. And without pretending to assign to Pye a plethora of traits that might be subconscious in Roe, one could point out that Roe once saw in the offing a chance for a sexual encounter, only to renege because he felt cumbersome and dirty in his fireman's clothes. So instead he returned to the station and, without thinking, put Pye onto those girls, setting in motion a train of gears that help catch Pye up in a foredestined trap. And Pye, we find, hearing of the girls, "went straight up" (p. 51). But even if Pye turns out not to be Roe's sexual surrogate, in the larger sense he "completes" Richard as Septimus "completed" Mrs. Dalloway. Pye succumbs to the tensions of environment mainly because he *is* concerned for those around him; Richard, more impervious to those tensions, is led from critical disengagement to awareness and commitment as a result of Pye's death.

By a sort of poetic logic, finally, Green disturbs us into assenting to the indivisibility of Pye and Roe. Roe's son, after all, was abducted by Pye's sister, who, childless, thinks of herself as the boy's mother. Next Pye believes himself to have forced his sister; the suspected incest seems to suggest he is her husband, hence the boy's father, hence Pye is Roe. Perhaps this is farfetched; yet the patent unreality of the equation does not destroy the complex of feelings it engenders, which yoke those alphabet symbols, Pi and Rho, and generate a third entity embracing both.

DISASTER FOR ALBERT PYE

Philip Toynbee has epitomized Pye's predicament in two accurate sentences: "He is the benevolent, bewildered and suspicious proletarian, for whom authority proves tragically too sudden and indigestible. He wishes—how he wishes—to understand and be understood, but his intelligence is just inadequate, and that bare inadequacy leads to outrageous failure." [4]

If Pye's inadequate intelligence dooms him, those above and beneath him likewise display ignorance that heaps misfortune on him. But what Green portrays most harrowingly in *Caught* is the autonomy of events that conspire to bring Pye down. Every episode that bears on his disintegration arises out of compulsive human behavior, behavior that cannot be tolerated by institutions like the London Fire Brigade.

The two chief human agents in Green's fatalistic plot are people from Pye's substation toward whom he is warmhearted: Piper, the old sycophant who bears tales to Trant, and Mary Howells, a headstrong old scrubwoman whom Pye has hired as third cook. But before these two undo their superior, Green employs two scenes that fuse Pye's personal and official problems. That is to say, his concern for his sister, rooted subconsciously in his suspicion of incest, becomes intertwined with his dread of being found remiss in his duties.

At a fire-house debate, first of all, Pye reveals his sense of exposure as a public servant when he defends the Brigade's action in the case of a Regular whose sister had been found shoplifting. On being told that the man's sister lived with him, Pye explains that the authorities must take a short view of stolen goods found in the home of a public servant having the right of entry. The men carry this logic a step further. "And if my sister had a bastard," a Welshman roars out, "would these head officials put me bloody inside for it, the druids" (p. 77). At which Pye, deeply moved, delivers a spontaneous and moving speech on circumstances that may have been to blame for the hypothetical illegitimacy—and leaves them, white-faced. That reference—"if my sister had a bastard"—foreshadows the deepest source of Pye's guilt: the suspected incest. Then the very next scene, of the substation's first civilian fire, presents a terror-stricken Pye, disgraced by his crew but also self-disgraced through his precipitate, compulsive action.

The fire itself is so small that an old lady puts it out unaided. What is worse, the actions of the Regulars, Pye and Chopper, are witnessed by some regular firemen who have arrived on the scene. The incident is told through Roe's eyes:

> Pye and Chopper plunged through a peacefully open door. . . .
>
> Regardless of what they had been taught, both [their] crews dashed in.
>
> . . . Then, in the way two dolphins will breast a wave and curve, Chopper and Pye hurled themselves downstairs past these lads coming up. [Roe] had a flash of their two set, dead-white faces. The crews turned round. They followed them out, three stairs . . . at a time, right to the next front door, also ready open.
>
> They had been in the wrong house. (pp. 79–80)

This piddling fire is a nuclear episode, and after it Pye is "never the same." The picture of the man, white-faced as he rushes downstairs, recalls his blanching two pages earlier, when the mention of the "sister's sin" touched his subconscious guilt. Having Pye go dead white at recognizing the "wrong house" may be Green's early symbolic equivalent of the kind of terror that strikes Pye's mind when he begins to think that he forced the *wrong girl,* in the deceptive moonlight of an evening far back in the past.

The civilian fire, which on the literal level initiates Pye's downfall (for Trant gets news of the fiasco), presents also in symbolic epitome the concept of man's tragic frailty that invests *Caught.* What constitutes that frailty is a pattern of compulsive behavior, error, and recognition—a pattern revealed brilliantly through the men's actions at the civilian fire, but informing as well other actions, earlier and later, that lead to Pye's suicide.

Immediately after that fire Pye has an encounter that casts the die of the plot. The demented daughter of cook Mary Howells, it happens, has left her husband in an army camp in Scotland, and returned home with a newborn baby. Getting wind of the cook's intention to beard this husband, Pye magnanimously offers to cover her absence. But when Howells mistrusts him, and goes off without his knowledge, he is forced to "post her adrift" up at Number Fifteen. This legitimate report by Pye counts more heavily against him than his own similar transgressions. (Three times, as Piper duly reports, Pye himself has for various urgent reasons been adrift.)

Poor Pye's compliance with orders, in reporting Howells absent, crushes him for a significant reason. Green is never one to pose against a character the intangible barriers of a baffling social system —not without assigning cause to individuals, even for events that become autonomous. And in *Caught* he assigns individual responsibility by allowing *conformity* to regulations to sink Pye, because of the whimsical and aberrant behavior of his superiors.

Mary Howells, duly reported absent, is summoned before Superintendent Dodge. To Pye's horror, she launches into a discussion of her daughter's dementia, not waiting on formalities. "But Mrs. Howells had made no mistake," Green writes. "Behind a front of purple, whisky-drinking ferocity, under wide shoulders, beneath the show he made of great strength for a man of his age, she had smelled the gossip in Mr. Dodge. At the first pause in the rattle of her narrative he said, 'You can go, Pye, dismiss.' Once Pye was out of the room he began, 'You know I 'ad a niece get just like it.' Before long they were deep in the topic of afterbirths" (p. 131).

One of the funniest scenes in *Caught,* this exchange spells doom for Pye and he knows it. With Mary let off, he expects to "catch it." And no sooner, some pages later, does Trant carry down the "traditional warning" than Green shifts montage-fashion to Pye at the asylum, about to be interviewed by a psychiatrist—"a man at ease behind a large desk, who might have been, and wasn't, Mr. Dodge, but who was properly imposing" (p. 137).

Pye fears such men's authority, whereas Green implies that they endanger him because of their single-tracked stupidity. Dodge has stranded Pye by greedily swapping tales with Mrs. Howells, and the psychiatrist maroons the poor man by forcing him into an erroneous review of his past. This doctor suggests to Pye that something must have happened in the sister's youth to prevent her marrying, then goes on to tell a patently slanted story of his own youth. Presumably the doctor had been responsible for his sister's breaking a

leg, with which she suffered greatly, since their mother's being a
Christian Scientist forestalled medical care. "Well, that is why I
chose this profession," the psychiatrist concludes, "why, to this day,
my sister stutters which, in turn, is, to a great degree, the reason
that she never married" (p. 140). Upon which, rapid-fire, he asks
Pye why he joined the Fire Brigade and why *his* sister never married.

Pye is immediately shocked into recollecting his first sexual encounter (with the daughter of a country neighbor), on which night
he had seen his own sister sneaking home. "He had never before
thought of his sister's creeping separate from his own with Mrs.
Lane's little girl. In a surge of blood, it was made clear, false, that
it might have been his own sister he was with that night. . . . So in
the blind moonlight, eyes warped by his need, he must have forced
his own sister" (p. 140).

The word "false," oddly placed here, implies that Pye did *not*
commit incest. Green earlier had stated as much, almost incontest-
ably, by pursuing Pye's thoughts and then adopting, a rare thing
for him, the omniscient point of view. Admitting that the sister had
had a lover the same evening, Green says of Pye, "He did not even
pause at the thought that she might afterwards, for the rest of her
life, have suffered from a violent distaste, *as had Mrs. Lane's little
girl at the time*" (p. 42; my italics).

True enough, Pye's psychological guilt obviates the necessity of
his having actually committed incest. His suicide can be equated, for
instance, with the suicide of Quentin Compson in *The Sound and the
Fury*. However, Green seems here to be asserting that memory (conscious or unconscious) is manipulative, hence unreliable. And abreaction,* supposed to exorcise guilt, here instead by a wry twist solidi-
fies Pye's guilt.

And so Pye goes down, as Green liberally assigns responsibility

---

* Defining "abreaction," A. A. Brill says, "It means 'to act off' or 'to work
off' something by reliving it in speech and feeling." (*Lectures on Psychoanalytic Psychiatry* [New York, 1955], p. 32.) In *Back*, Charley Summers is
saved by willfully *repressing* the memory of the traumatic experience of losing a leg.

to numerous individuals, all blind, none able to support Pye any more than he can himself. The final action that leads to his suicide shows him so driven and guilty that he misinterprets his own tenderness. Having been jilted by one woman, he is prowling in the blackout in search of others and finds instead a snot-nosed urchin. He brings him back to the station, his humane instincts prevailing over his lust. But he is led to regard his sheltering of the boy as a criminal act—not illogically, since Piper carries the tale up to Number Fifteen, where it is received as such. To escape this last and all the other quandaries, Pye takes his life.

SEX AND THE STRUCTURE OF ''CAUGHT''

Although Pye's activities maintain a sense of crisis throughout *Caught,* we follow Richard Roe for the greater part of this novel, and its structure seems to illustrate his progress through four stages. This progress ends with Roe's renunciation of women ("all you bloody women with all your talk")—as if through Pye's story Green would indict male authority, and through Richard's story, female interference, in time of war. No foreshadowing is blunter in *Caught* than one that punctuates one of Roe's earliest reflections. "As he walked away he thought the women would cause endless trouble. He was right" (p. 57).

Roe is far from renouncing women—he is far even from being entangled with them—during the novel's first half, which comprises two of the four structural movements. The first deals with his attachment to sister-in-law and son, those links with his insular past; the second traces his acclimatization to the new life at the station, which finds him mistakenly considering himself "a labourer . . . one of the thousand million that toiled and spun" (p. 51). At this point Roe has not yet forged bonds with the firemen, to whom he soon afterwards refers slightingly as the "proletariat."

The mid-point of the novel is marked by a description of an actual raid, during which Roe wishes poor dead Pye could witness the doings of a soldier and a prostitute in a street shelter. The banal reflection actually foreshadows his later sense of comradeship. This description pushes *Caught* momentarily forward in time. The regular time scheme of the novel, meanwhile, has given ample evidence of the general sexual promiscuity to which threatened London has fallen heir. Aviators and firemen especially have become recipients of sexual gratuities. And Roe, beginning to feel fledged as a fireman, has let himself be "caught up in what he understood to be the way other people acted at this time" (p. 50). His lascivious imaginings impel him, as the third movement begins, to take up with Pye's dispatch driver, Hilly. "What he might be missing," says Green, "haunted him" (p. 99).

For the space of a quarter of the novel Roe indulges himself with Hilly, experiences great physical relief, and tumbles into a new kind of insularity—her bed. Theirs is a false position, self-gratifying on either side, starting with Roe's opening gambit, their first nightclub kiss. " 'Oh darling,' he said, low and false, 'the months I've waited to do that' " (p. 111). Their later conversation reveals their bland satiety:

> "Darling," said Richard, "I thought it would kill me," while she thought well anyway I never snored or did I, it was such heaven I shan't know unless he tells; or would he have noticed, but it certainly didn't seem as if he could. She said, "Oh it was worth the candle." (pp. 119–120)

The last quarter of the novel begins shortly after Richard has quarreled with Hilly. "Secretly, and he had not even put it to himself, he was irritated, mainly because she had gone to bed with him. He found it made her of no account" (p. 130). Roe's sister-in-law brings Christopher to the station, and is noticeably impolite to Pye. Richard disguises his resentment, but we sense his feelings engaged for the first time in Pye's behalf. Meanwhile, Green has subtly indicated Richard's growing close to the firemen in various ways. On his first leave, Roe had thought of his life in the Fire Service as "easily forgotten" (p. 27); now, near the last quarter, "Coming back after his second spell of leave, Richard found he could not remember what his home life had been only a day or two before" (p. 134). Also, his speech has undergone transformations, as Dy notices on the day she visits him. She hears him call into the firemen's dormitory to explain that the boy who has run in there is his son. " 'It's all right, cock,' he cried, 'it's only my nipper.' Dy thought, what horrible expressions he does use nowadays" (p. 145).

At this point Hilly disappears from the novel. The action centers on Pye's disintegration—on his prowling the streets, lust-goaded, only to be caught adrift by Trant. From a last view of Pye dreading the consequences of his actions, *Caught* leaps forward through time to its conclusion—Roe's painstaking recollection of fires fought and manhood won.

There is definite logic in Roe's condemnation of women at the end of *Caught;* for Green has portrayed a sexuality gone sinister in these women who anticipate that the war, not yet felt, will bereave them. Their softness of sentiment for men in uniform turns to greed, as Roe perceives:

> . . . he saw them hungrily seeking another man, oh they were sorry for men and they pitied themselves, for yet another man with whom they could spend last hours, to whom they could murmur darling, darling, darling it will be you always; the phrase till death do us part being, for them, the short ride next morning to a railway station; the active death, for them, to be left alone on a platform; the I-have-given-all-before-we-die, their dying breath. (p. 63)

That such a glut of giving is artificial, self- as much as war-in-duced, Green emphasizes through his portrait of Prudence, the English girl who becomes Pye's mistress, and who has no illusions that she is pitying anyone. Prudence's simple thesis is, "War is sex"; by having her interrupt one of Roe's reveries, Green is able to con-trast Prudence to Roe's wife, and through imagery to suggest how fittingly the girl and the atmosphere of danger accord. Richard is sitting on the step of a fire truck, watching "a mangy kitten swiping at flies attracted by a cod's head in the gutter at his feet." But his past still controls him, and in memory he is back in his mother's rose garden, remembering how he first saw his wife, in her white clothes:

> Roses had come above her bare knees under the fluted skirt she wore, and the swallows flying so low made her, in his recollection, much taller than she had ever been.
>
> Back in his present, he heard a tap of high heels. Looking up, he saw Prudence, dressed in green as of dark olives like to the colour of that cod's head. She smiled, but did not stop. Still under the influence of his memories, he thought how sharp she appeared against the black wall with AMBULANCE painted in grey letters three foot high, knife sharp compared to the opulence [of] his darling. . . . (pp. 64–65)

Flowers and birds embellish the unnamed wife in the garden retreat; * ambulance shed and fish head adorn the kingdom of the girl who seeks "danger . . . in this lull of living" (p. 122). And if Prudence is special, she is only less deluded than other war-struck women, who despite their "daze of giving," as Roe perceives, are quite as detached as Prudence. "He invariably found these girls had no fear but that the Auxiliaries would come out all right. At first he supposed they took this line to still his fears. But whenever he bothered to be honest he had to admit they were a long way from paying attention to his final bit of trouble" (p. 70).

These sentences record Green's deepest probing into the hearts of women who lament their men in war; they complete the logic by which Roe excludes women in the end. Dy herself shows the same attitude when she explains her reaction to the news that Richard had been knocked out by a bomb.

---

* The natural image of roses coming under the girl's skirt recalls a striking artificial image in the first description of Prudence: "An acetylene lamp triangle of sunlight cut into the floor. . . . This light, reflected up the bell of her skirt, made her translucent to the waist" (p. 50).

"Were you very worried?" he asked.

"No. We knew you'd be all right." He looked at her. He was irritated to find she was laughing.

"Did you? I wish I had." (p. 173)

War being beyond their experience, the women of *Caught* consistently fall back on such clichés of the mind. Between the attitudes held by Dy and Prudence a whole range exists, yet no English-woman in *Caught* comprehends war any better than these two do. A Norwegian girl, though, does understand war. She is Prudence's friend Ilse, who goes to bed with the man who proves to be the most heroic of the Auxiliaries, Shiner Wright. At a fire-house party, Ilse daunts Richard with her penetration to the heart of the deadly game all in London are playing. She makes comment on the skeletons the firemen have drawn on the station-house walls, and on Richard's rather calculated allusion to the "gigantic death roll" the Brigade has been warned to expect after the first raids. Richard, we find, was

expecting the usual "Oh, you will be all right" . . . when she said, "Yes, and it is my thought that your people in this country have not done enough, not nearly, no, you are such a long way far to go even yet, you will not realise," she said. "I was so surprised," she said, "to see those death bodies, skeletons, up there, such a lot think bombs do not explode because they come from Czechoslovakia. . . . I'm sorry," she said, "but you have chosen, ach, so dangerous a thing, this fire, and I wished I could tell you. . . . Prudence, she is English like you, she does not agree with me, she thinks this is all good fun. . . ." (pp. 70–71)

Ilse's prescient attachment with Wright (who is to be killed) is joyless and resigned; Prudence chafes to find her friend going "coldly . . . almost publicly" to bed with the man (p. 142). But Ilse, knowingly sombre, has unmasked the debilitating properties

of sex when it is adjunct to war, and alone among the women has
made a drear offering at war's altar.

To distinguish *Caught* most sharply from Green's other novels,
we might set atop its heap of women that daughter of Mary Howells, Brid, the only married girl in the novel. Demented, suspicious,
forlorn, she is estranged not only from husband but from mother
and child, and splits Green's revered family structure into frag-
ments. Brid is totally denied the composure or direction of Edith or
Lily Gates, her counterparts, in age and social station, from *Loving*
and *Living*. Brid's chaotic mind may be an emblem of the fact that
under unnatural pressures women no longer sustain others, but only
add to chaos. In this book they are simply incapable of coping with
war, at least in its incipient stage. Their interference—their insular
trap of sex—keeps men sundered meanwhile, until, having at last
to cope with war, the men can become truly interdependent.

THE STRUCTURE OF ''BACK''

Back is constructed much like *Caught* in that one may discern four
general movements in the novel, which follow poignantly and humorously Charley Summers's undulating course toward reality in buzz-
bombed England. The overall pattern may be charted as follows:
As Charley gradually grows to forget his past dead love, Rose, he is
quickened by resurgent sexual impulses. These are directed at his
secretary, Dot Pitter (the two are employed by an engineering
firm), but Charley's plans for Dot twice take unexpected turns, and
he is by these accidents led to Nancy Whitmore. (Old Grant, Rose's
and Nancy's father, has given Charley Miss Whitmore's address.)

In the first quarter of *Back*, Charley guiltily berates himself as
he is reminded that Rose is slipping from his memory all too pain-
lessly. But then, one day, having kissed Dot on the temple to smooth
over some office altercation, he is electrified by the brief contact,
and is driven to walk home that evening, "so as to see girls. . . . So
it was that he found himself, by chance, within a few yards of the
address Mr. Grant had given" (p. 52).

The second movement of the book is touched off when Charley finds Nance, and is bowled over in thinking she is Rose. The girl, primly indignant, will not stand for his raving and turns him out at the first opportunity. Charley recognizes her animosity, and is afflicted with a desperate love for her. Misinterpreting everything he sees and hears, he imagines her to be a whore, and, upon learning she had married a flyer now dead, a bigamist. In a misconceived effort to deliver "Rose," he confronts Nancy with Rose's widower, James Phillips. This interview all but ruins Charley, for he decides that James and "Rose" are in collusion. To assuage Charley, James sends him a curious memoir, and here at the center of the novel Green interrupts his story to present another very brief one.

The memoir, composed by an eighteenth century French gentlewoman, recounts a young woman's love for two half-brothers, the legitimate and illegitimate sons of a French marshal. The young countess's attachment to the untitled man, begun after the death of the brother, provides Green with a rather contrived parallel for his story of Charley's love for two half-sisters, one dead and one living. At the same time, as Giorgio Melchiori says, the "pre-romantic setting" of this document "enhances . . . the shabbiness of the contemporary world." [5] These are abstract functions, but the memoir has also a local function, to my mind more interesting. Charley is somehow relieved when he reads the countess's story, and the memoir becomes the first of many markers that chart his deliverance from his hallucinations about the dead girl. Subconsciously, that is, if not yet consciously, Charley recognizes his delusion, whereupon the third movement of the novel begins.

This involves anew the waning of Charley's passion for Rose. Ironically, Charley feels Rose's absence least when he is at James's house for a week end—at the place where he used regularly to cuckold James. The account of this visit Green stuffs with squalid humor, for Charley has brought Dot Pitter along with him, and James turns the tables on him by scrambling into bed with her. Once Charley learns of this transaction, a mute jealousy stirs him to seek out Nancy again. Nancy has by this time written Charley an apologetic letter. Not only does this letter reopen his access to her but also it starts him on an enterprise of symbolic significance. He decides to have Nancy's handwriting analyzed. In order to give the analyst a sample of Rose's writing, he inadvertently destroys all her old letters. (He snips them to pieces, thinking their contents to be too revealing.) The incident is to prove psychologically curative. Just beforehand, Charley "knew Nance was really Rose" (p. 141); shortly afterward, he finds himself "thinking of Nancy's mother as of someone quite separate from Mrs. Grant" (p. 163).

Although Charley grows ever more at ease in Nancy's presence, and knuckles down to work at his firm, he is not to be initiated into a genuine love for her until the book's final nuclear event, the paralysis and death of Mr. Grant—on which the last section pivots.

Old Grant is the progenitor of all villainies in *Back,* in a remote but decisive way. His own adultery has produced Nance, who has suffered by it. (Grant's paralysis frees her, though, because in coming to tend her father she gains the recognition she had always been denied.) Charley, who had dabbled in the vice, suffers from Grant's adultery because the resemblance between the girls stuns him. Rose's son, Ridley, becomes the last victim of what old Grant has propagated; for as in a Greek tragedy, suffering in *Back* is transferred to progeny. The same deep and baffled pain that seared Charley sears Ridley when he sees Nancy, who reminds him of the mother he knows only by a photograph.

In concluding this account of the book's structure, we may note two reflections of *Back*'s dull people that reveal exact truths to the reader, and constitute principles governing the action in *Back.* "Life has a funny way of getting back at us, sometimes," James Phillips unwittingly tells Charley, just before James steals Charley's girl in cosmic retribution (p. 147); the phrase applies also to Grant, who had worried his wife to become in turn worried by her as he lies helpless, and who had denied his daughter only to have her present in all her bloom at his deathbed. (The book's title refers not only to a soldier's getting back *to* a place, but to life's getting back *at* the characters.) And while life's way of getting back is curious, it is also continuous. Charley, "with surprising intuition," supposes that "one crisis in this life inevitably brings on another, that

[Nancy] wouldn't have kissed him if Mr. Grant had not been having a relapse . . ." (pp. 212–213). Just as in *Caught,* the crises generated by original compulsive behavior (Pye's and Grant's sexuality, for example) are hardly exhaustible. The boy Ridley, in fact, assumes the final symbolic burden of an initial action that is never rectified. But by an occult transference of that burden to Ridley, Charley is released from it.

BETRAYAL AND REDEMPTION: THREE DENIALS

Devoid of subplot aside from that central memoir, lacking the many images and juxtapositions that characterize the other novels, *Back* is the most simply conceived of Green's books. In it he keeps so close to the feelings of Charley Summers that Charley is present in every scene but two, which involve brief dialogues between minor characters. What makes Charley much more than a victim in this story, and gives him a moral complexity without which the novel would doubtlessly fail, are the clashing qualities with which Green endows him. We notice he is both diffident and self-sufficient, unconscionable and conscience-ridden, acquisitive and self-effacing; and gradually we come to associate the former qualities with his prewar life, and the latter with the life he has salvaged after having been wounded and imprisoned.

The qualities of self-absorption, possessiveness, and jealousy indicate the wantonness and fickleness of Charley's relationship with Rose; they also enable him readily to forget her. In forgetting her, of course, he betrays her. At the end of *Back,* Charley makes restitution for his denials by crying out Rose's name when he has "under his eyes the great, the overwhelming sight of the woman he loved, for the first time without her clothes" (p. 246). But by this time it is Nancy he loves. It seems to be one of the ambiguities of *Back* that Charley must atone for his infidelity to Rose, yet that his own salvation depends upon his denying her. Nor is it that a prolonged emotional attachment to a dead loved one amounts to a warping of vitality—the theme of, say, Tennessee Williams's *The Rose Tattoo*. Rather, Charley must escape from an attachment that, despite his own conception of it, was trivial and unwholesome while Rose lived.

Charley is not only a perplexed lover but a disabled veteran returning to a life in which he needs to relocate himself. His war experiences are not responsible for what proves to be a crippling introversion; for we learn in the first scene, when he cannot find his girl's grave, that he is "in his usual state of not knowing, lost as he always was, and had been when the sniper got him in the sights" (p. 6).

The sniper makes all the difference, however. Not only is a man without a leg, who has been kept behind barbed wire, entitled to some measure of self-concern—his condition makes it almost impossible for his people to receive him adequately. They cannot get beyond the standard clichés, any more than the women of *Caught* could get beyond them; and it is Charley's reception, taken up in the first forty pages of *Back,* that disposes the reader to exculpate the man, even though he mopes and does little to help himself in the early sections.

Of Charley's different encounters early in the book, the reception sententious old Grant gives him is the most repellent, for the man has invited Charley to the house that he may be used "as a guinea pig on Rose's mother" (p. 15). This lady has forgotten Rose and thinks the year is 1917, and Grant hopes to shock her back into the present by confronting her with Charley, whom the Grants had liked best of all of Rose's old suitors. "Not that we wouldn't have been glad to see you, any day," he reassures his visitor. "After what you've been through" (p. 15).

Small wonder that when Mrs. Grant confuses Charley with a brother killed in '17, "Charley hardened his heart" (p. 16). (But one notices that when Charley outrages Nancy, who has been in grief over her lost husband, out of pity for him she asks him to her flat once more to set things aright. The episodes are antithetical: Mrs. Grant mistakes Charley for another, at which he hardens his heart; Charley mistakes Nancy for another, but is rescued by her kindness.) Always, then, the fact that Charley has been barbarously received at home mitigates the unproductive self-pity or moral turpitude Green exposes in him. Nevertheless the exposure is complete, and often very funny. Green satirizes Charley's grandeur of purpose, for example, when he tries to reform "Rose." "Never knew such filth existed," he mutters disgustedly at one point, referring to Nance's "bigamy" (p. 102). Yet Charley is morally outraged according to conventions he himself had so freely abrogated when he cuckolded James; through innocent Nancy, he is in effect chastising the real Rose, whom he had sported with, never once reflecting that he was a party to her offense.

In the midst of his recriminations, Nancy is quick to perceive that Charley's self-righteousness keeps him impervious to the truth. "Why, you're so proud you can't see out of your own eyes," she challenges (p. 104). A similar kind of pride leads him to believe, erroneously, that Ridley is his son; indeed, this belief figures in the second of three acknowledged denials of Rose.

We learn there are to be three denials when, at the end of the opening scenario (in which Charley has accidentally met James at the cemetery), James points out Rose's grave to him. "Charley bowed his head, and felt, somehow, as if this was the first time that he had denied her by forgetting, denied one whom, he knew for sure, he was to deny again, then once more yet, yes thrice" (p. 12).

Green here announces a motif that is to have a counterpart. Charley's second denial accompanies his braggart's boast to his fellow repatriate, Middlewitch. " 'Had a child by her as a matter of fact,' he boasted, denying Rose a second time" (p. 28). Last, he denies Rose when Dot Pitter, who has been fired and suspects Charley has maligned her, refers tauntingly to the dead girl and to his "martyr ways":

> It was water off a duck's back. . . . She could not hurt him through the war, or through Rose. Then he denied his love for the third, and last, time.
>
> "Rose?" he said. "Her? Oh, she was just a tale." (p. 176)

The counterpart that gives purpose to this rather casual motif is generated by Nancy's three affirmations of her dead pilot-husband.

These occur in different contexts. First she is infuriated when cynical Charley refers to her "bigamy":

> "You swine," she yelled, coming up to him. "You keep Phil's name out of this, d'you hear? He died fighting for you," she shouted and, bringing her hand up, she slapped his face hard, and it hurt. (p. 101)

She explains Phil's sacrifice next, when, at Grant's death, she reveals to Charley her deepest hurt—that she could not have been with her husband when he died, as she had just been with her father. "She had told him this before but it was very different now, it was as if she were making him a gift" (p. 195). But if Nance is to offer Charley that gift of a redeemed life (which is what she will offer him as his wife), she must remind him once more, when he is brooding and querulous, of the airman.

> "That's all right then. For you know, no matter what others suffered, it was his life he gave." This was the third time she had said it, and it had been different each time. (p. 234)

Surely Green wishes here to intone the deep message of immolation accepted—a meaning that loses its import through all-too-common voicing. The gratitude due the war dead he is able to express by this careful double motif—Charley's infidelity being counterbalanced by Nancy's loyalty; Rose, in her self-absorption having fostered nothing, deserving Charley's denials, Phil's sacrifice having earned the homage of the widow. Green has formalized what otherwise could have been trite—an example of the power of abstract art to ensure the proof of commonly diluted emotions.

THE GUN BENEATH THE ROSE

To say that Rose deserves betrayal is to say that Charley must escape an insular past, without having verified that Rose was herself largely responsible for Charley's introversion. My interpretation of *Back,* differing from the interpretations of others, seems to require such verification.*

There are only two sentences in *Back,* occurring on the first and second pages, that refer to Charley Summers's actual experience under fire. The first describes the amputee searching for Rose's grave. "He might have been watching for a trap, who had lost his leg in France for not noticing the gun beneath the rose" (p. 3). The second pictures the man laboring uphill toward gravestones, "when came a sudden upthrusting cackle of geese in panic, the sound of which brought home to him a stack of faggots he had seen blown high by a grenade . . ." (p. 4). Charley remembers, then at once forgets the grenade. "But there was left him an idea that he had been warned."

The rose in the French field that had failed to warn "lost" Charley of the gun beneath it seems to refer, on the novel's thematic plane, to the dead girl, who concealed behind natural beauty the lethal quality of her hold upon Charley. The second sentence reinforces this notion. The screams of those geese are much the same as the screams of the peacocks in *Loving* when they panic at the approach of the sensual couple, Mrs. Jack and the Captain. Charley senses a warning not to pursue this quest, a warning that reaches him through association with another death agent, a grenade. He senses he should beware, but then forgets. What he remembers is "oh Rose, best of all in bed, her glorious locks abounding" (p. 5).

We are privileged later to see Rose in bed on two occasions

* A typical interpretation is discovered in this sentence from Jean Garrigue's review of *Back:* "Rose, both dead and alive, becomes, it is obvious, more than herself—a symbol of goodness, love, and just Rosiness—around which all who knew her revolve." (*New Republic,* CXXIII [Nov. 6, 1950], 20.) Similarly, though Kingsley Weatherhead does say that "in *Back* betrayal is the good," he holds this view because betrayal marks a progress "away from the ideal." ("A Critical Study of . . . Green," pp. 146, 147.) H. P. Lazarus is the only critic I have found who takes an opposite viewpoint, the one to which I am committed. Love, says Lazarus, is "symbolized by the mundane rose, not the Rose of Charley's obsession—really a stinkweed that rose in the nursery of his mind—but the real rose, Nancy." ("Henry Green's Technique," *The Nation,* CLXXI [Nov. 4, 1950], 16–17.)

Charley recalls. What makes the visions rush upon him are some comments of people in the street who see Charley woebegone and recognize him as a war victim.

> A woman behind said, "They're like flies those bloody 'uns, and my goodness are they bein' flitted." Then he saw Rose as he had once seen her, naked, at sunset, James away, standing on the bed which was so soft it nearly tumbled her down, laughing and flitting mosquitoes on the ceiling above, and with her hair . . . a flaming rose.
>
> . . . "Lost 'is leg in the war I'll bet," another voice came, and he knew Rose as she had been one afternoon, a spider crawling across the palm of a hand, the hair hanging down over her nose, telling him how many legs they had, laughing that red spiders were lucky, dear, darling Rose. (p. 64)

By these bald but telling conjunctions Green thrusts together Rose and the war, suggesting the lethal effect of each: men's lives flitted as a girl flits mosquitoes, men's legs lost as a girl laughs at the surplus legs of a lucky spider. (Wreaths of pigeon's blood had contrasted similarly with wreaths of scented steam in *Party Going*.) What is suggested remains concealed from Charley, who gorges himself on the glorious darling, the soft bed. Charley can never be undeceived. This we know when we look into Rose's letters he has saved—notes that reveal her asperity, her acquisitiveness, her mockery. The contents of one of these five precious letters is as follows: "Dear Stinker. I must say I think it's a bit lopsided your simply making up your mind you'd forget when I asked you especially to get me those mules we saw in the advert. Don't be a meanie darling. From Rose" (p. 140).

The others do not differ (except that she forgets to sign one)— they consist of an excuse to put Charley off, a reprimand for not having sent some goody, a teasing "bet you wish you were here," and even a request that Charley visit and mollify the Grants, to whom Rose has not been able to find time to write. Charley's later denials are made in the same spirit of self-concern as Rose's directives in these sacred letters; life again has got back.

Not laboring the point, Green makes the letters as diverting as they are revealing, in that Charley values them for their intimacy. Yet from these remains we know enough of Rose to recognize that she has kept Charley in thrall so as to use him. As for their brand of love, Nancy brings this up when she alludes to her own plans for him—children of their own, a house, hard work—and notices Charley wincing.

> "Not much of a lookout for the husband, then," he had the courage to say.
>
> "What d'you mean?" she asked. "What is there that's wrong for him, in all I've just said? I don't see life as sitting in another person's lap, as you and your Rose seem to have done, from what Mother tells me. It's starting a home and working for it, that's what I call it," she said. (pp. 242–243)

Nance has the domestic fire of Raunce's Edie, and Charley wavers under its blast. But she has not mistaken her man. She has perceived in him the quality that Rose may have stunted, but that has taken new root in the very desperation of his homecoming: his self-sufficiency. "For what she liked about Charley was how he did not ask for anything, however small, although his need was desperate, a child could tell it" (p. 236).

The crippling war and disheartening return, which have made Charley diffident, passive, maudlin, have also struck deeper at him and met resistance; they have forced him to be capable. It is surprising how well Charley gets about in this novel. And at his work, for a time, he has coped successfully with what is an asinine complex of priorities, circumlocutions, face-savings, and evasions. To keep track of his company's orders and receipts, he has devised a card-index file—a system that indeed breaks down later, but to which Green refers early as "the system . . . which had kept him sane throughout the first reflowering of Rose" (p. 43).

This is no cursory reference to Charley's method of protecting his sanity. The same power of will that produced the card-index file is summoned again, in by far the most important passage of *Back,* when Charley hears old Grant die above him, and locks out the past —the night in France we never learn about. Over his head, Mrs. Grant has been calling out hysterically.

> She was yelling now. "Gerald." After which the most frightful sobbing. "Gerald darling, Father, where are you?"; then, in a sort of torn bellow, "Father," then, finally, "Come back," and the culmination of all this was about to remind Summers of something in France which he knew, as he valued his reason, that he must always shut out. He clapped hands down tight over his ears. He concentrated on not ever remembering. On keeping himself dead empty.
>
> He made himself study the living room. He forced himself to stay clear. And he saw the cat curled up asleep. It didn't even raise its ears. Then, at the idea that this animal could ignore crude animal cries above, which he had shut out with his wet palms, he nearly let the horror get him, for the feelings he must never have again were summoned once more when he realized the cat, they came rumbling back, as though at a signal, from a moment at night in France. But he won free. He mastered it. And, when he took his streaming hands away, everything was dead quiet. (p. 218)

And by this magnificent winning free, which marks the highest point of the self-sufficiency we have been talking about, Charley not only locks out the past but admits the future, wins through to Nancy, and first learns his love for her. As at a signal, Nancy comes immediately to him on his couch in the dark living room, bearing news of Grant's death, and also, most mundanely, a sedative. "He took the glass. It was when he saw her as she was looking at that moment, when, finally, she brought him peace, that he knew he really loved her" (p. 219).

That there is need for wilfully blotting from one's memory the traumatic incidents of the past is an idea Green conveys in both *Caught* and *Back*. Certainly Pye's erroneous recapitulation, prompted by a psychiatrist's gambit, results in his self-destruction; just as certainly, Charley's victory over memory results in his salvation. A sub-current in *Back* affirms the same idea. Mrs. Grant, we recall, had suffered from a loss of memory after Rose's death. She seems jolted back after her husband's stroke, and the family doctor, whom Green freely satirizes as he had the psychiatrist, gives Charley a most erudite account of the recovery. But Mrs. Grant herself has something other than a scientific opinion about the onset of her amnesia after Rose's death.

> "You know for a long time after that happened I couldn't bear it, I had to put the whole thing behind me or lose my reason. Then the doctors gave Father some wrong counsel, and he used to keep on to make me remember. Oh, things weren't easy for me, I'm sure."
> "I came down, d'you recollect?" he said. . . .
> "I don't know whether I do or I don't," she replied, and he was horrified to find a look of sly cunning begin to spread over her placid face. (p. 202)

Green seems to be affirming that people know instinctively how to protect themselves, and that in extremity they are able wilfully to do so. (We notice his eighteenth century, virtually Johnsonian, view of the human will.) This is not to say that moral repercussions of past errors dissolve away. Grant is dogged to death by the secret he tried to conceal. Even Charley, who has paid for mental and moral obtuseness through the agency of a gun beneath a rose, is relieved of that burden of the past only when Ridley intervenes.

Charley and Nance, on Christmas day, have been walking in James's village, where they are taking a holiday. In their talk, Nancy has been bearing down hard on Charley for his unconscionable attitude toward progeny. He has confessed that Ridley might be his own child. "But Charley," she admonishes, "it would be living a lie" (p. 239), and she goes on to explain how Grant himself had lived just such a lie through her. This sally prepares a means by whicḧ Green can recapitulate and roll into one the offenses of both Charley and Grant—for just afterwards the couple come upon Ridley.

> Then, absolutely without warning, stepping out of a surface shelter in the roadway, and not three paces from them, was Ridley, his eyes fixed on Nance. Afterwards, when Charley went over it in his mind, he thought he had never seen such pain on any face. For the boy had blushed, blushed a deep scarlet in this snow-clear light. He must have thought he was seeing his mother step, in her true colours, out of his father's micro-films. And Nance, who did not know him, passed him by.
>
> Charley managed to turn round, without attracting her atten-tion, in order to make the child a sign. All he could think of, and he did not know why, was to put a finger to his lips. At that, Ridley turned, and ran off fast. (pp. 244–245)*

In the very next passage, Nancy proposes to Charley, and he is saved.

COLOR AND ROSES IN ''CAUGHT'' AND ''BACK''

I have withheld discussion of some scenes in *Caught* and *Back* until I could present an interpretation of both books, which may serve as a context to support a few remarks on the imagery of the two. I think the imagery to be basically the same in each, and the novels them-selves to be complementary.

Green's careful use of colors—particularly of rose and other reds —reinforces his theme that war checks feminine capacities for pro-moting life as it incites women to make uninhibited sexual responses. Earlier I noted occurrences of red in the novels as signifying fulfill-

---

* It may serve to show Green's eclecticism with regard to psychoanalytic theory if we mention that the shift of burden from Charley to Ridley con-forms with the phenomenon called "transference" by the psychiatrists.

ment and concord (opposed by green, which indicates deprivation, anxiety, and need).* In *Loving,* for example, the "blushing rose" of a turf fire, investing Edith's eyes with "rose incandescence that was soft and soft and soft," signals breathtaking promise to Raunce (p. 157). But a different effect is gained from a related scene in *Caught,* in which Richard and Hilly, naked on a sofa, make a "pleasant brutal picture" as they are showered by "rose petals" of firelight, which spreads a flush "over contented bodies" (p. 120).

Here the effect is partly insidious, not mainly because the lovers are spent and gratified (in contrast, *Loving* celebrates a potential), but because flames play over that couple, and fire in *Caught,* its aspect alluring, is all-consuming. During the central conflagration in *Caught,* which also sheds rose-colored light on streets and buildings, Richard enters a surface shelter to find a drunken soldier and a tart who have just finished copulating. "He had been kissing her mouth," Roe sees, "so that it was now a blotch of red . . ." (p. 97). This image sticks in the mind when some lines farther down we are shown a looter dragged along by police, "drooling blood at the mouth," and someone dying on a stretcher laid down next that shelter: "The twisted creature under a blanket coughed a last gushing, gout of blood."

In *Back,* similarly, the color red, even when it apparently revitalizes, is insidious. There is a scene near the end of *Back* in which Nancy kisses Charley in a blitzed rose garden. It is autumn, the garden is bare of roses; a red sunset suffuses the scene and appears to transfigure it. But what the redness may symbolize is ambiguous. First of all, the place is cold; second, the red glow settles upon a scene of decay: Nance and Charley enter the garden by passing the chimney and staircase of a ruined house, and look back at "the red

---

* For examples from *Living,* see above, pages 86, 93, 96. In *Loving,* green is emblematic of Raunce's needs, but is perhaps most suggestive in the description of "Kate's greenish body" (p. 214), when Edith covers the girl up and comforts her. The color green occurs rarely in *Caught* and *Back.* We have noticed Prudence's olive-colored dress; just before Grant's death, we find Charley in great terror, feeling "as though something dirty was at work which might at any time come out in this darkness, and be green" (p. 216).

mound of light rubble" soon afterwards. Yet turning back to the garden they find the roseless briars "aflame, as alive as live filaments in an electric-light bulb, against this night's quick agony of the sun" (p. 207).

The imagery of life-amid-waste seems too complicated to present one meaning, especially when next Nance kisses Charley, "her breath an attar of roses on his deep sun-red check . . . her blood-dark eel fingers [fumbling] at his neck" (p. 208). Yet, and this may explain it all, Nance's purpose has been to get back at Rose. "Was it like that?" she asks, her question aimed at Rose. And Charley, uncomprehending, is stunned, lost again:

> . . . his arms hung at his sides, and he could not speak, paralysed, for an instant, as Mr. Grant.
>
> "I'm sorry, dear," she said, annoyed with herself. He did not move, or speak.
>
> "It's too cold to sit. We'd best go back," she said.
>
> So they walked home in silence. In the dark she took his arm once more, pressed close. But he said and did nothing at all. He couldn't even feel. (pp. 208–209)

By no means, here, has life begun anew for Charley. Nancy is to bring him peace only later, after that horrific evening of death—not with a kiss, but with a sedative.

Red then, in these war novels, seems to have allure but conceals something sordid. A feminine color, in *Loving* it was an emblem of promise, but it betokens the carnal wherever carnage has displaced fruition. War reveals some powerful destructive agent at work; no longer does rose or lily, in Lawrence's phrase, tell triumphantly of "the incarnate disclosure of the flux." War breaks the delicate pattern of continuity and fruition, thrusts men into some unreal region between life and death. I know of no passage in Green's work that attests this conviction more eloquently than one from a story, "Mr. Jonas," which describes plumes of water—traditional sources of life —directed against a conflagration: "The plumes, when all pressure was spent, dipped weakly to those flames in a spatter of drops. It was as though three high fountains which, through sunlight, would furl their flags in rainbows as they fell dispersed, had now played these up into a howling wind to be driven, to be shattered, dispersed, no longer to fall to sweet rainbows, but into a cloud of steam rose-coloured beneath, above no wide water-lilies in a pool, but into the welter of yellow banner-streaming flames." [6]

The lily image that helped *Living* burgeon with life is undone here, rose color is portentous, a "howling wind" drives the spent plumes of water so that all tendency toward natural composure is checked. Lawrentian rainbows give way to clouds of steam topped by "yellow banner-streaming flames." The whole passage seems an image for war's effect on normal creative processes, and may explain why, in *Caught* and *Back*, Green blends white with heretofore promising reds in those scenes in which Roe and Summers are granted breathtaking revelations of what their wives-to-be are to mean to them. In the rose garden where Roe first understands "this heavy, creamy girl turned woman" is to be his, his wife is virginal in white clothes. "Her bare legs had been the colour of white roses about them, the red toenails, through her sandals, stood out against fallen rose leaves of a red that clashed with the enamel she used . . ." (p. 65). And in the last scene of *Back*, Nancy, with whom Green had earlier associated the color pink, is "lying stark naked on the bed, a lamp with a pink shade at her side": "And because the lamp was lit, the pink shade seemed to spill a light of roses over her in all their summer colours, her hands that lay along her legs were red, her stomach gold, her breasts the colour of cream roses, and her neck white roses for the bride" (p. 246).

Not that Green translates the significance of action or resolution to a spiritual plane. Even in his closest approximations of the absolute he stops short of the extreme position Eliot takes in the rose garden imagery of *Ash Wednesday*, say, or "Burnt Norton." He stops short of Joyce, too, who in the *Portrait* used separate images of white rose (signifying Stephen's devotion to the eternal) and red (signifying his commitment to mortal beauty). Green will go no further than to blend the two symbolic colors. The conjunction of red and white, though, is intriguing in *Caught* and *Back*. Especially in these novels Green seems attracted by the stabilizing appeal of the absolute. His whiteness signifies virginity, purity, serenity, some kind of spiritual capability, finally, that he finds necessary to blend with natural instincts; these alone cannot contend with war because war looses them in gales. Roe's wife, the only woman in *Caught* untouched by war, suggests a state of womanly perfection. And virginity is explicitly associated with Nancy, the only girl in the wartime span of either novel who is not demented or selfish or promiscuous. She says once she doesn't want to die an old maid, and when Charley reminds her she is a widow, she replies, "But if you live on long enough without a man, you go back to be a virgin" (p. 242).

The conflicts in *Caught* and *Back* are resolved when Richard and Charley, after purgative experience, make commitments respectively to men and to a woman. It is relevant that both end in seasons of snow. At the end of *Caught* all personal tragedies, as Miss Jean Howard points out, are "composed now and settling to winter in Roe's convalescent mind." [7] And when Ridley assumes Charley's burden, we recall that "the boy had blushed, blushed a deep scarlet in this snow-clear light." But the solutions of the two novels are opposite. What makes them complementary, one serving as prelude to war, the other as aftermath, is the location in time of the two heroes' real loves. Charley's past love was physical, his later love more selfless and promising; Roe's past the true love, his blitz affair with Hilly one of physical release, and (by implication) blasted before the book's end. But part of Roe's new commitment involves his disengagement from the past, so that, convalescing at the estate which had formerly revived his nostalgia, "In his pre-occupation with air raids he could even let his son run on ahead without sentimentalising over the boy." And, "He had forgotten his wife" (p. 178). The war still confronts Roe, but it is over for Charley.

Green's use of the color blue in *Caught* and *Back* is also significant. In its variations—sapphire, gentian, indigo, grape, violet, purple—it is the color most evocative of the unreal atmosphere war creates: a color of danger, compulsion, disguise, false exultation. It draws people hypnotically to one another, to their own pasts, to objects of their desire. In night clubs in *Caught* we learn of a "hyacinthine, grape dark fellowship of longing" (p. 112); by day we find the boy Christopher entranced by blue light settling over toys in the store from which he is abducted; again at night Green describes Pye's last walk through indigo streets in blackout—or Dot Pitter when she leaves her bed, in Eton blue moonlight, to fornicate with James in his. The unreal blue causes Pye, after talking suggestively to "gentian hooded doorways," to drag from one of those doorways what he takes for a girl, only to find he has that urchin, from whose nostrils snot pulsates, "almost Eton blue in this brilliant light . . ." (pp. 167, 168).

As Pye is fooled in his walk, so are he and the other two main figures in *Caught* and *Back* fooled in their desperate attachments to their pasts, and once for each man a compelling memory is accompanied by the image of a blue road. The roads confine and bound them, *mis*lead them. Bound up with Pye's recollection of the escapade with Mrs. Lane's girl is "that winding lane between high banks, in colour blue" (p. 40); when Roe is with Christopher and their dogs, and is trying to cling to the estate of both present and past, we read that the road they walk on "was like a dark glass bottle" (p. 31); on the first page of *Back,* Charley dismounts from a bus to a road near the cemetery that is "asphalted blue."

Blue never sustains, never rectifies. When Charley, searching for Rose's grave, comes upon a nest, he reaches to touch the eggs (symbolic of his longing for renewed life). "But the eggs were addled, blue cold as moonlight" (p. 7). The empty bed in James's house, since Charley grows jealous after discovering it, brings nothing for Dot except the loss of her job. And the fusion of the debilitating force of war with that of sexuality, so powerfully suggested throughout *Caught* and *Back,* culminates in one image when Charley watches bombers fly over Grant's house. "The moonlit world was Cambridge- and Eton-blue, as he saw again in his mind the filthy moonlight on Dot's bed" (p. 217).

Yet for all the duplicity and lust he has exposed in *Caught* and *Back,* Green is not recriminating. He is more compassionate in these novels than in others. His description in *Caught* of a Negress singing in the gentian light of a night club attests to the depth of his understanding of the fellowship of longing; for in the mood this woman creates, in time of war that surrounds singer and listeners, what is real becomes patently and deservedly unreal, what is unreal becomes truth, and for once we hear Green's voice assent:

> As she stood there . . . as she pretended to remember the south, the man who had gone . . . music floated her, the beat was even more of all she had to say, the colour became a part, alive and deep, making what they told each other . . . simply repeatedly plain, the truth, over and over again. . . .
>
> . . . When she had done, and the lights went up, the singer stood revealed as what she was not, a negress with too wide a smile. (pp. 111–112)

Blue, falsifying light becomes temporarily a real medium; plain light reveals all as what they are not. Once then at least the acknowledgment of a new reality neutralizes the distortions blue has been responsible for in *Caught*. (Once also in *Back,* on the last page, we find that electric light has converted the outside dark to "a marvellous deep blue.") Although Green has portrayed sinister cupidity and sexuality, which prevent the growth of lasting bonds, he has shown reluctance to judge where these exist. He is like Richard Roe, when Roe imagines his boy pointing a finger and shouting, "I want, I want," and thinks to himself, "it is not for us to measure the dark cupidity, the need" (p. 14).

RECALCITRANCE AND CONFORMITY

Before *Concluding* came out in 1948, Green had published three *-ing* novels and three novels of catastrophe. One can differentiate the two kinds of books by saying that in the former, much is threatened, with the characters' predicaments continuing unresolved, whereas in the latter, serious losses are sustained, and ensuing catharsis contributes to the novels' resolutions. With *Concluding*, the pattern of continuing struggle is resumed; yet this book, shunted into a future dominated by a Welfare State, bounded in space by the grounds of an English estate that has been turned into a school, and in time by the rising and retiring of an old man, represents a totally new, and perhaps philosophically conclusive, achievement for Green. It strikes between the merry pursuit and disorder of *Loving* and the record of muddled suffering in *Caught* and *Back*. Its hero, Mr. Rock, is as isolated as the young men bereaved in the serious novels, because the threats *Concluding* poses are more genuinely dangerous than those in the comic novels; yet threats remain undelivered, and crises unresolved.

Old Rock, though guaranteed his cottage on school grounds in return for an undisclosed contribution to the State, stands to lose the place by being elected to a "scientific poor law sanatorium" (p. 9). Should he be elected and forced to reside at that institution, along with his cottage would go his granddaughter's security. Liz is recuperating from a breakdown presumably due to overwork, and Rock is trying to prevent her carrying on with her neurotic lover, Sebastian Birt: "she would never get well while she could see that man, he knew" (p. 7).

On this Founder's Day at the Institute for state servants, Liz capitalizes on so many opportunities to see that man that by the end of the day she is ready to announce her engagement. Meantime, to the consternation of all, two pupils have been discovered absent, their beds unmussed. One is found in the forest, but explains nothing; the other, Mary, remains missing throughout the novel. For Miss Edge, the dominant co-directress, Mary's absence constitutes a serious threat. Humane considerations pale, however, in the face of other consequences in the Directive-and-Report controlled state, which destroys careers upon surmise. The burden of caring about Mary's safety shifts to Rock, who becomes Miss Edge's antagonist in a double sense; for the woman covets his cottage, and has done nothing about finding Mary. Miss Edge does, however, carry on with plans for the traditional anniversary dance; for her greatest dread is of disruption to her smooth-running operations. She fears this, not for her own sake, but for the sake of the deified system itself.

How the lost girl affects the plans of Rock (for preserving his cottage) and Edge (for preserving a dance)—herein lies the mainspring of *Concluding*'s plot. Rock and Edge are both trying to maintain a *status quo.* (Her name suggesting agency, Edge is the resolved instrument of the state, just as Rock, not agent but object, represents personality dedicated to itself.) Edge is trying to continue operations that will produce state servants in her own image, while Rock wants to cling fast to the granddaughter, as well as to the cottage to which he feels rightfully entitled. Just how the two fare gives the measure of difference between *Concluding* and Green's earlier novels. Comparisons from *Living* and *Loving* clarify this difference.

Mr. Craigan of *Living,* for example, Green's closest counterpart for Mr. Rock, tries to hold together a pseudo-family he has founded, and this involves his opposing Lily's courtship. Lily does return to him after being jilted by her callow young man. It is true that Craigan's bid to hold things fixed is doomed, but still his Lily, unlike Rock's Elizabeth, remains placidly devoted to him. Rock's struggle is more desolate, for Liz has in her heart consigned their cottage to Birt; she does little more than wheedle promises from the old man that jeopardize a holding already precarious. The reason Rock fares worse than Craigan is related to the reason Edge has success keeping a *status quo* which the state has ordained should be kept. She manages, for example, much better than those earlier matriarchs who tried to rule the servant kingdoms of *Loving.* Housekeeper Burch, cook Welch, nurse Swift all designed taboos to prevent life forces from asserting themselves in the young ladies under them. Yet Burch's housemaids escaped to Raunce and Paddy; Welch's girls kept trysts with tradesmen; and the nanny's charges watched doves murder and make love while the old lady told her tale unheeded. Designs that would keep the matriarchs in power in *Loving* are impeded by instinctual self-assertiveness. Not so in *Concluding,* where rebellion takes perverted form (in a secret, gossip-ridden cult of schoolgirls), and where, at Edge's successful dance, "the first waltz would send each child whirling forward into her future, into what, in a few years, she would, with age, become" (p. 180).

What lies in store for the girls seems already reposited in Liz, who is licentious, greedy, and, worst of all, too cunningly self-protective to be capable of even the feeblest gesture of aid to another. When one of the lost girls, Merode, interrupts the lovers near a fallen beech tree, her cry for help makes Liz "at once put on her vagueness for protection in the circumstances" (p. 56). Liz is merely demonstrating one of many defense mechanisms adopted by the state-whittled lesser figures of *Concluding*. But in doing so she indicates how far removed she is from the capable young women of Green's former books.

In all of the earlier novels except *Caught,* men distressingly self-conscious are buoyed up by women of domestic fervor. The qualified optimism of these books was bound up with their heroines' assertions of biological instincts, these checked only by their wholesome (even prudish) respect for matrimony. But in the impending war of *Caught,* femininity lapsed, in the name of giving, into licentiousness, and Roe's commitment to the firemen depended upon his last-page repudiation of women, who had been a divisive force in the novel.

Caught then looks forward to *Concluding,* since it presents women basically modified through pressures from without. Echoes of war do not disturb *Concluding,* but it has as the source of its deepest pessimism a perturbed intimation of change. Nature seems to have changed, women have changed: not so that they are unrecognizable, but so that what is deadly in them is no longer counterbalanced by what is vital. A doctrinaire state, giving outlet to women's organizing, ambitious drives, has shackled their capacities for lending emotional or physical support to others. (Green's view of such change is more depressing than Orwell's in *1984,* since Orwell presents some women—Winston Smith's mother and the proletarian washerwoman—who are unmodified and who nurture their loved ones and endure.) Accordingly, Rock alone can assume the burden of action and endurance; and Rock, like *Concluding*'s day, is headed for the dark. We meet no one who will succeed him.

In his grumbling, dogged way, though, old Mr. Rock is belligerent enough not to be pathetic. In fact, there is no pathos in *Concluding* —principally because nothing is concluded. Were it not for its unsolved mysteries, one could say, as Mark Schorer did, that "dissolution is complete," [1] and that Rock's being survived by no one gives the measure of Green's despair. But Mary's disappearance is never explained.

It is on the missing schoolgirl that readers of *Concluding* must peg their optimism. She can possibly be akin in spirit to Rock, and late in the novel we learn that she had been to see the old man, and that he had expected she would fly the place (p. 173). Being the favorite of the directresses, Mary had been privileged to serve them and overworked in the process—so goes the policy of favoritism in the Welfare State. Her escapade may be prank or rebellion, she may be alive or dead; but if this girl, quiet and reliable as she has been reported (and the only girl in school who keeps a doll), has indeed revolted against totalitarian authority, *Concluding* confirms Green's faith in the ascendency of the individual, the power of the will, and the resistance of some human beings to forces that would overmaster them, and denature them. The question is whether *Concluding*'s intimations of change generate too insistent a motif to allow Mary to take a place alongside Green's earlier heroines.

One thing we must remark is that *Concluding* does deal with human qualities that seem changeless. In Mary perhaps, and in Rock and Edge definitely, Green locates two familiar attributes of man—his recalcitrant individualism, as opposed to his zealous conformity. This scheme of contending forces requires a confrontation between Edge and Rock, whom we see by turns succumbing to human weaknesses, then mastering them. Edge's strength is best revealed at a luncheon when, before staff and students, she has a hallucination that Mary's body is among some floral decorations, but makes a "stupendous effort" and wins through; she then is able to preside at High Table till the meal's conclusion (p. 104). Rock, who faces up to or ignores threats all through this novel, weakens once when he is physically fatigued. He opens a letter, departing from his usual practice of stuffing mail unopened into a great trunk. But his fears of being elected to the home for old scientists are not confirmed by this letter, and he weakens only once more, again when fatigued.

In a curious scene at the height of the dance, when Edge and Rock meet in the woman's sanctum, their strength has ebbed. There,

Edge has succumbed to "a special, exceptional indulgence," tobacco, so that at Rock's unexpected appearance, "she now had nothing but pity for the old man" (p. 234). For his part, "he no longer seemed to hate the woman, all the go gone out of him" (p. 235). What ensues is summarized as follows by Robert Phelps: "For a gently fatigued ten minutes, their defences relax. They confess that they are both old, they try to accept each other. But then some imperfection of human intercourse intervenes. At some slight misunderstanding, they shy, bristle, and resume their barricades. Their parting is cold. Mr. Rock makes his way through the darkness and wet grass to his cottage; lonely, truculent, self-deceived; a summary image of everything that unloved, unloving, uninnocent man must be." [2]

Though Phelps reports accurately, he tends to misconstrue the import of this meeting. In the first place, the misunderstanding he alludes to is both funny and functional. Because "All this sympathy was so unexpected," Rock has lapsed into self-pity, and, nearly sobbing, confesses his love for Elizabeth. "I love her. She's all I have," he says (p. 237). But Edge, misunderstanding, believes him to be admitting an affection for one of the schoolgirls, Moira. No sooner does this come out than Rock, "suddenly and finally disgusted," retorts that they have been at cross purposes (p. 238).

What follows is quietly revolutionary. Rock goes to the door, ready to escape, Edge complains she cannot see the man in the gloom, and then, grown curious about Edge's allusions to the day's events, Rock comes forward "a second time . . . only to sit, without thinking, in her own place, behind the great desk of office" (p. 239). From there, virtually usurping her authority, he cross-examines the directress, about Mary, about mysterious Adams, the woodman who may be involved in sexual offense. His attention riveted on the disappearance, Rock is formidable again, and self-forgetful. As if recognizing how really dangerous he has become, Edge makes a preposterous proposal of marriage. "—What a desperate expedient to gain possession of a cottage, she laughed to herself, almost completely out of control" (pp. 241–242). With this, she flips a cigarette and her State Kidderminster rug begins to smoulder.

In these seconds Rock has vanquished her, as, with dignity, he rejects the marriage offer. True enough, he wins no total victory, not even a symbolic one. Edge shows no haste in stamping out the blaze, once he has left. (The Institute will not burn down.) Yet she does hear his disdainful parting laugh. And what would have incapacitated Rock has been averted. He has, by accident, circumvented sympathy.

Rock's contest with Edge and the forces of organization, epitomized in this odd scene, ends in deadlock. We discover this when Rock leaves to begin his walk home. "He even turned round to view the hated mansion which the moon, plumb on it, made so tremendous that he spoke out loud the name, 'Petra' " (p. 245). It is his own name he speaks here.

The estate and all it stands for may be permanent foe, yet in Rock a kind of permanency of spirit is embedded—spirit nearly given over to itself when sympathy is extended unexpectedly. But continuing vigilance and hostility are mandatory at the conclusion of a book in which the name "Mar . . . eee" is bandied between bright house and dark woods to fall loud on the old man's deafness. For all the while Rock has been summoning ethical reserves, *Concluding* has insinuated, through structure and imagery, that man has undone himself and nature; that, having thrown nature's forces into imbalance, he has unwittingly brought her darkness upon himself.

GREEN'S MOST EXPRESSIVE STRUCTURE

Concluding is divided into three sections. The first runs from dawn fog to luncheon at noontime; the second from teatime to dusk; and the third from the opening of the dance to late night, and Rock's return home through terrifying moonlit forest. It is worth pausing over the patterns of each section. In the first, nature awakens man, only to have him impose upon the natural order of things his ritual of luncheon. In sections two and three, the pattern has been reversed: each begins with man's artificial ordering of time (afternoon tea, the evening dance), only to conclude with nature's reasserting her control (with sunset, then deep night). This three-part structure conforms conventionally enough to diurnal sequence, but barely any space is given over to the splendors of afternoon. A sentence at the beginning of the second part announces the theme for this structure and justifies the prevalence of dimness and darkness. "Day was committed to night; the sequence here is light then darkness, and what had been begun in this community under the glare of morning, is yet to be concealed in a sharp fresh of moonlight, a statuary of day after sunset, to be lost, at last, when the usual cloud drifts over the full moon" (p. 109).

The sentence both recapitulates fully and foreshadows fully. Its language is allusive and indeterminate. What had been begun will be concealed, then lost. What that is we cannot creditably tell, and hence the sentence accounts for the structure of a book that runs a single day out, with the promise that all shall be unfathomable.

Elements of the supernatural, of hallucination and fantasy, are worked into *Concluding,* and cannot be dislodged without damaging the ground on which its events transpire. Nevertheless, for every event that seems caused supernaturally, or to come about as a result of melodramatic and sinister complications, there is a perfectly plain and ordinary explanation. The mysterious forest voices, heard at the beginning and end, may only be girls searching for lost Mary; and a doll that turns up, painted in Mary's effigy, seems to be a schoolgirls' prank to frighten a schoolmistress. To the same girls, conceivably, can be traced the slipper fixed round the neck of Rock's pet pig, Daisy, and the terror-stricken flight of Ted, his goose, who had never flown before. Even surly forester Adams, who makes Cassandra-like predictions, may be hiding in lakeside rushes all afternoon because he has been caught loafing by Miss Marchbanks, and because he too is a widower possessed of a cottage that Miss Edge may have designs on.

As for two admissions by the girls that seem to implicate Adams, these again may be laid to the claustrophobic effect of the state. When old Rock asks about Adams at a meeting of the girls' secret society to which he has been taken, "Him?" one girl answers. "We call that man the answer to the virgin's prayer" (p. 228). But very

likely all such allusions are prompted by the children's need to pre-
varicate, to create excitement through a semblance of intrigue along
lines rigorously tabooed. And when Merode admits a man partici-
pated in her and Mary's escapade, it is only after her interrogator,
Marchbanks, has supposed as much. "—What's the use? Merode
asked herself. Let them tell it" (p. 171).

Extortion, taboo, disembodied threat, the source of which is universal fear of Directives and Reports—such compose the intolerable
atmosphere that *Concluding* propounds, through the poetic logic of
action unclarified and menace that is hallucinatory. The children are
driven to lie and scandalize. Adams is driven to hide in a weed bed.
His fears are commensurate with those of others round the Great
Place, and literal explanations of the characters' phobias make for
high comedy at their expense. At the same time, hints of supernatural tamperings enrich the book, explaining, on a metaphoric
level perhaps, why everyone cowers (subject as all are to death,
which the state for all its guarantees of security cannot repeal).

The ubiquity of death is the part of *Concluding*'s dark theme that
mystery enhances. Consider how Rock and Sebastian are differentiated when, on the night of the dance, Birt rises from shadows to
guide the Rocks to a back entrance of the Institute. The old man
demands that they enter by the front way. What follows, the kept
promise of announced thematic structure, is the imagery of moonlight, illuminating what the dark holds, for Rock soon perhaps, but
for all in their turns: sundering, and death.

> They turned, and at once became aware of the new powered
> moon . . . a huge female disc of chalk on deep blue with holes
> around that, winking, squandered in the void a small light as
> of latrines. The moon was now all powerful, it covered every-
> thing with salt, and bewigged distant trees; it coldly flicked the
> dark to an instantaneous view of what this held, it stunned the
> eye by stone, was all-powerful, and made each of these three
> related people into something alien, glistening, frozen-eyed,
> alone.

"I'll leave you now," Sebastian said, as if to announce the
moon had found him out.

"Thank you, I don't fancy that," Mr Rock objected. "They
shall not come upon us unawares in this light." (p. 189)

"They," on the anecdotal level, are the directresses whom Sebastian
fears and Rock defies; but this scene has been transformed, as an
alien moon disfigures living substance, and "They" may be agents of
death about to strike man, rendered vulnerable. Sebastian would
hide, but Rock, once exposed, will only stand expectant, combatant.
That he does convert the sundered trio of "related people" to "one
hydra-headed body," which mounts the steps of the Institute (p.
190), attests the composing power of his courage. Ordinarily in
Green's work the human force that reassures and unites people derives from a feminine concordance with nature's regenerative processes; but in this image the sundering moon is "female," the "la-
trine" light of the stars seems filthy, organic nature is "bewigged"
with salt—and individual obstinacy stems a tide but temporarily.

THE GIRLS OF "CONCLUDING"

Nature's potential regenerating force, which brings Green's earlier
novels to fruition, is warped in *Concluding* into league with unnatural powers. Although physical drives bid fair to defy prohibitive
regulation—although nature endows young girls with growing
bodies, and instinctive needs—the woods they fly to harbor old
Adams and the corrupt lovers, and may hide Mary's body. Nature
is even responsible for old Rock's sexual susceptibility, which he
must overmaster. Sex in *Concluding*, connected with greed and depravity, is a dark contributor to "The sequence here [that] is light
then darkness."

The obvious sexual maturity of the Institute's young girls in no
way offsets the fact that they are stripped of sustaining, composing
powers. And because of what the girls are, *Concluding* is what it is.

Brilliant as they are, they are sinisterly non-individuated. (All their names begin with M; they have no surnames.) When we see them first they are consigned to darkness; a great shaft of sunlight bisects the kitchen, and beyond it in the dark the girls move, out of sight of Rock and the cook, fetching their breakfasts, "their low voices . . . just a female murmuring, a susurration of feathers" (p. 21). We last see them drugged by their Founder's Day Dance. In between times, when they appear as individuals, they are petulant, anxious, bored, ready to gratify themselves at others' expense. Mary's absence, for example, exhilarates them. They intimidate the animals they profess to admire, just as they intimidate Rock, whom they profess to admire.

Oppression does drive the girls underground, to their cabalistic sorority in the mansion's cellars, but depravity seems manifest even in their rebellion. Their motives for enticing Rock to their meeting, for example, are uninnocent. He is pushed forward, "an old lamb offered up" (p. 224); the club rules call for initiatory kisses, which offend Rock. "At the same time he began to have a gross feeling of immoderate amusement, such as had not come his way in years" (p. 226). Moira is possessive of him, and when he inquires about Mary, only to be shushed, Moira pouts with jealousy. The girls' allusive talk verges on the indecent, they giggle at Rock's embarrassment (as they had giggled behind their hands at the spectacle of the old man at breakfast). Finally we learn they have brought Rock down to query him about Liz's prospective wedding, and once this is apparent, fresh wounds open. He reacts instantly. He thunders out at them and quits them. "Then someone said, 'oh Gosh,' and laughed" (p. 230).

Rock's escape is crucial, for he has been susceptible to these children—especially to Moira, and "the endless prize of her fair person" (p. 202). Earlier Rock had escaped from Moira, after he had followed her belowstairs too early for the society's meeting, and she had implanted on his lips a ceremonious kiss. Breaking from her in dismay, he had led the way out of the fearful passage, controlling himself from responding to attentions mutely sexual in character. "She followed immediately," writes Green, "in immodest silence"

(p. 205). Yet Rock did go down to that cellar a second time; and mention of Liz's engagement, reviving his gruffness, saved him then, as an accident would save him from surrendering to self-compassion in Miss Edge's room. In escaping entanglement with the children—who, predatory and secretive, seem as far beyond hope as Henry James's innocents—Rock resumes his truculence. He returns to his granddaughter, trumpeting that he and she are unwelcome there, then in leaving encounters Edge in her sanctum, and lastly stomps from the Institute, through frightening woods, to the cottage—disenchanted, his integrity intact. Green has in effect provided him with a state of mind approximated two hundred years earlier by Jonathan Swift, who resolved when he should come to be old, "Not to be fond of children, or let them come near me hardly." [3]

When Philip Toynbee assesses the reader's reaction to *Concluding,* he remarks its erotically enchanting girls, but also the reader's "uneasy suspicion that the magic was black." [4] This may account for the rightness of Rock's ultimate disaffection for the children. Toynbee goes on to differentiate *Concluding* from its forerunners by saying, "There is not only no compassion in this book; there is, for the first time, a subtle assault on compassion." The sentence penetrates to the heart of the novel, yet by no means devaluates it. Granting the atmosphere, one can see that Rock deserves no compassion from *author* or *reader,* simply because the futuristic world is such that compassion extended by any *character* would devastate him. In place of compassion there seems to exist, between author and reader, a silent agreement that only if nothing softens Rock, in the crumbling civilization of this novel, can his contest be deadlocked.

A WORLD UNDERSEA

Green does refer once to innocence, momentarily present when *Concluding*'s girls begin to wake from an afternoon nap. Their eyes, he writes, "like jewels enclosed by flesh coloured anemones beneath green clear water when these yawn after shrimps, disclosed great innocence in a scene on which no innocence had ever shone, where life and pursuit was fierce, as these girls came back to consciousness from the truce of a summer after luncheon before the business of the dance" (p. 109).

But the admitted innocence is conveyed in the image of a predator; even before the girls are conscious, imagery operating "metaphysically" announces what will soon be resumed—fierce life and pursuit. The anemone image reappears when, at the ball, Rock is mobbed by children desiring him to dance (he being the only available male): "Mr Rock could feel their moist fingers' skin, the tropic, anemone suction of soft palms over rheumatic, chalky knuckles" (pp. 222–223).

Admittedly bizarre, these images are functional in *Concluding*. Just as bizarre, for example, is the description of Sebastian's and Elizabeth's first kiss at the fallen beech. Liz, we read, "helped his heart find hers by fastening her mouth on his as though she were an octopus that had lost its arms to the propellers of a tug, and had only its mouth now with which, in a world of the hunted, to hang onto wrecked spars" (p. 55).

But putting the separate images together, we note correspondences: each metaphorical action takes place under sea, in a world of hunters and hunted. And just as that image-world conforms to *Concluding*'s world, one other aspect of the sea corresponds as fittingly: the sea *transforms* matter, and in *Concluding* nature has in some way undergone a sea change. Notice the phrases I have italicized in the passage which describes the fallen beech Merode lies under, as Elizabeth and Sebastian come upon it.

> A great beech had fallen a night or two earlier, in full leaf, lay now with its green leaves turning to pale gold, *as though by the sea. . . . The wreckage* beneath standing beeches was lit at this place by a glare of sunlight concerted on flat, dying leaves which hung on to life by what was broken off . . . all now an expiring gold of faded green. A world through which the young man and his girl had been meandering . . . on *a sea bed* past grave trunks, was now this dying, brilliant mass which lay ex-

posed, a hidden world of spiders working on its gold, the webs these made a field of wheels and spokes of *wet silver*. The sudden sunlight on Elizabeth and Sebastian . . . was *a load,* a great cloak to clothe them, *like a depth of warm water that turned the man's brown city outfit to a drowned man's clothes,* the sun was so heavy, so encompassing betimes. (pp. 54–55)

The passage, perhaps the richest in all of Green's prose, has counterparts for its spiders and gold and silver in *Loving*'s description of King Paddy asleep in dead Ireland. But the slow transmutation by sea establishes a motif new to Green's work. The stricken beech, and what it harbors, seem to represent organic nature subsiding. Merode is a live girl when found there, yet even her vitality has the quality of mirage: her knee sticking from a torn pyjama leg makes what is static seem kinetic, yet hints of the stasis of bone beneath—"A knee which, brilliantly polished over bone beneath, shone in this sort of pool she had made for herself in the fallen world of birds, burned there like a piece of tusk burnished by shifting sands, or else a wheel revolving at such speed that it had no edges and was white, thus communicating life to ivory, a heart to the still, and the sensation of a crash to this girl who lay quiet, reposed" (p. 56).

Conflicting imagery makes the passage seem ambiguous. Like a dead tusk one moment, that burnished knee communicates life the next. We need only look back to *Loving,* however, to perceive an intention here that resolves the ambiguity. In the three crucial passages in *Loving* of arrest-and-motion, the static (and suffocating) element is invaded by heedless and vitally engaged servants: Raunce hunting for corn while Paddy snores in his bog-reflecting kingdom, Kate and Edie dancing in the unused ballroom, Edie and the children playing blind man's buff in the gallery of statuary. At the beech tree, on the other hand, Merode is in repose, as if at one with an element of decomposition so unhurried as to seem static. Imagery of sea change seems propitious for suggesting the slow transformative power, in force for an undisclosed period of time, that has made the natural unnatural, the organic unable to support life. And that

Merode is at one with such a power seems asserted when, after being extricated from the beech, "with an absent, ceremonious look," she combs out her "heavy hair a colour of rust over a tide-washed stove-pipe on a shore" (p. 58).

What is best about Green's use of sea imagery is that it appears but sporadically, and infiltrates rather than dominates the novel. Nor shall we find point by point correspondences within analogies or between separate analogies that maintain the motif. The description of Merode in a bath (rules require a comforting bath before grilling) may induce us to change our terms from "sea change" to "transformation by water": "In next to no time the bath was run, with Merode stretched out under electric light and water, like the roots of a gross water lily which had flowered to her floating head and hands. This green transparency was so just right, so matched the temperature of the hidden blood, that she half-closed her eyes in a satisfied contemplation of a chalk white body. She felt it seemed to sway as to light winds, as though she were bathing by floodlight in the night steaming lake, beech shadowed, mystically warmed" (p. 63).

Once again repose is charged with sinister overtones. "Gross water lily," "chalk white body," * the final sentence as well suited to a drowned body as to one bathing—all these insinuations urge that opiates, State-administered, keep these girls euphoric, volitionless, only to be drowned out of all touch with instincts maternal, compassionate, generous, responsible.

The Founder's Day Dance proves to be the most desensitizing opiate of all. "There's anaesthesia in a valse," says lovelorn faculty member Winstanley (p. 201), dancing with her partner in a room in which everyone is given over to music, and in which great affection starts in all the white-clad children's breasts for the belles of the ball, Edge and her colleague Baker in black. The dance is deadly in

---

* The recurrence of chalk imagery in *Concluding* seems to pertain to the sea change motif, since chalk is composed of the calcareous remains of marine organisms. We have already seen Rock's "chalky knuckles" and a chalk moon; it is perhaps worth observing that when Rock recoils from Moira's kiss, his back becomes covered with "powdered whitewash" (p. 205).

that it projects the children comfortingly into their futures; at the first false alarm of music, they marshal "as women but in couples, what had been formless became a group," until the trial needle is lifted: "At once these students broke away disappointed, years younger again" (pp. 186, 187).

For the duration of the dance the image pattern of drowning persists. "Then Moira whirled past, hair spread as if by drowning over Marion's round, boneless shoulder" (p. 196). The music even works on Mrs. Blain, the grouchy, unservile cook in whom one earlier had detected a ray of hope. (Green has stereotyped her, as much as to say that the totalitarian state will not modify the likes of her, so long as it chooses to eat.) Only from her dance partner does Mrs. Blain learn of Mary's disappearance. " 'Lost?' she yelled, but it was *drowned by music.* 'What's this? So that was it, then? Oh, you wicked things' " (p. 197; my italics).

Her protest is muffled for good once her partner complains of Mary, " 'We think it's pretty rotten of her to want to spoil this heaven evening.' " " 'Well then,' the cook said, quietened at once, and folded the child to an enormous bosom. Upon which both gave their two selves over, entire. As they saw themselves from shut eyes, they endlessly danced on, like horns of paper, across warm, rustling fields of autumn fallen leaves" (pp. 197–198).

The music itself is an autumnal flood, spreading to summon dancers from remote places in the mansion, "the water wheel turned by a rustling rush of leaf thick water" (p. 199). Only deaf Rock, impervious to music, and fresh from his experience belowstairs, can leave the place. But outside the moon has continued, where the sun left off, to work a sea change. Now Rock,

> . . . again in difficulty on account of the treacherous light, but glad of his escape, waded much as though the moon had flooded each Terrace six inches deep. For the spectacles he used seemed milk lensed goggles; while he cautiously lifted boots one after the other in an attempt to avoid cold lit veins of quartz in flagstones underfoot because these appeared to him like sunlight

that catches in sharp glass beneath an incoming tide, where
the ocean foams ringing an Atlantic.

So much so, that when he came to the first flight of stone steps
Mr Rock turned completely round and went down backwards.
(p. 245)

This climb down a "cliff face," as if to a sea, followed by Rock's
walk through moonstruck forest, reveals a competitive grimness
that has stood by the man at every threshold. The final section may
be an analogue for death and how Rock will face it; he seems pains-
takingly to make headway against every threat, and then, as Ted
flies at him, to have a premonition and to resign himself; he kneels,
trembling, fearing a collision. "Then Ted was gone" (p. 252).

Might Ted's coming "noisily by at speed six foot off the ground,"
straight for the old man, symbolize the flight of a soul? One forbears
to say; yet Ted's rush is on the literal level of the story portentous
enough, for the animal seems driven at last by instincts long before
suggested (when it hearkened to the cries of wild geese in flight).
Rock cannot expect to see Ted again, so that here he does seem
finally to be stripped bare. Yet Rock and the reader are to learn that
Ted, unaccountably, has not really flown off. And, following the
crisis, Rock settles to rest peaceably, astonished perhaps that on his
return the goose is in its kennel, yet well satisfied with his day.
"Everything settles itself in the end," he had said earlier (p. 176).

Just after he had said so, while walking with Liz toward the mansion and the dance, he had paused to watch legions of starlings
crossing the sky at dusk, then settling in trees: "as they descended
through falling dusk in a soft roar, they made, as they had at dawn,
a huge sea shell that stood proud to a moon which, flat sovereign red
gold, was already poised full faced to a dying world" (p. 177).

This is a cumulative image. The all-powerful moon is there, and
the sea shell emblem of mutation and death, yet these birds sing in
unison. A second, then a third concourse descends, and Rock, wondering "if this were not the greatest sound on earth," acknowledges
aloud, "I'm glad I had that once more" (p. 177). Here for once in
Concluding is evidence that animate nature has not been corrupted,

and that living trees continue to shelter living things. At the all-conquering dance Rock had heard a trial waltz begun and stopped, and had "caught the last echoes of this music sent back by the beeches, where each starling's agate eye lay folded safe beneath a wing" (p. 187). The fact of this safety is important, for it means that against its intimations of change, *Concluding* does finally pose prospects of a restoration of balance between nature's consuming and sustaining forces.

Only the animals of *Concluding* are untroubled by diurnal processes. On the first page Alice, Rock's cat, could keep herself dry "where every blade of grass bore its dark, mist laden string of water"; and his goose, we notice, was "not ringed in by fog" (p. 5). Even these creatures, however, come to partake of the excitement that fills the day. They seem both hostile to regulatory agencies (Ted makes advances on a policeman) and terrorized by things happening in their forest (Daisy snorts in panic while the slipper is round her neck). Yet goose, cat, and pig are waiting quietly for Rock when he reaches home at last. The old man may profess that "No-one has to keep silent under persecution, except dumb animals of course" (p. 252); but his animals have expressed protest, and, finally, a kind of unpredictable attachment to him.

In the beginning, when Rock *was* ringed in by fog, an image suggested why man is more confined and uneasy than unattached animals. Describing sun striking into the ring of fog, Green wrote that Rock "might have been inside a pearl strung next the skin of his beloved" (p. 8).* But toward the end, creatures have begun to seem human, in consequence of the default of humans like Liz. If Rock has any triumph in the unresolved day, it lies in his satisfaction (and astonishment) that his animals are home. Their odd and mute expressiveness seems to purport that nature will not allow its law of mutual dependence to be destroyed, although another of its laws allows that "life and pursuit" shall be "fierce." Meantime, that the bewitched girls will continue to live by the latter mandate seems incontestable. "Mary's a curse," they agree (p. 183). And even their

---

* In *Living* Green was more explicit when he said, "We are imprisoned by that person whom we love" (*Living,* p. 250).

championing of Sebastian's and Elizabeth's engagement smacks of depravity. When someone asks, in fun, what Edge will give for a wedding present, three answers come spontaneously. They help make *Concluding* the stylized fairy tale it partly is, but they also proclaim the abiding unnatural allegiances of the girls:

> "A stuffed goose."
> "One of those lucky cat charms."
> "Or a black and white china pig money box." (p. 182)

Postulating, with mirth, changes to come to *Concluding*'s three principal animals, the answers can be read as the culmination of Green's frightening vision of the future.

GREEN AND WALLACE STEVENS

At the beginning of this chapter I said that with *Concluding* Green may have reached a philosophically conclusive position; yet in emphasizing that the novel is steeped in mystery, and that the presence of sheltered, gloriously singing birds seems to be set against otherwise predacious imagery, I seem to have precluded any definite, unambiguous view on Green's part. Still there seems no doubt as to the direction of his attitude. Even dismissing the sea change imagery, we can recall phrases that label the world of *Concluding* a "dying world," a "fallen world of birds." Nor is the sequential structure of the novel ambiguous. Now it may be charged that Green has been oversensitive to signs of the times, and that the changes he has insinuated in *Concluding* are not intellectually convincing. It is for this reason—that Green's futuristic subject matter may not be strictly defensible as the source of his pessimism—that I have chosen to end with a speculation on his philosophy. This may be independently responsible for *Concluding*'s dark themes. My idea takes rise from a recent article by Louis L. Martz, entitled "Wallace Stevens: The World as Meditation," [5] because of some passages Mr.

Martz examines from Stevens's "Owl's Clover." This poem was first published in 1936, revised in *The Man with the Blue Guitar* (1937), then excluded by the poet from the *Collected Poems* (1954).

Presenting as its chief early symbols a magnificent statue, embodying man's accomplishments and hopes, which is ignored by "a woman so depressed that she cannot apprehend the statue's action," "Owl's Clover" goes on, as Martz says, to postulate what course may be taken in life to allay the effects of such depression and suffering. No statue, no static approximation of an ideal will serve. Instead, Stevens in the original poem urges "Mesdames" to

> Dance, now, and with sharp voices cry, but cry
> Like damsels daubed and let your feet be bare
> To touch the grass and, as you circle, turn
> Your backs upon the vivid statue.[6]

This admonition contains the materials of two symbols in *Loving,* to which I drew attention earlier—of Kate and Edie dancing in oblivion, and of Edie and her young charges circling indifferently beneath "stone-cold bosoms" and "damp streaming marble bellies." Both Green and Stevens in these passages present oblivious concord with the flux as a resolving agency.

Indeed, one is amazed at the similarity of materials "Owl's Clover" and *Loving* employ for similar purposes. Green's novel both celebrates and associates decay with peacocks, doves, and the solitary Irish keeper, who live on the grounds of the spoiling castle. Toward all of these the servant girls display reverence, astonishment, even love. Notice Stevens's treatment of like elements in the composition of his long poem:

> And if you weep for peacocks that are gone
> Or dance the death of doves, most sallowly,
> Who knows? The ploughman may not live alone
> With his plow, the peacocks may abandon pride,
> The dove's adagio may lose its depth

And change. If ploughman, peacocks, doves alike
In vast disorder live in the ruins, free,
The charts destroyed, even disorder may
So seen, have an order of its own, a peace
Not now to be perceived yet order's own.[7]

The results of sympathy and engagement on the part of the girls
Stevens addresses, and on the part of Green's servant heroines, are
equivalent. To the abiding disorder "in the ruins" is brought "a
peace" that contains the seeds of order, something substantial and
positive, to which the artist may commit himself.* Green's novels
from *Blindness* to *Back* are sustained by this kind of conviction. He
and Stevens praise hieratically their heroines' obliviousness. But a
year after Stevens had written the lines just given, he revised
them; and also in the 1937 version he deleted the passage exhorting
the dancers to "turn / Your backs upon the vivid statue." He was
following a policy, Mr. Martz holds, of cutting away remnants of a
hedonism that had buoyed his earlier verse. It is not enough, says
the 1937 version,

. . . It is not enough
That the vista retain ploughman, peacocks, doves,
However tarnished . . .
And that, heavily, you move with them in the dust.
It is not enough that you are indifferent,
Because time moves on columns intercrossed,
And because the temple is never quite composed. . . .
. . . It is only enough
To live incessantly in change.[8]

---

* An identical vision is achieved, through the help of his wife Anna, by Will
Brangwen in *The Rainbow*, who rejects his former belief in the absolute,
symbolized by Lincoln Cathedral, and who assumes the attitude I have just
explained in Green and Stevens: "He thought of the ruins of the Grecian
worship, and it seemed, a temple was never perfectly a temple, till it was
ruined and mixed up with the winds and the sky and the herbs." (D. H.
Lawrence, *The Rainbow* [New York, n.d.], p. 193.)

A much flatter view, this—and it seems equivalent to the view Green comes to take in *Concluding*. The temple—the bringing of pattern to completion and rest, aesthetically satisfying—is really "never quite composed." Hence the singleness of direction that uniquely (for Green) determines *Concluding*'s structure. As early as *Living*, Green had shown he was sensitive to the idea that pattern, repeated until it could approximate stasis and perfection, was but an illusory comfort seized by man. (This idea was best conveyed when Dick Dupret daydreamed by the autumnal Thames, watching a launch and wondering, "Why did they turn it there.") However, when the heroine, Lily, makes an emotional commitment to the continuum on the last page, *Living* strikes a qualified note of optimism. Its author was young, and autumnal notions did recede. Not so in *Concluding*, in which that culminating dance of drowning is replete with autumnal imagery, and in which man's imposed patterns of luncheon, teatime and dance depend first upon his being awakened, and are then eclipsed, by a directional force that is one way ever.* And here Green's vision seems mature, considered, conclusive —a vision, says Giorgio Melchiori, of "everything . . . swayed by fluctuation, not temporary and seeking a consummation, but self-sufficient and permanent." [9] This tallies with Stevens's disheartening vision of the flux in the revised "Owl's Clover"; and Stevens went on in both versions, says Martz, to grant "less and less sustenance for the troubled mind trying to feed in the dark. . . ."

What Stevens went on to consider is once again strikingly related to what Green did, this time in *Concluding*. In both versions of the poem, after the section with which we have been concerned, Stevens set about contrasting two ways of life—a way, like that of Mr. Rock, of humanistic or religious loneliness, wherein each man "walked alone / Noble within perfecting solitude"; and a way of

---

* A highly compressed image in *Concluding*, which may suggest the same directional force as in the Thames sequence, occurs when a policeman lays his bicycle on its side: "Mr. Rock noticed, with a dreadful reluctance, that its uppermost pedal still revolved" (p. 74). This and the image of Rock's being ringed in by fog, compared to the more apparent statements in *Living*, suggest Green's progress from impressionism to expressionism—a progress Giorgio Melchiori briefly noted.

life wherein physical nature (Stevens's "Africa"), unresisted, dominates all. Here is a world like Henry Green's world of the hunted, a kingdom in which

> Death, only, sits upon the serpent throne:
> Death, the herdsman of elephants,
> To whom the jaguars cry and lions roar
> Their petty dirges of fallen forest men,
> Forever hunting or hunted, rushing through
> Endless pursuit or endlessly pursued,
> *Until each tree, each evil-blossomed vine*
> *Each fretful fern drops down a fear like dew. . . .*[10]

Of this passage, the lines I have italicized are as applicable to *Concluding* as any other. They condense, for me at least, all the inchoate suggestions in Green's prose of the evil forest and menacing lake, which spawned fear where they did not spawn depravity; which took even the measure of fearless Rock, who would not walk alone through the woods by night. What then of the benediction of the starlings at sunset? In the light of the intellectual pessimism that preponderates in this novel, they seem to marshal that consummate, unsullen emotion that accompanies clearest disclosures of transience—the joy to which Keats gave expression in the "Ode on Melancholy."

EIGHT : *Six and six* :
NOTHING, DOTING

RESIDUE OF ''CONCLUDING''

The novels that follow Green's masterpiece, *Concluding,* are *Nothing*
and *Doting.* Their titles and even their jacket blurbs suggest that
they do not explore the same depths as *Concluding,* and one finds on
reading them that they consist of dialogue scenes, presenting members of London's Mayfair set stricken by middle age and postwar
taxation. These scenes, laid in hotels and flats and restaurants, are
rampant with the ingenuities and self-betrayals of genteel folk, who
pursue their wants deviously out of lasting regard for propriety.
The scenes articulate with near-mathematical precision, and because
of this precise treatment of lightweight material, *Nothing* and

Doting pose an evaluational problem that explains their mixed critical reception.

The problem is to decide whether Green has despaired of humane values, and resorted to the emotional consolations of abstract art, or whether in these comic novels he has retained his gift for enjoying the human beings he mistrusts and for accepting cheerily the combinations of pleasure and pain that come their way in lieu of happiness. The title *Nothing,* for example, could refer to an airiness of subject matter, or it could reflect the nihilistic view of life that Giorgio Melchiori has attributed to Green in the later novels.

After a book like *Concluding,* it is a bit astonishing to come upon *Nothing* and *Doting,* in which descriptive prose is drastically curtailed. They seem to demonstrate the philosophical conclusiveness of *Concluding;* at least we may begin to evaluate the rationale behind the two novels by examining some relationships between them and it.

Beekman Cottrell has remarked in Green's fiction up to *Concluding* an increasing drift toward unreality, a progression so radically terminated that Cottrell feels that "the nightmare of Mr. Rock's world may account for the sharp move into the bright, commonplace light of the two novels which followed." [1] In the fantasy of *Concluding* I have attempted to show a new kind of dismay, centering in Green's vision of the demise of organic nature. And although *Nothing* and *Doting* return us to recognizable country, they repeat danger signals sounded for the first time in *Concluding,* in such a way that the pessimism Melchiori and Cottrell find in them may derive from the pessimism registered through *Concluding*'s "sea change."

One relationship concerns the stultifying atmosphere of Welfare Statism. In *Nothing* the conflict between generations results largely from the over-responsible attitudes of its youths. How soberly Mary Pomfret and Philip Weatherby treasure their government jobs reflects a gauche earnestness that causes them to disapprove of their parents (who are victims of low cash as their children are of high seriousness). Once when Mary bemoans being regimented, "You wouldn't want to go back to the bad old times Mary," Philip remonstrates. "Not when we're making this country a place fit to live in at last" (p. 55). (In *Concluding,* Sebastian once related Rock to the same "bad old times": "Any man as old stretches back to the bad times. He's suspect just because of the years he's lived" [p. 46].) As for the young females of *Doting,* also on a bureaucratic treadmill, and given to doting on older men when they can, J. D. Scott has summarized their plight in terms that remind us immediately of *Concluding:* ". . . the particular symptom which starts [*Doting*] off is the inability to provide a mating machinery to replace the over-elaborate machinery of presentation at Court, London Season, country house entertaining, and so on." [2]

The combination of job earnestness and an insufficient "mating machinery" prevent *Nothing* and *Doting,* like *Concluding* before them, from spawning women capable of enriching their worlds. Plotting females of the older generation do win funny victories over younger antagonists, and do manage their men with ease—yet they only exploit others to gratify themselves. Although Jane Weatherby of *Nothing* and Diana Middleton of *Doting* have redeeming qualities (involving their attitudes to marriage, as we shall see), not one woman appears in *Concluding, Nothing,* or *Doting* to promise that continuance of support, through giving, that brightened the novels from *Blindness* to *Back.*

A feature of those earlier novels was the prose that seemed to burst forth spontaneously with praise of birds and animals and plants. But with *Concluding,* nature's sinister qualities prevailed, and the one deeply moving passage of this kind, describing the settling starlings, was elegiac in tone. In *Nothing,* only one fleeting intrusion hints that organic nature is still a self-fostering thing: the Weatherbys' Italian maid has bought a mouse for her cat, and to Mrs. Weatherby's shocked surprise the two animals drink from one saucer. In *Doting* there are no such intrusions. The only extended prose passages in these novels describe wholly artificial phenomena —a silent, mirrored hotel room standing in readiness for a party (in the middle of *Nothing*), and two night clubs, with dance floors and wrestling arenas, strippers and jugglers (at the beginning and end of *Doting*).

These passages are strategic, because they intensify scenes that determine each novel's structure. *Nothing* builds toward and away from the central engagement party; *Doting* supplies parties at the beginning and end of Peter Middleton's school vacation. And all dynamism appears canceled by the processional quality achieved (as in no other of Green's books) when partners measuredly exchange one another as a result of what happens at the parties.

The fact that Green has deployed six characters in each book, in relationships that can be diagramed, tempts one to detect in his construction a negation of organic principle, which is ostensibly replaced by inorganic (therefore lifeless) schematization. For instance, the six characters of *Nothing* can be arranged hexagonally so that each person exhibits emotional ties to right and left, all more or less minor relationships attending the bond of a central axis linking Jane Weatherby and John Pomfret:

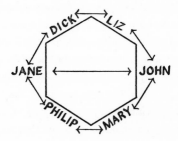

Similarly, a hexagon can be constructed for *Doting,* its top half grouping the older characters, its bottom half the younger, and again we can mark interior and peripheral "lines of force":

It is well known that inorganic material takes hexagonal shape in the formation of a snowflake; with this in mind, consider in connection with *Nothing* and *Doting* the passage in *The Magic Mountain* during the climactic ski scene, when Hans Castorp examines some snowflakes before his dream-epiphany: "Yet each, in itself—this was the uncanny, the antiorganic, the life-denying character of them all—each of them was absolutely symmetrical, icily regular in form. They were too regular, as substance adapted to life never was to this degree—the living principle shuddered at this perfect precision, found it deathly, the very marrow of death. . . ."[3]
The nature of Green's structures in the other novels makes it in no way farfetched to attribute such suggestive force to his arrangements. But I intend to go no further in substantiating the viewpoint, of Giorgio Melchiori especially, that Green's attitude in the end is nihilistic; for I believe that such recapitulations of structure are based upon *impressions* received from scenario devices Green employs—devices that give an idea of geometric precision.* Such precision cannot *really* be demonstrated. When a critic borrows terms from another art or a science—as here from geometry—he is speaking metaphorically, and his conclusions claim only a general kind of validity. A term like "hexagonal" may help explain the structural pattern by which, very formally so to speak, Liz Jennings and Dick Abbot form a new alliance after they are given "marching orders" by John and Jane respectively. In a general way this pairing maintains conformity of structure. But meanwhile there is always the novel's specific texture. When V. S. Pritchett wrote that *Nothing* and *Doting* go back to one of the novel's sources, the

---

* In *Nothing*, for example, the first three scenes introduce the six major figures as they are originally paired: John Pomfret with Liz Jennings; Jane Weatherby with Dick Abbot; Philip with Mary. The novel is to conclude with the contented alliance of John and Jane; hence Green ends the three scenes drolly by showing all the *others* contented: Liz's "sad face was beaming" (p. 13), Dick's "great face was beaming" (p. 23), the young people were "well contented it seemed" (p. 29). In *Doting* Green goes so far as to duplicate an entire introductory sentence to suggest the resumption of the same old round when characters are rejoined. Here is a sentence he uses twice: "Her day's work done, Annabel Paynton had a drink in the pub outside the office with her confidante, Miss Claire Belaine" (pp. 63, 129).

theatre, and likened Green to a "quietly raging Congreve," he observed that "The matter and machinery of classical comedy is always deceptively trivial; what counts is the texture. In *Doting* this
lies in Mr. Green's phenomenal ear for talk." [4] And if we focus on
texture, we perceive that a dynamic principle prevails, after all, in
the variety of dodges and slips of the tongue Green concocts for our
entertainment. Symmetry may satisfy aesthetic demands, and repetition of situation may symbolize stagnation of spirit; yet within the
working limits defined by structure, the novelist may achieve the
gratification of creating life that endures beyond his book. This has
always been Green's first aim.

In his postwar comedies of manners, despite their being touched
with *Concluding*'s pessimism, Green achieves this aim—better, say,
than he achieved it in *Party Going*. This is true even though the last
novels, having nothing to do with class conflict, have no proletarian
fellow-feeling to pump vitality into them. (They do re-embody
Party Going in other respects: Arthur Morris in *Nothing,* dying by
degrees, substitutes for Miss Fellowes, and on the first page of
Doting another dead bird is mentioned—the goose Peter Middleton
is to carry back to school after vacation.) The trouble is that the
Mayfair pleasure-seekers have aged but have not changed. They are
sad extensions of their affluent selves of the thirties. Parties are few
and far between in postwar London, since Pomfrets and Middletons
and Weatherbys wince at the thought of paying for them; nevertheless, they can conceive of no other way of expressing the feelings
they would like to have, and hence, to celebrate the rearing of their
offspring, give in one novel a "twenty-firster" (for Philip Weatherby), and in the other a tour of night clubs (to Peter Middleton).
These parties are really for the grownups. At them they are able to
reassume the old manners, so connected with flair and free-spending
—a way of life that had bankrupted them emotionally two decades
earlier.

But because parties can be arranged but rarely, one seems to find
mild sympathy extended to the jaded middle-aged of these novels.
At least the brunt of ridicule is reserved for their offspring. The
young people may be stuffy and deferential like Philip Weatherby,

glad to have circumstances relieve him of deciding whether to marry or not, or glib and dissatisfied like Annabel Paynton in *Doting,* who, vowing herself "expendable," lets older men wine and dine her, until in boudoir crises they find her by no means ready to return favors on the only scale that matters to them.

The youthful rich of *Party Going* were satirized for similar reasons. The males in *Party Going* were, like Philip, incapable of the tiniest decisiveness. And hangers-on like Angela and Julia promised sex and delivered none, their real motives conditioned, like Annabel Paynton's, by their hopes of being squired about expensively. Nevertheless, one female in *Party Going, Nothing,* and *Doting* is vested with total sexual control over her men. These are Amabel, Jane Weatherby, and Diana Middleton. But in 1950, in contrast to 1939, Green has made his important males a bit wistful and reflective, definitely intelligent, even at times capable of real passion and self-assertion. Although they are staggeringly deficient in will, they are capable of an intermittent resilience, a kind of daily gusto, that may make them heroes of sorts in the end.* Totteringly, they skirt the brink of despondency. Whatever sympathy we can detect Green extending them would seem to imply a queer, undaunted heartiness, on his part, in the face of all the intellectual misgivings that *Concluding* broached and with which these conversation pieces abound.

APPEARANCES, DEIFIED

The plots of *Nothing* and *Doting* are governed by the characters' considerations for appearances. In the absence of any deeper-founded integrity, the sanctions of their fast depleting social set become the only standards for conduct to which John Pomfret and Jane Weatherby, or the Middletons, have recourse. It is both sad

---

* Green's treatment of these men (not of the women) marks a significant difference between him and representative contemporaries. Compare, to the men of *Nothing* and *Doting,* Tony Last of *A Handful of Dust,* for example, or Thomas Quayne of *The Death of the Heart,* to whom his wife Anna says accurately, "Your lack of gusto's your particular thing." (Elizabeth Bowen, *The Death of the Heart* [New York, 1955], p. 334.)

and funny that the older generation remains faithful to its specious conventions: funny that everyone's sense of duty makes grim business of the parties; sad that John Pomfret, out of real feeling, can speak as follows of Arthur Morris while Arthur undergoes piecemeal amputations of his leg: " 'If I lay in bed about to be amputated [he says to Liz Jennings] I wouldn't expect you to laugh of course my dear and naturally Mary couldn't, but I'd lose a certain amount of resistance if I thought our acquaintances weren't roaring their beastly heads off! I'd even forgive you a grin or two,' he said smiling at her" (p. 9).

Nothing is the story of the rekindling of an old flame between Jane Weatherby and John, widow and widower, who had a well-known affair about the time Jane's Philip was conceived. As the novel opens, they have been encumbered for some time with partners, Dick Abbot and Liz Jennings. But for some time also Jane has been quietly trolling for John, the two having kept on good terms in the intervening years. When their children, Philip and Mary, fall in love (in consequence of their working at the same government office), a conflict between generations ensues, characters' loyalties are tested, and *Nothing* fashions a yardstick to measure the absolute sexual and social dominion of Mrs. Weatherby.

In the first third of the novel, before the children surprise their parents by announcing their engagement at Philip's twenty-firster, we have learnt humorously of Jane's abiding interest in John. Jane's six-year-old daughter, Penelope, supremely reactive to all sorts of traumatic experience, is Jane's alter ego; and Penelope's mock wedding to Mr. Pomfret, performed at his instigation one evening at Jane's flat, has left the child desperate (because husbandless), according to her mother. "I've got to act, rid her of this somehow," is one of Jane's typical alarums over Pen (p. 31), but we may fix the source of her agitation in her own frustration. Her concerns for Penelope recede measurably once she has properly netted John.

Jane's capacity for taking action helps keep *Nothing* the untrammeled frolic it partly is. When her frantic son pursues her to Brighton, demanding to know the truth about his parentage, she evaluates his motives instantly, apprehending that an affair between Philip and Mary would endanger her plans. So to gain time, she orders him to take a bath in her hotel room (he is dripping wet, and she cries pneumonia), then whisks his clothes off to be dried, thus preventing—so she imagines—an elopement. Resourcefulness of this sort is what makes the middle-aged Englishwomen of *Nothing* and *Doting* too great a match for their lovers or rivals. If nothing else, they have direction to their lives, a purposiveness we have known Green to respect in Mrs. Haye in *Blindness,* in his young heroines, even in Mabel Edge of *Concluding.*

The fear of possible incest, not very well grounded as far as their parents are concerned, keeps Philip and Mary at an impasse. Philip, succumbing to the aura of pressure, ill-temperedly places blame on the scandalous elder set, meantime remaining gratified that his decision can be postponed. But Jane's opposition to the marriage is not at all connected with fears of incest; in fact the most interesting feature of *Nothing* is that Jane sets out to wreck the engagement, and John in the end complies, only because a double marriage seems inexpressibly vulgar to them, and would make them ridiculous before their friends. Fanfare for Mary and Philip would draw attention to the ages of Jane and John, and would make any subsequent union of theirs inelegant (because libidos would obviously be getting preference over what society expects of parents—attentiveness to their children). Jane's reasons for blocking the marriage, which crumble under logical examination, are nevertheless insinuated so deftly that the reader accepts the central situation of *Nothing* without question, and it slips without splash into the realm of the absurd.*

---

* By the absurd I mean the fictional attitude lately associated with Camus, but relevant also to Green. In his interview with Green, Terry Southern gave a working definition when he asked Green about the absurdity of having English servants staff an Irish castle. "For a situation to be, in the literary sense, genuinely *absurd*," said Southern, "it must be convincingly arrived at, and should not be noticed by readers as being at all out of the ordinary." In reply, Green assented that "the whole of life now is of course absurd." ("The Art of Fiction XXII," *Paris Review,* V [Summer 1958], 75–76.)

Her heart set on preventing one embarrassing series of appearances from materializing, Jane nevertheless responds to the engagement announcement with a studied graciousness that provokes one of Green's finest passages of emphatic rhetoric:

> And when Jane came to their table she folded Mary Pomfret into so wonderful an embrace while the child half rose from her chair to greet it that not only was the girl's hair not touched or disarranged in this envelopment, but as Mrs Weatherby took the young lady to her heart it must have seemed to most the finest thing they had ever seen, the epitome of how such moments should be, perfection in other words, the acme of manners, and memorable as being the flower, the blossoming of grace and their generation's ultimate instinct of how one should ideally behave. (p. 111)

This passage, with its interminable qualification, its periodicity broken, then resumed for a final lift and thrust, marks Green's most telling disclosure of deified appearances.* Jane's action tests the shallows of her set's belief in manners, yet is performed elegantly and receives a measure of praise through syntactical climax: at the moment of ethical penetration the prose will not deny grace and poise, and we understand how formidable the woman is.

John Pomfret, not knowing Jane's plans for him, is genuinely exhilarated by the betrothal. Later in fact, after he is told Jane opposes the match, he breaks forth in the one passionate outburst of *Nothing*. He turns a temperate argument into a heated one, losing his temper for once:

> "I don't want us to look ridiculous Jane!"
> She raised her eyebrows and stared coolly at him.
> "I'm not sure what you mean?" she said.

* Twice Mrs. Weatherby is described with "heavenly" superlatives. Once she gives "two nods that seemed to promise paradise" (p. 6), and another time a waiter gazes at her "as though he might never see another promise of heaven" (p. 228).

In a trembling voice, with an obvious and complete loss of temper he cried all at once "By trying to stop this marriage by saying as I'm told you are that Philip is my son." (p. 188)

Jane of course has done no such thing, her ways being more subtly lethal, and unassailable. She has simply refused to discuss wedding arrangements with John, meanwhile disengaging him from Liz by having him to numerous dinners, on the pretext of discussing that wedding. Two large tears and a studied exit and re-entry are all Jane needs to overpower John at this crisis. But notice that he is moved to passion by a regard, not for his daughter's happiness, but for appearances. "I don't want us to look ridiculous Jane!" is his rallying cry, and it explains also the lather he works up over the cheap ring Philip has bought Mary.

In the same tenor as John's protestations are those of Arthur Middleton in *Doting*. Because Arthur has been kept in sexual fever by young Annabel Paynton, his wife has had to threaten taking up with their old friend Charles Addinsell in retaliation. Arthur's gravest fear is of being made ridiculous:

"And, in addition" she went on "I may be forced to do what I warned you I might have to. Reprisals!"

"Now, look here, Di—" he pleaded.

"Something with, say, Charles which I could afterwards regret."

"With my best friend?" he burst out. "Why, you'd make me a laughing stock." (p. 178)

Diana Middleton wishes to torture her husband back into obsequiousness, and accomplishes her job, as Jane Weatherby had hers, for the same reason: both sets of male and female protagonists want to cling to the baubles their generation does not tire of, sexual gratification and social approbation. In *Doting*, as V. S. Pritchett says, the Middletons' double bed is "the centerpiece of the book," and their love-making is refreshingly spontaneous. But meantime

Arthur and Diana are intent on accrediting their marriage as a purposeful, intelligent union—so as to justify all of Arthur's tireless work, and Diana's loneliness.

They honor therefore their special "arrangement," by which either may go out on his own. And they comfort themselves by agreeing that every sacrifice they make, every boredom they endure, is for their son Peter. Mutual trust, then, and a belief in the contributing importance of their marriage, are the values Arthur and Diana profess to live by. It is ironic that these nominal values are responsible for the disruptive nonsense of *Doting*.

For it is on pretext of duty that the elders give Peter his vacation parties; and at the first of these Arthur becomes infatuated with Annabel, an old friend's daughter whom Diana has paired with Peter. The special "arrangement" subsequently gives Arthur grounds for treating Ann to weekly luncheons. Ultimately, on a night Diana and Peter are supposed to have left for Scotland, Arthur brings Ann to the Middleton flat for dinner. There he spills coffee on her in an awkward attempt to embrace her, and during the cleaning up at a bedroom washstand, with Ann standing in her knickers and Arthur kneeling beside her, Diana walks in. She is fresh from a cab accident that has put Peter in the hospital, and is more than ready to believe the evidence of her eyes.

Raffish Charles Addinsell emerges as an important figure at this stage of the novel. Arthur sues to Charles to square things with Diana, but Charles elects to try for Diana's favors instead. He is unsuccessful; meanwhile the discrepancy between doting and loving is made clear by Arthur's agitation, once he finds Di has visited Charles "three times in five whole days" (p. 98). He deals Annabel right off to Charles, for the sake of regaining Diana.

Doting is not very far along before Mrs. Middleton's control over her husband becomes fairly predictable, their squabbles invariably being settled by their periodic joy over Peter's fishing prowess up in Scotland. What continues to flavor the novel's intrigues is the thoroughness of Diana's planned vindication. Although she has permitted Addinsell no liberties, she warms herself knowing that Charles and Arthur both wait at her beck and call. Hence she is

doubly antagonized by Annabel, who first threatened her husband
and then her loyal Charles.

Diana's plan is to "safeguard" both Charles and Arthur from
Annabel by arranging a last vacation party for Peter that will in-
clude Claire Belaine, Ann's plain but rotund confidante. The aim is
to divert Addinsell to Claire so that Diana may take conspicuous
revenge of Annabel at Peter's party. But in vanquishing the girl,
Mrs. Middleton overreaches: widower Charles falls too heavily for
Miss Belaine. Here *Doting* teems with bawdy poetic justice. Diana
had kept respectable with Charles, Annabel had proved an icicle to
him as well as to Arthur—but Claire tumbles into bed with him with
celerity.

A clue to the tone and purpose of *Doting* may be gained from
Green's merry countenancing of Addinsell's success with Claire,
poised as the two are against plaintive Peter and "unexpended"
Annabel, who are miserable as the last night club party ends. In the
serious novels *Caught* and *Back,* one recalls similar situations in
which widowers in physical need (Richard Roe, James Phillips)
were gratified by plump and eager young women (Hilly, Dot Pitter). But whereas those temporary unions granted a measure of
relief, they pointed to lust always debilitating, and were opposed
thematically by the genuine loves of Roe and Charley Summers, one
past, the other new found. In *Doting,* on the other hand, Addinsell's
success gives a positive lift to a novel that protracts anxiety and
unfulfillment for its doting males. So many juicy promises remain
undelivered that a kind of condolence mixes with the drollery of
such descriptions as Annabel's leave-taking of Charles, after the
man has made a pass at her: "And within twenty minutes she'd got
out of that flat, and left him behind, as though she'd done Mr Addinsell the greatest imaginable favour. Indeed, from the expression on
his face, while he handed her into the taxi, for which he'd phoned,
it seemed he was fully conscious of his merit. He looked old and
sad" (p. 188).

For the author to seem delighted over shrewd and vegetable-like
Miss Belaine serves to highlight the sympathy that shares space
with his pessimism. Sexuality may have been deleterious in the

serious novels, but in the emotional vacuums of *Nothing* and *Doting* it emerges as the best of few consolations. It would seem, too, that Green views his sad profligates more sympathetically than he views straitjacketed idealists like Philip or prudes like Annabel Paynton —simply because the profligates make more headway and get *some* satisfaction, however trivial.

When Diana Trilling reviewed *Nothing,* she spoke of "Mr. Green's refusal to choose between the generations"; but in qualifying her statement she refutes it, I think, by drawing this accurate comparison: "Seen beside their offspring, Mr. Pomfret and Mrs. Weatherby are frivolous and selfish, and very dangerous in their ruthless manipulation of other people's lives. But seen beside their parents, Mary and Philip are rather a pair of prigs, and natural victims." [5]

All the characters of *Nothing* and *Doting,* indeed all the characters of Green's novels, may be said to be natural victims—of time, if not of circumstance. But Green has invariably had most fun at the expense of those, like Jim Dale and Raunce's Albert and Sebastian Birt and the young of the Mayfair novels, who have not been able to chop even a resting place out of the blockhouses that confine them; and conversely he has always shown respect for people, however hedonistic, who are wily enough to see their small schemes through. Ruthlessness hardly alarms him—especially in the last two novels—for the pleasure he takes in people who are capable of gaining their own ends remains constant, regardless of what he demonstrates to be the source of their actions. In *Nothing* and *Doting* the blockhouses of postwar living have been made absolute; the consolation is sex. There are no more extraordinary combatants like Mr. Rock, who can eschew such consolations.

ACUMEN AND UNSTRUNG WILLS

Lionel Trilling once wrote that the novel at its greatest is the record of the will acting; with such a guide we can say that *Nothing* and

Doting, like many modern "examples which do not deal with the
will in action," become "secondary in their genre." [6] (This is
another reason for saying that *Concluding,* superior to the others
though most dismaying, is the novel with which Green "concluded.")
The male characters in *Nothing* and *Doting* come nearest, perhaps, of
all Green's people to being victims of modern lassitude, in the face
of wearying facts.

Charles Addinsell's philosophy of life, for instance, amounts to a
distaste for binding emotional attachments. Having lost his wife in
childbirth, he shies from talk of remarriage, and at one point pro-
fesses that he will not love his son Joe too much "on account of if he
dies" (p. 143). The fact that Charles's philosophy is also his formula for decoying girls into bed, combined with the wonderfully
sententious language Green puts in his mouth, makes him a kind of
mock Hemingway hero. "Not her fault, good God!" he can say of his
wife's death. "If anything, might have been mine, or equally the
fault of each of us, in actual practice. No, what I have against living,
is the dirty tricks fate has in store. No good blinking facts. Do
better to realize, they probably will be coming to you. I couldn't
stand a second kick in the pants of the kind" (p. 226).*

Despite the maudlin humor here, Addinsell's phrase "No good
blinking facts" has a pernicious formative influence on the older men
of *Nothing* and *Doting.* Their conviction in its merit gives rise to
their resilience, but also to their self-exculpation and passive wills.

Green's males will not blink facts, whereas his women will. After
Dick Abbot and Liz Jennings have teamed together, Liz crows about
having escaped from John Pomfret; but as for Dick, "Never was
good enough for Jane," he admits reluctantly (p. 226). Similarly,
Green's males often show disinterested curiosity, whereas his women
are self-protective and try to shut out unpleasantness. In one scene
in *Doting,* Peter, just returned from the hospital, announces that
some patients had died during his stay. "Don't, darling," says his
mother.

---

* Quite different is the intended effect of Catherine Barkley's deathbed remark to Frederick, "It's just a dirty trick." (Ernest Hemingway, *A Fare-
well to Arms* [New York, 1929], p. 342.)

"Yes, at least three people died" Peter interjected.

"No, don't" was Mrs Middleton's earnest plea.

"What time of the day or night?" his father wanted to be told.

"Usually it seemed to be about four or five in the morning."

. . . "Curious" Mr Middleton remarked "it always seems that resistance is lowest at that hour of the night." (p. 92)

The reactions of husband and wife to this news are exactly matched in *Nothing* by John Pomfret's reflections on the dying Arthur Morris, as compared later to Jane's protestations on hearing of Arthur's death. Jane will not have the thing mentioned. It is her way of keeping doors shut on whatever is ugly or unappetizing. Perhaps this self-protective tendency is best revealed when Jane, having permitted her cook to bring a mouse for the cat, keeps clear of the house, fearful of the mauling. "I can't bear cruelty to animals John dear," she explains. ". . . Naturally I kept out of the house for a few days after that and forbade sweet Penelope the kitchen or I said I'd simply never speak to the child again" (p. 79).

Cringing from unpleasant contact, but inwardly unperturbed by others' misfortune, the women of *Nothing* and *Doting* make their openly curious men appear humane by contrast.

These men are of course controlled sexually by the two women. The fact that Green has not therefore made straw men of them is his greatest achievement in these novels, for hollow men could not have been vehicles for serious themes, nor could they have enabled Green to avoid tediousness in his plotting. After all, the subject of each book is the very stealthy ensnarement of these males. Yet well beyond the middle of *Nothing*, John Pomfret is still elusive enough to be able to speak with detachment to Jane of their torrid past. "Nonsense my dear," he quips once. "You never lived until you met me and that was years later" (p. 134). And well beyond the middle of *Doting*, Arthur Middleton has the gall to make love to his wife the day of her trip to Scotland, and that very evening to whisk Miss Paynton up to the flat (another unsuccessful gambit).

The reason these men prove at first difficult and at last easy quarries is that along with their pervasive curiosity goes a certain acumen. Observation—"not blinking facts"—has convinced them that their situations are essentially changeless. Arthur can warn Ann, for instance, "you needn't think your emotional life will ever not be in a tangle, dear" (p. 52); John can grimace over how embarrassing it is "when the parent has to implore his child not to be home at certain hours" (p. 100). But each seems convinced that such as the facts are, no corrective steps can be taken; so they take none. "That is the whole beauty of us," Mr. Pomfret cries in one place, "we never can seem to do anything" (p. 97).

It is not so much their sexual susceptibility that unstrings these men's wills as it is their cheerfully negative philosophies.* Although they would both have and eat their cake if possible, they are willing to settle for less. Hence at the outset, as Walter Havighurst has said, "There is always the same divided attention, part for the savoring of an old liaison and part for the forwarding of a new." [7] But when time comes for a choice, the men fly back to habit, so to speak. John will let his daughter's happiness slide, because the gaiety he finds in Jane allows him to "forget time and place" (p. 137). And for Arthur, the accepted alternative is to keep his marriage going as before. He will keep hard at work so that Peter may be schooled (though Diana has questioned the value of this aim), and he will continue the traditional parties for the boy (though he himself has recognized the parties are for the parents).

All of this exploration of the male characters of *Nothing* and *Doting* points to one of the most amazing things about the books: that their men understand they will not be happy. Indeed the principle of seeking enjoyment without happiness is one of what appear to be three serious themes in *Nothing* and *Doting*—the only one predicated on self-awareness. (The others, as we shall see, have to do with marriage and uncomprehended enjoyment.)

---

* Green never explains the incipience of these philosophies. The sense that the holders of them are undiagnosible is often harrowing. "Never will understand a man like that though," muses Richard Abbot over John Pomfret. "Good war record, plumb through the desert . . . must have had umpteen fellows killed right beside him. Did he laugh then out there—eh?" (pp. 15–16).

Both Arthur Middleton and Charles Addinsell indicate that they have definite ideas about a difference between joy and happiness. When Annabel uses the terms synonymously, Arthur protests, "Yet if you are enjoying yourself, you needn't necessarily be happy"— and assures her he is not splitting hairs (p. 166). Charles makes more expansive observations to Ann. She has protested she cannot fall in love, but he counters that love is unnecessary, going on to cite his wife's decision to marry him—which was made at the instance of a Victorian aunt, who told the girl "it didn't matter who you married in this life, you came to love them in the end" (p. 183). Says Ann:

> "Well then, Charles, I think that's the most extraordinary thing I've ever heard."
> "What's odd about it?"
> "Everything."
> "Why? Human nature's much the same from one person to another. So long as you don't expect to be happy, you can get to love anyone. Ours is still a very small proportion of the world that chooses their own wives." (p. 184)

With such statements of resignation as these, Green's male characters have in his last book drifted a long reach from the determined wishfulness of Mr. Craigan of *Living,* or the humane truculence of Mr. Rock in *Concluding.* But Addinsell, Pomfret, and Middleton, who approach Green's craggiest figures in intellect if not in will, are more consoled than Rock and Craigan, because they have reduced their hopes—however sententiously. We remember how Green wrote of much-admired Craigan, in *Living's* penultimate scene, "He thought what was there now for him? Nothing, nothing, He lay." How different is the mood of the last sentence of *Nothing,* in which Mrs. Weatherby ministers to her now betrothed Mr. Pomfret:

> "And how's your wicked diabetes my own darling?" she whispered.
> "All right" he barely answered.
> "And is there anything at all you want my own?"

"Nothing—nothing" he replied in so low a voice she could barely have heard and then seemed to fall deep asleep at last. (p. 250)

The ministrations of the middle-aged, one to another, may be terribly funny in *Nothing* and *Doting,* and the quality of the relationships may boil down to nothing in essence, yet the consolations of doting are the one recourse against time's encroachments. Terrible reminders of death, some very funny, infiltrate both novels. When I compared Green to Céline in the first chapter, I mentioned the yellowed place card of a man long dead, which turns up at the "twenty-firster," and Dick Abbot's choking convulsions (caused by food and sex, the two indulgences that permeate these novels); then there are John's diabetes and Arthur Middleton's unnamed sickness, both of which become salient near the end, as Raunce's dyspepsia had become. "How are you physically?" "How d'you feel in yourself?"—questions like these trip to the tongues of nearly every character with a vested interest in another, for years have set about breaking them all down in different ways. So, despite the hard, clear light that illuminates the follies of *Nothing* and *Doting,* do we sense the dimming of people until they fade out as smudges. And the most poignant scene of these novels is undoubtedly that in which John Pomfret is lulled to sleep by his daughter, she sitting on the arm of his chair, their voices growing progressively lower as light recedes. "She looked down but could make out no more than the dark top of his head. She glanced up at the framed reproductions and in this light they were no more than blurs in frames" (p. 41). That is what one senses, having laid the books aside, about the characters of *Nothing* and *Doting.* They are blurs in frames. And the men seem to know that they are substanceless.

EPITHALAMIA

To be willing to settle for enjoyment without happiness demands a condition of mind observable in the men but not in the women of

Nothing and *Doting*. The women, not content with limited objectives, might be expected as in *Party Going* to carry out the most complete depredations. But in Jane and Diana, Green seems to detect a devotion, frivolous to be sure, that makes their impact on these novels less divisive. This is their devotion to the idea of marriage.

Mrs. Middleton, quick to threaten Arthur with reprisals, would never carry out those reprisals because of her respect for the appearances of matrimony. When Addinsell advises her to teach her husband a lesson, "Oh," she replies, "I think mothers, of grown-up boys, who go to bed are pretty squalid, don't you?" (p. 174). Nor would Diana consider ending her marriage. "What d'you maintain we ought to do, then? Separate?" her husband asks in one fit of exasperation. At which she screams, "Arthur!! Arthur! You're never to say that again, d'you hear, even as a silly joke!" (p. 116).

To Jane Weatherby, marriage and the rituals that lead up to it are equally sacred. "And of course when Penelope's little time comes," says disgruntled Philip, "there'll be thousands of young men Mamma will have in, all that part of it is in my mother's blood" (p. 53). Philip has reason to know. Consider his mother's animation as she implores her stuffy son to arrange a tête-à-tête dinner with a girl he knows:

> "No you must really have pity on the poor fainting souls Philip! Just imagine them sitting by their telephones bored to tears with their sad mothers who're themselves probably only dying to have an old flame in, waiting waiting to be asked, eating their lovely hearts out!"
> . . . "I might" he said.
> "In a little sweat of excitement in their frocks!!" she said turning swiftly away the beautiful innocent eyes soft with what seemed to be love, her great mouth trembling. (pp. 34–45)

When we recall that all the young girls of *Nothing* and *Doting* are just the sort that sit by telephones, we recall that no mating machinery operates in the upper-class milieux of *Nothing* and

Doting. This may cause us to view Mrs. Weatherby as an adjunct to nature after all.

Certainly some peculiar incidental situations relate to Jane's reverence for "magic marriage" in *Nothing,* a book that is concluded with a betrothal. The novel opened, for example, with Mr. Pomfret's description of Penelope, dolled up as a bride, who had so captivated him and Jane that they decided on a mock wedding on the spot. As the child stood there, veiled in window muslin, "in adorable humility," John had felt "that all this spelled magic marriage, heralded a bride without music by firelight, a black mouth trembling mischief and eyes, huge in one so young, which the fire's glow sowed with sparkling points of rose" (p. 4).

The concluding scene returns to this imagery, confirming Penelope as Jane's alter ego, as John Pomfret looks down into Jane's fire-sown eye, "into the two transparencies that veiled it, down to that last surface which at three separate points glowed with the fire's same rose . . ." (p. 248).

These two scenes, early benediction and late consummation, span the novel with a kind of homage to magic marriage. Yet a budding marriage is wrecked in the interim proceedings. And just at the time of John's decision to urge his daughter off to Italy, Arthur Morris dies—his death signifying perhaps the destructiveness inherent in his friends' action, for their union does not hint of future offspring, as the younger couple's would have. With these remarks in mind, let us turn to one final, apparently innocuous passage, that may create a summary image of *Nothing*'s conflicting themes. This has to do with Jane's line of questioning when Dick Abbot confides some of his war experiences. Their conversation is overheard by her son, who recounts it to Mary. Says Philip,

"Imagine what I overheard between Mamma and that old Abbot. He was going endlessly on about his war experiences out in Italy. She'd said how wonderful she found white oxen, I expect someone once said those great eyes of hers were so like. . . . But anyway he said he'd spent night after night out with them. That made Mamma scream all right. So he came back that a night in a stall with an ox was a damn sight better than one out in the open alone under stars. Then she asked did they snore? Would you believe it? And there's worse coming. Because when he didn't reply Mamma said 'Do they dream Richard?' Honestly I was nearly sick" (p. 76).

Her mind darting to the customary bedfellow, known in the intimacies of snores and dreams, Jane pops these mischievous questions, and they may be appalling. At least the presence of oxen here —devoid of color, castrated, bulkily neuter—may symbolize the direction of that final union between Jane and John. The very deepest theme in *Nothing* may be contained in that phrase of dubious preference, "a night in a stall with an ox was a damn sight better than one out in the open alone. . . ."

At the same time, it is Philip who is disgusted, not necessarily the reader, so busy laughing. In neither *Nothing* nor *Doting* do any young people marry; and the solutions (not resolutions) of the novels involve, in the one, the establishment of a middle-aged marriage and, in the other, the continuance of one. These unions, selfish, nevertheless thrive within the bounds of man's invention, matrimony —these women's upbringing, responsible for their bondage to social convention, has implanted in them a regard for wedlock that no code of canceled decency can impair. Such indications possibly reassure Green that by a fluke the edicts of cyclic nature will be upheld.

Self-deceit abets both novels' solutions. John Pomfret feels himself swell importantly at the prospect of being Penelope's guardian. The Middletons hold their party and will continue to go grumbling on enjoying themselves. No one ever realizes that the turbulence in which he finds himself is the direct source of his temporary satisfaction. And therein lies the only definitely optimistic theme in *Nothing* and *Doting*.

The theme can be stated in the generalization that depression, mistrust, and contention providentially enable people to find their way to each other. It can be documented from the closing lines of many scenes in the two books. One, describing the onset of Philip's and Mary's love affair, is a scene in which the two drive themselves into despondency, only to end as follows:

> There was a pause while he crumbled bread into pellets. He looked at her again. The face he saw seemed even younger, wore an expression of childish obstinacy.
>
> . . . "But we've got everything before us haven't we?" he moaned as if he were looking down into his own grave.
>
> "Year in year out" she assented.
>
> "Sometimes it seems hopeless" he said and in his turn took on an appearance of obstinacy younger even than his years. As she watched him she visibly brightened.
>
> "Cheer up Philip" she encouraged. "Things may not be as bad for all that."
>
> "Here" he demanded, obviously puzzled. "I thought you were the one who saw no hope."
>
> "Oh come on" she cried. "Let's not sit any more, glooming Sunday afternoon away! What about a film?"
>
> "I'd love to if you would" Mr Weatherby replied, back at his most formal, and in a short time they were off. . . .
>
> They hardly spoke again that day, a kind of blissful silence lay between. (pp. 56–57)

Or we may select from *Doting* a scene recounting a protracted quarrel between Arthur and Diana at a restaurant, which Green concludes by saying, "When they came home, it was plain the two of them had had, on the whole, a very pleasant evening" (p. 152).

Green's pessimism thus stands qualified by two themes: one, in which characters settle knowingly for enjoyment without happiness; the other, in which women's inbred attitudes toward marriage promote some form of concord. But the most optimistic thrust in *Nothing* and *Doting* develops from Green's belief that people further their happiness unintentionally, by creating dilemmas. Only if one realizes that Green finds psychological therapy in worry, in the

continuing conflict his best people grumble under, can one receive
heartily the excellent summary H. P. Lazarus has made of Green's
characters. "They never change," says Mr. Lazarus, "and if they
end up happy, as they often do, it is almost in spite of themselves.
They destroy the whole fiction of self-knowledge." [8]

HOBBY-HORSES

In the first chapter of this study I compared Green's humor to that of Laurence Sterne and Lewis Carroll; now, since I have just been speaking of a kind of benefit that Green assigns to obsessions and dilemmas, it seems appropriate to return to that comparison. In a study of Sterne, Norman Holland noted a similar benefit accruing to Sterne's characters. "Sterne's comedy," says Holland, "centers on the hobby-horse, the preoccupation of a character on which he rides through life. . . ." [1] Often, of course, the characters of Sterne or Green or any comic novelist are bumped off their steeds. Holland gives the illustration from *Tristram Shandy* of Phutatorius, preoccupied with abstract discourse, being upset by the presence of a hot chestnut in his britches.

Reality then, in the form of hot chestnuts down one's pants leg and the like, impinges and knocks one from one's hobby-horse. But being preoccupied also helps these people over really formidable barriers. The deaths of Le Fever and Yorick, for example, are "quickly submerged in Tristram's peregrinations," says Holland, and he goes on to give related examples: the mother thinking of winding a clock at the instant of Tristram's conception, Slop worrying about his forceps when Tristram is delivered (Slop on less auspicious occasions has trouble untying knots from his medical kit). "This is the paradox of Sterne's humor," Holland concludes. "Hobby-horses are ridiculed (in their vulnerability to little things, hot chestnuts, or knots), but respected (in their resistance to big things, birth, and copulation, and death). Sterne ridicules reality by juxtaposing it with hobby-horses that refuse to take it seriously unless it is a squeaking hinge; but since the hobby-horses are themselves ridiculous, some seriousness, even about death, remains." [2]

The summary applies perfectly to Green, and explains the paradox of his own humor, the combinations of grimness and merriness with which his novels are replete. With Green, too, "some seriousness remains"; meanwhile examples flock to mind of preoccupations or reflexive actions that enable his characters to get the best of "big things": birth, copulation, the vicissitudes of pain, loss, and sickness, death. When demented Brid bore a child in *Caught,* as Mary Howells tells Piper, "She 'ad a terrible time 'aving it, really" —but when Mary went to attend her, the girl showed only one interest, that of justifying her philandering husband. "Not a word against Ted, mum" is her preoccupation (*Caught,* p. 58). In *Concluding,* when Elizabeth lies stark naked with Sebastian behind the beech, and, Miss Baker happening by, the young man nearly bursts a vein in his forehead, Liz imagines what the principal's expression would be like "if this lady had come upon her lover as he now was"; and she laughs a "loud, gurgling laugh of cruel, delighted ridicule" (*Concluding,* p. 153). Here for once Liz gets beyond herself and her concerns for winning Sebastian through copulation; in her scorn she is marvelously juxtaposed with the man, gone "wooden with horror," and the principal, who almost breaks into a trot in her effort to get away from that laugh-haunted wood.

People bypass pain and death similarly. In *Back,* Mrs. Frazier's "hobby-horse," a place near the front of a queue, keeps her from grasping the horror with which poor Charley is struck upon first seeing Nancy, and Mrs. Frazier remains invulnerable. As for death, this needs bypassing more often than other serious threats in Green's books. Raunce, heir-apparent to Eldon's position, can get by death in two sentences, when he asks "When's the interment?" and then wonders what will be on for dinner (*Loving,* p. 11). Mrs. Grant gets by it by clucking at her husband on his deathbed; Mrs. Weatherby by covering her ears "with two fat white hands," when Pomfret would tell her about Arthur Morris (*Nothing,* p. 198). Green's most profound or most injured characters, it is true, cannot so easily ride over hurdles. We remember Charley Summers covering his ears with "streaming" hands, or Craigan grappling with despair, whereas a man like Gates "could never be sad" (*Living,* p. 256). But most of his people are of the other stamp, and react like the people of Sterne and Carroll. "The horror of that moment I shall never, *never* forget!" cries the White King in *Through the Looking Glass.* "You will though," replies the Queen, "if you don't make a memorandum of it." [3]

Tiny obstacles that people magnify and then cannot get around loom up more frequently in Green's books than the realities of birth, sex, and death. This befits the comic spirit. Miss Marchbanks makes a shambles of grilling Merode because, Edge and Baker being away, she yields under the sudden load of authority vested in her as deputy. Impending war causes the same kind of thing to happen at every echelon in the London Fire Brigade. Mary and Philip in *Nothing* cannot act because they cannot get facts. "No one tells me anything," moans Philip, on one of his endless rounds of question-plying. Miss Jennings's reply to him—"You're one of these talkers Philip. You don't go out and do things" (*Nothing,* p. 215)—applies handsomely to Green's gallery of flustered young men: to Jim Dale, Robin Adams, Raunce's Albert, Sebastian Birt. These and others, stuck on the dead centers of themselves (themselves their own hobby-horses), afford Green much merriment and little chagrin.

In the -*ing* novels, the people who "don't go out and do things" are most often those of the foundering leisured class. One is reminded of Huxley's aphorism in *Those Barren Leaves* about modern, emancipated young people, who do what they wish, namely, "nothing; for the demurest and the most 'old-fashioned' can and do act. . . ." [4] But Green's novels are peopled with the old-fashioned too, and he is bent on demonstrating their ability to act, whereas Huxley, having a different purpose, is content simply to make the statement. This is why I find it difficult to relate Green to contemporary English satirists, although I do think he has an affinity with Anthony Powell. Consider this curiously relevant passage from Powell's *The Acceptance World,* in which the narrator, Nick Jenkins, describes the action of the boorish businessman Widmerpool:

> Widmerpool acted quickly. He strolled to the kerb. A cab seemed to rise out of the earth at that moment. Perhaps all action, even summoning a taxi when none is there, is basically a matter of the will. Certainly there had been no sign of a conveyance a second before. Widmerpool made a curious, pumping movement, using the whole of his arm, as if dragging down the taxi by a rope. [5]

Not only does the phrase "a matter of the will" echo a concept we have seen suggested in Green but also we find a familiar contrast between Jenkins, a reflective man stricken with inertia, and Widmerpool, here and elsewhere a man of no acumen but capable of gearing action to the demands of circumstance. Green's mundane heroes and heroines have something of the narrow assurance of Widmerpool and impulsively cope with immediate situations. From his observation that they get by—accidentally but all the same capably—by refusing to remain concerned with peripheral threats, Green seems to have made an intellectual commitment in favor of such a response to life. This is why he does not get tormentedly involved in his characters' predicaments. Wallowing in quandaries, they do not distress him so long as they can and do act. The bumps they receive as they ride their hobby-horses into action are usually minor and funny; meanwhile Green "ridicules reality," because his activists have no time to take it seriously.

Green's irresponsible attitude toward his characters' predicaments results in an approach to life more freewheeling than that which uplifts much modern fiction—the faith in man's ability to endure. Endurance implies the Promethean struggle, to which Green does not subscribe. It implies that the problem of man's existence has been solved, and that man is obviously and tragically trapped.

We could call Green's non-Promethean attitude a traditionally British one, no doubt. Certainly his themes are the antitheses of American themes, as Paul Pickrel indicated when he reviewed *Nothing* and *World Enough and Time*. Robert Penn Warren, said Pickrel, "holds the Promethean view of life which most serious American novelists have held," and he went on to apply the opposite adjective, "Olympian," to Green's view.[6] "Olympian" does point to the fact that Green's view, though it lacks austerity, is the limited, classical view of man that has permeated one tradition in English fiction from Swift, say, to Forster.

To Green existence is an enigma, not a trap. "We shall never know the truth," says Mr. Rock at the end of his day (*Concluding*, p. 253); quieted by this knowledge, he settles down "well satisfied," behaving in a manner characteristic of most of Green's ordinary people. Walter Havighurst observed this manner to be unchanged even in the wartime environment of *Back*. "V-bombs . . . fall from time to time in the story," says Havighurst. "But the people do and say and think and feel only the usual things, as though it were any other time in history. People cannot sustain any sense of crisis or extremity. They fall quickly back into the pattern. At least these people do."[7]

These are the woolly-minded Londoners, preoccupied with ration coupons, from whom Charley Summers feels estranged. Does a man like Charley, different from most in that he has taken life's blows directly, subside "back into the pattern," get aboard the same kind of hobby-horse as his neighbors, and with new preoccupations ignore loss and sorrow? Essentially, yes, Green says, though the process takes time. Notice that during Charley's period of alienation, for all his self-pity over Rose, he never takes notice of the fact that he's lost a leg. Then think how astonishingly mobile he is. His obsession is similar to the obsessions of people *not* stricken; he is similarly protected by it; he is at bottom the same as they are. And when Charley does complete his readjustment, he acts like Green's other successful people. He can wink like the butler Raunce, and put his finger to his lips, and his arm in the arm of his girl. These are the gestures which Green associates with the happiness that is possible in this world.

Marlow, in *Lord Jim,* commenting on Jim's inability to get "out from under the shadow" of his guilt, says once that "the truth seems to be that it is impossible to lay the ghost of a fact. You can face it or shirk it—and I have come across a man or two who could wink at their familiar shades. Obviously Jim was not of the winking sort. . . ." [8] Obviously, we might say, Green is. A symbolist novelist in the twentieth century, he is virtually unique in his predilection for figures who can wink at their familiar shades, before they gird themselves to meet the trivia with which they are besieged.

THE TRUTH OF BANALITIES

Green is understandably disengaged from characters who manage in spite of themselves, or who, rushing after enjoyment or not daring to move at all, impale themselves on their great greeds and fears. But granting as he does that men are antic, incorrigible beings, he by no means minimizes their emotional needs, which are usually supplied when they partake unconsciously of fellowship or consciously of love. Their love is often strongly sexual, but when it sustains them, it is never wholly sexual. Indeed, the emotional revelations granted even the best of his men all but overwhelm them, so steeped are their girls in sexual promise. Raunce moans "Edie," as the dying butler had moaned "Ellen"; Summers buries his face in

Nancy's side and bawls like a child; Roe is "caught fast" by the "impermanence" when his wife-to-be first seems to be his in the rose garden. Less resilient characters are in similar situations wholly undone—Jim Dale, for instance, equally "caught" when half moons of light fix on dishes Lily is washing, or Raunce's Albert, dazzled and rooted to the spot after the briefest contact with Edith in the blind man's buff game. This is why, when Nancy brings one Charley a sedative, or Edith worries about the other Charley's swollen glands, the kind of love that includes but subordinates sex becomes that most promising of support.

Then there are the unloved—who also need consolation. Joan and Lily in the early novels may have cared for the old vicar and Craigan, but by the third novel we find Miss Fellowes having to draw on her own reserves. Her determination not to appear ill before the young people is spiced with the comic flavor, but it is well that she has some fund of self-sufficiency. The older people in the later novels are constantly remanded to cells, so to speak, to shift for themselves as they decline.* What their needs are, what they will settle for, we hear once from Agatha Burch, when she tells Nanny Swift how the young housemaids "look at us old women and they say to themselves they don't wish to end up like us. I was the same at their age. It's only after they've lived a few years longer that they'll come to realize there's worse than sleeping alone in your own bed, with a fresh joint down in the larder for dinner every day" (*Loving,* p. 133).

Notwithstanding Green's customary comic withdrawal, a sentiment like this, deriving from a very candid pessimism, could be said to be *his* sentiment. The novelist's recognition of emotional needs, especially of such needs as are satisfied by the presence of a fresh joint in the larder, points to a serious attitude of Green's which suggests his departure from current fictional dogma. I mean his championing, however shruggingly, the homeliest traditions—marriage, faithfulness, loyalty to the aged, duties devolving on people

* Nancy and Edith, cut from one mold, do divide their generosity between their elders and their husbands-to-be, but these are only two from a group of seven novels.

bound within family structures (at least within "archetypal" families). The modern zeal for rebellion, for the setting free of the individual, seems to find no champion in Green, whose rebellious youths, youths devoted to causes, joy-seekers, fornicators, end up frayed of nerve and discomfited. His characters find most happiness in commitments that bind people—even if, in the end, they are reduced to being bound to "the service," as Miss Burch is, or to pets and a cottage, as Rock is.

Although most serious twentieth century novelists share the tragic, Promethean vision, it is perhaps not uncommon to find commonplace virtues championed. Joyce Cary's *To Be a Pilgrim* offers a clear example. Here are Tom Wilcher's reflections after his sister-in-law Amy has whispered to him from her deathbed, "Got to die sometime": "Amy . . . had the penetration of innocence, which can see the force of a platitude. Amy's 'got to die sometime' has been on the lips of every private soldier since the first army went into battle. For her it was still profound." [9]

Green's work commonly yields sentiments like this, but his method of presenting "the force of a platitude" is uncommon. When his people come out with statements like Amy's, they are usually being not profound but sententious, and instead of resorting to a labeled post-mortem reflection like Wilcher's, Green works through the comic obtuseness of his speakers to a serious verification of the force of their platitudes in spite of these speakers. He does this by following up the homilies with symbolic episodes, leaving the reader to work out the connection. Thus, when Richard Roe ingratiates himself with the regular fireman Chopper, treating him to drinks long before any bombings and fires, he tells Chopper, "It brings everyone together, there's that much to a war" (*Caught*, p. 48). Absurd when Roe utters it, the statement foreshadows a theme to be worked out in the novel through Roe's very participation with the men. Nor does James Phillips have in mind that he will bed down with Charley's girl, Dot Pitter, when he tells Summers, "Life has a funny way of getting back at us, sometimes" (*Back*, p. 147). Yet again, a theme of the novel is broached, to be confirmed both in James's success with Dot and Charley's denials of Rose.

Shifty Charley Raunce once found a banality convenient for divulging news about the missing ring to the servants. He began by saying, "Well we're all one family in this place, there's how I see the situation" (*Loving,* p. 170). The truth of this banality was verified in the scene of "family loving," touched off soon after by Albert's decision to enlist. The scene in which Raunce thinks of his rival Albert as "me own son" and the earlier one in which he and Edie protect Albert from the insurance assessor remind me of a related sequence in *The Castle,* which may provide a basis for some last remarks on Green.

The episode I have in mind occurs after K. has been appointed school janitor, and has removed to the schoolhouse with his "pseudo-family"—his fiancée Frieda and the two mischievous assistants. On the first morning there, having used too much firewood the evening before, they have overslept and are found undressed by the woman teacher. She reviles them on the spot: "A janitor's family that loll in their beds far into the forenoon! Faugh!" [10] K. drags some parallel bars across the floor, throws blankets over these, and from behind the barricade he and Frieda and the childlike assistants watch their belongings destroyed by the schoolchildren.

Shielded from the hostile eyes of the teacher and her class, Frieda and K. dress the assistants, and he allots the morning's work, after which he decides "to issue from their shelter himself first, the others were only to follow when he called them." [11] His motives are to prevent any silliness on the part of the assistants from jeopardizing them further, and to protect Frieda. (Raunce acts from these motives when he drives the assessor from the castle after Albert's silly confession.)

Later, when the more dangerous schoolmaster arrives, Frieda confronts him in defense of the assistants—"they're only children," she says.[12] In the end even K. outbraves the master, taking the blame for burning so much wood, and retorting that the Mayor "certainly never gave me this post so that I and my dependents should freeze here. . . ." [13]

My point in reviewing this scene has been to illustrate what we have seen often in Green's books: unplanned self-sacrifice and, above all, the change under stress of a disorganized, squabbling group into a cohesive "family." In the light of later developments in *The Castle* —K.'s jealous dismissal of the assistants, for instance, which leads to the rift with Frieda—Kafka's purpose seems to be that which I have claimed for Green. Kafka seems to affirm that harmony results from outward-directed, generous behavior, and that the harmony is broken when K. tries in self-assertion to appropriate Frieda as his own.

But Kafka's characters and Green's are in these parallel scenes acting more as archetypal figures than as free agents, and they are doing so almost in spite of their individual personalities. Because scenes like these tend to interrupt or contradict character development, one finds the authors allowing so many incongruities to accumulate that the reader cannot be sure of what a given scene or symbol means. If Kafka's sanction of instinctive subordination were not debatable, I should not have ended with this comparison between *The Castle* and *Loving*. I think Kafka and Green do sanction the commonplace, we might say "communal" responses, and do minimize the chances of the individual who acts in the interests of the self. Still one could argue that K., in making his late decisions, has grounds for being jealous, and that Kafka has him choose the *heroic* alternative in dismissing the assistants, thereby precipitating the breach with Frieda, instead of continuing the "familistic" relationship, which could only involve unheroic compromise.

This would be the existentialist view, and Kingsley Weatherhead makes this very argument in examining every book of Green's; that is, he argues the individual's need to reject familial ties and reassurances in the interests of "self-creation," regardless of what terrifying estrangement results. That he finds Mrs. Haye, Craigan, Miss Fellowes, and even Rock to be inimical parent-figures who retard the growth of young people, and that he finds Hilly, the girls of *Concluding,* Max and Julia, even Sebastian and Liz to be potential or real heroes and heroines, is not so much an evidence of Weatherhead's misconstruing Green as it is a commentary on Green's obliquity. Hence, though the serious themes I have here been summarizing were nineteenth century themes too, I have had to return to

Kafka in order to suggest Green's ultimate ambiguity. He has abided by his dictum that "the function of narrative prose is not to be clear," and his work does seem to become, as he would hope, "as diffuse and variously interpretable as life itself." [14]

I think then that Green, as Thomas Mann has said of Kafka, has "yearned after the 'blisses of the commonplace.' " [15] And because his characters are autonomous though impulsive, a kind of traditional hero and heroine emerge from Green's novels, as they emerge in Forster perhaps, but in few other twentieth century novelists. I mean heroes different from the rebellious individuals called anti-Heroes by Sean O'Faolain in *The Vanishing Hero*. To use the words O'Faolain applied to nineteenth century novelists, Green is satisfied, with themes of "Marriage, love, domestic happiness . . . to bring [his] novels to an intermediate destination rather than to expound an ultimate destiny." [16] His protagonists are caught heroes and ensnaring heroines, or lonely, unbowed old heroes like Craigan and Rock, invariably representative of the virtues found in homilies, or turned that way in the end, like the two Charleys, by their women.

Wholly mundane and unideal, these themes of Green's are not so much convictions that "here is the way to get through life" (rather the way is to ride the hobby-horse) as observations that age-old, unindividualistic conformity allows for the greatest extension of mutual support. It is almost the natural correlative of his non-Promethean outlook that he emphasizes fatigue rather than endurance. *Living*'s thematic symbols, we recall, involved first the pattern of escape-and-return (what we might call the pattern of individual self-assertion), which was supplanted by the pattern of fatigue-and-support, enforced by a number of "leaning" images.

Green was once moved to write, in *Pack My Bag*, of the inclination of one head against another as "the oldest gesture" (p. 211). Alone in a movie house, regretting a hangover, he was able to notice how tranquil were "those heads more intent on each other's breath as in the oldest gesture they inclined one to the other against the lighted screen. . . ." It was a typically Green-like vantage point.

Notes :

The quotations from Henry Green's nine novels and autobiography were made from the editions indicated in the list of Green's works in the next section.

O N E :

1 New York *Herald Tribune Book Review*, October 8, 1950, p. 14.
2 These theories were made public in an article in *Contact*, I (August 1950), 21–24; in three broadcasts printed in *The Listener:* XLIV (November 9, 1950), 505–506; XLV (March 15, 1951), 425–427; XLVI (August 23, 1951), 293–294; and in three interviews: with Harvey Breit, New York *Times Book Review*, February 19, 1950, p. 29; with Terry Southern, *Paris Review*, V (Summer 1958), 61–77; and with Alan Ross, *London Magazine*, VI (April 1959), 18–24.

3 Philip Toynbee, "The Novels of Henry Green," *Partisan Review,* XVI (May 1949), 489.

4 James Hall, "The Fiction of Henry Green: Paradoxes in Pleasure-and-Pain," *Kenyon Review,* XIX (Winter 1957), 85.

5 Green, "Communication Without Speech," *The Listener,* XLIV (November 9, 1950), 505–506.

6 Green, "The English Novel of the Future," *Contact,* I (August 1950), 24.

7 Green, "An Unfinished Novel," *London Magazine,* VI (April 1959), 11–17.

8 Walter Allen, "An Artist of the Thirties," *Folios of New Writing,* III (Spring 1941), 152.

9 Nigel Dennis, "The Double Life of Henry Green," *Life,* XXXIII (August 4, 1952), 92.

10 Henry Reed, *The Novel Since 1939* (London, 1946), p. 29.

11 Terry Southern, "The Art of Fiction XXII," *Paris Review,* V (Summer 1958), 67.

12 Virginia Woolf, *The Voyage Out* (London, 1949), p. 266.

13 Theodore Kalem, "Green: Ironist of the Human Heart," *Christian Science Monitor,* October 27, 1949, p. 11.

14 R. W. B. Lewis, *The Picaresque Saint: Representative Figures in Contemporary Fiction* (New York, 1959), pp. 24, 28.

15 "Art of Fiction XXII," p. 68.

16 Harvey Breit, "Talk with Henry Green—and a P.S.," New York *Times Book Review,* February 19, 1950, p. 29.

17 Lewis, p. 31.

18 Sean O'Faolain, *The Vanishing Hero* (London, 1956), p. 193.

19 "Art of Fiction XXII," p. 71.

20 Louis-Ferdinand Céline, *Death on the Installment Plan,* tr. J. H. P. Marks (Norfolk, Conn., n. d.), p. 386.

21 Aldous Huxley, *Point Counter Point* (New York, 1929), p. 118.

22 V. S. Pritchett, "Green on Doting," *New Yorker,* XXVIII (May 17, 1952), 141.

23 William York Tindall, *Forces in Modern British Literature 1885–1956* (New York, 1956), p. 106.

TWO :

1 Nigel Dennis, "The Double Life of Henry Green," *Life,* XXXIII (August 4, 1952), 92.

2 *Ibid.,* p. 86.

3 Green, "The English Novel of the Future," *Contact,* I (August 1950), 24.

4 These sentiments make up the burden of Green's article in *Contact* and of his first broadcast, which carried the subtitle, "Communication Without Speech."

5 V. S. Pritchett, "A Literary Letter from the British Capital," New York *Times Book Review,* January 7, 1951, p. 14.

6   "The English Novel of the Future," p. 21.

7   Terry Southern, "The Art of Fiction XXII," *Paris Review,* V (Summer 1958), 72.

8   "The English Novel of the Future," p. 21.

9   Giorgio Melchiori, *The Tightrope Walkers* (London, 1956), pp. 188–212.

10 *Ibid.,* p. 209.

11 *Ibid.,* p. 211.

12 *Ibid.,* p. 209. My italics.

13 Green, "A Novelist to His Readers—II," *The Listener,* XLV (March 15, 1951), 425.

14 Melchiori, p. 193.

15 William York Tindall, *The Literary Symbol* (New York, 1955), pp. 217 ff.

16 "A Novelist to His Readers—II," p. 425. Tindall uses the same words, talking of "telescoped montage or montage by superimposition." (*The Literary Symbol,* p. 206.)

17 Sergei Eisenstein, *The Film Sense,* tr. Jay Leyda (New York, 1942), p. 11.

18 *Ibid.,* p. 35.

19 Green, "Communication Without Speech," *The Listener,* XLIV (November 9, 1950), 506.

20 "The English Novel of the Future," p. 22.

21 *Ibid.*

22 *Ibid.,* p. 24.

23 Mark Schorer, "Introduction to Henry Green's World," New York *Times Book Review,* October 8, 1949, p. 1.

24 Martin Greenberg, "Two Novels by Henry Green," *The New Leader,* May 14, 1951, pp. 25–26.

25 Melchiori, pp. 205, 198, 200.

26 Edward Stokes, *The Novels of Henry Green* (London, 1959), pp. 191, 193.

27 Green, "Apologia," *Folios of New Writing,* IV (Autumn 1941), 44–51.

28 Quoted in D. G. Hogarth, *The Life of Charles M. Doughty* (London, 1938), pp. 114–115.

29 Charles M. Doughty, *Passages from Arabia Deserta,* ed. Edward Garnett (New York, 1931), p. 34.

30 *Ibid.,* p. 21. Cited in "A Poet of Fear," anon. rev. of *Concluding, Times Literary Supplement,* December 25, 1948, p. 726.

31 Theodore Kalem, "Green: Ironist of the Human Heart," *Christian Science Monitor,* October 27, 1949, p. 11.

32 Doughty, p. 56.

33 *Ibid.,* p. 180.

34 *Ibid.,* pp. 76, 23.

35 *Ibid.,* p. 57.

36 Stokes, p. 190.

37 Doughty, pp. 138, 142–143.

[38] *Ibid.*, p. 24.

[39] Diana Trilling, ". . . the Comic View," New York *Times Book Review,* March 26, 1950, p. 1.

T H R E E :

[1] Harvey Breit, "Talk with Henry Green—and a P. S.," New York *Times Book Review,* February 19, 1950, p. 29.

[2] Beekman W. Cottrell, "Conversation Piece: Four Twentieth Century English Dialogue Novelists," unpub. diss. (Columbia University, 1956), p. 79.

[3] Anon. rev. of *Party Going, Atlantic Monthly,* CLXXXVIII (October 1951), 86.

[4] D. W. Brogan, rev. of *Blindness, New Republic,* XLIX (December 4, 1926), 174.

[5] T. S. Eliot, *The Waste Land,* lines 22–23, in *Collected Poems, 1909–1935* (New York, 1936).

[6] James Joyce, *Dubliners* (New York, 1927), p. 103.

[7] Fyodor Dostoyevsky, *Crime and Punishment,* tr. Constance Garnett (New York, 1923), p. 492.

[8] Anon. rev. of *Blindness, Saturday Review of Literature,* III (December 25, 1926), 472.

F O U R :

[1] Ruth Chapin, rev. of *Party Going, Christian Science Monitor,* September 13, 1951, p. 13.

[2] Edward Stokes, "Henry Green, Dispossessed Poet," *Australian Quarterly,* XXVIII (December 1956), 89.

[3] "A Poet of Fear," anon. rev. of *Concluding, Times Literary Supplement.* December 25, 1948, p. 726.

[4] D. H. Lawrence, *New Poems* (New York, 1920), pp. iii–iv.

[5] *Ibid.*, pp. vi–vii.

[6] Lawrence, *The Rainbow* (New York, n. d.), p. 125.

[7] *New Poems,* p. ix.

[8] T. S. Eliot, "Burnt Norton," V, lines 140–143, 159, in *Four Quartets* (New York, 1943). See also the line from section III of this poem, "With slow rotation suggesting permanence" (l. 95).

[9] I owe my concept of the gap between Lawrence and Eliot to Giorgio Melchiori, who compared the two in *The Tightrope Walkers* (London, 1956), pp. 89–103.

[10] Green, "The English Novel of the Future," *Contact,* I (August 1950), 24.

11   Harvey Breit, "Talk with Henry Green—and a P. S.," New York *Times Book Review*, February 19, 1950, p. 29.

12   R. M. Linscott, "Cinematograph," New York *Herald Tribune Book Review*, August 11, 1929, p. 2.

13   David Garnett, rev. of *Party Going, New Statesman and Nation*, XVIII (October 7, 1939), 489.

14   *Ibid.*

15   In his brief examination of *Party Going*, William York Tindall appears to assign chief values to the same three symbols when he says, "Another reading might almost fix the relationship of artichoke, station, and bird that baffles and delights me, but 'almost' is the important word." (*The Literary Symbol* [New York, 1955], p. 95.)

FIVE :

1   Green, "The English Novel of the Future," *Contact,* I (August 1950), 23.

2   Lionel Trilling, *The Liberal Imagination* (Garden City, N. Y., 1953). "The novel, then," he says, "is a perpetual quest for reality, the field of its research being always the social world, the material of its analysis being always manners as the indication of the direction of man's soul" (p. 206).

3   John Pendy Kirby, "Tradition and Experiment," *Virginia Quarterly Review*, XXVI (Winter 1950), 148.

4   James Hall, "The Fiction of Henry Green: Paradoxes in Pleasure-and-Pain," *Kenyon Review*, XIX (Winter 1957), 82.

5   John Farrelly, "The Success of Form," *New Republic*, CXXI (December 26, 1949), 19.

6   Hall, p. 83.

7   William York Tindall, *The Literary Symbol* (New York, 1955), p. 97.

8   Hall, p. 77.

SIX :

1   The phrase is John Bardin's, from his review, "Fire and Flight," in *The Freeman*, May 7, 1951, pp. 509–510.

2   Mark Schorer, "The Real and Unreal Worlds of Henry Green," New York *Times Book Review*, December 31, 1950, p. 5.

3   Frederich Wyatt, "Some Comments on the Use of Symbols in the Novel," *Literature and Psychology*, IV (April 1954), 20–21.

4   Philip Toynbee, rev. of *Caught, New Statesman and Nation*, XXV (June 26, 1943), 422.

5   Giorgio Melchiori, *The Tightrope Walkers* (London, 1956), p. 203.

6 Green, "Mr. Jonas," *Folios of New Writing,* III (Spring 1941), 11.

7 Jean Howard, rev. of *Concluding, Horizon,* XVIII (November 1948), 366.

SEVEN :

1 Mark Schorer, "Introduction to Henry Green's World," New York *Times Book Review,* October 8, 1949, p. 22.

2 Robert Phelps, "The Vision of Henry Green," *Hudson Review,* V (Winter 1953), 617–618.

3 Jonathan Swift, "Resolutions When I Come to Be Old," in *Swift's Satires and Personal Writings,* ed. W. A. Eddy (New York, 1956), p. 405.

4 Philip Toynbee, "The Novels of Henry Green," *Partisan Review,* XVI (May 1949), 496.

5 Louis L. Martz, "Wallace Stevens: The World as Meditation," *Yale Review,* XLVII (Summer 1958), 517–536.

6 Wallace Stevens, *Opus Posthumous* (New York, 1957), p. 51.

7 *Ibid.,* pp. 48–49.

8 Stevens, *The Man with the Blue Guitar* (New York, 1945), p. 48.

9 Giorgio Melchiori, *The Tightrope Walkers* (London, 1956), p. 206.

10 *Opus Posthumous,* p. 55.

EIGHT :

1 Beekman W. Cottrell, "Conversation Piece: Four Twentieth Century English Dialogue Novelists," unpub. diss. (Columbia University, 1956), p. 95.

2 J. D. Scott, rev. of *Doting, New Statesman and Nation,* XLIII (May 10, 1952), 564 (566).

3 Thomas Mann, *The Magic Mountain,* tr. H. T. Lowe-Porter (New York, 1930), II, 606. See also Hermann Weyl, *Symmetry* (Princeton, 1952), pp. 63 ff.

4 V. S. Pritchett, "Green on Doting," *New Yorker,* XXVIII (May 17, 1952), 137.

5 Diana Trilling, ". . . the Comic View," New York *Times Book Review,* March 26, 1950, p. 20.

6 Lionel Trilling, "Art and Fortune," in *The Liberal Imagination* (Garden City, N. Y., 1953), pp. 254–255.

7 Walter Havighurst, rev. of *Nothing, Saturday Review of Literature,* XXXIII (March 25, 1950), 13.

8 H. P. Lazarus, "The Symbolical Apple," rev. of *Doting, The Nation,* CLXXIV (May 24, 1952), 506.

NINE :

1 Norman Holland, "The Laughter of Laurence Sterne," *Hudson Review,* IX (Autumn 1956), 422.

2 *Ibid.,* p. 425.

3 Lewis Carroll, *Through the Looking Glass,* in *The Complete Works of Lewis Carroll* (New York, n. d.), p. 152.

4 Aldous Huxley, *Those Barren Leaves* (New York, 1925), p. 60.

5 Anthony Powell, *The Acceptance World* (London, 1955), p. 204.

6 Paul Pickrel, "Outstanding Novels," *Yale Review,* XXXIX (June 1950), 766.

7 Walter Havighurst, "Search for a Dead Rose," rev. of *Back, Saturday Review of Literature,* XXXIII (September 30, 1950), 30.

8 Joseph Conrad, *Lord Jim* (New York, 1957), p. 126.

9 Joyce Cary, *To Be a Pilgrim* (New York, 1942), p. 339.

10 Franz Kafka, *The Castle,* tr. Willa and Edwin Muir (New York, 1954), p. 168.

11 *Ibid.,* p. 170.

12 *Ibid.,* p. 173.

13 *Ibid.,* p. 175.

14 Green, "The English Novel of the Future," *Contact,* I (August 1950), 22.

15 Thomas Mann, "Homage," introduction to *The Castle,* p. x.

16 Sean O'Faolain, *The Vanishing Hero* (London, 1956), p. 73.

Books, stories, and articles by Henry Green :

Blindness. London: J. M. Dent, 1926. New York: Dutton, 1926.*
Living, London: Hogarth Press, 1929.* New York: Macmillan, 1929.
Party Going. London: Hogarth Press, 1939. New York: Viking, 1951.*
"A Private School in 1914," *Folios of New Writing,* I (Spring 1940), 11–25.
Pack My Bag. London: Hogarth Press, 1940.
"A Rescue," *Penguin New Writing* (March 1941), 88–93.
"Mr. Jonas," *Folios of New Writing,* III (Spring 1941).
"Apologia," *Folios of New Writing,* IV (Autumn 1941), 44–51.
Caught. London: Hogarth Press, 1943. New York: Viking, 1950.*
"The Lull," *New Writing and Daylight* (Summer 1943), 11–21.
Loving. London: Hogarth Press, 1945. New York: Viking, 1949.*
Back. London: Hogarth Press, 1946. New York: Viking, 1950.*
Concluding. London: Hogarth Press, 1948. New York: Viking, 1950.*
Nothing. London: Hogarth Press, 1950. New York: Viking, 1950.*
"The English Novel of the Future," *Contact,* I (August 1950), 21–24.
Autobiographical sketch, New York *Herald Tribune Book Review,* October
    8, 1950, p. 14.

"Communication Without Speech," *The Listener,* XLIV (November 9, 1950), 505–506.

"A Novelist to His Readers—II," *The Listener,* XLV (March 15, 1951), 425–427.

"A Fire, a Flood, and the Price of Meat," *The Listener,* XLVI (August 23, 1951), 293–294.

Doting. London: Hogarth Press, 1952. New York: Viking, 1952.*

"The Spoken Word as Written," review of *The Oxford Book of English Talk, Spectator,* CXCI (September 4, 1953), 248.

Review of Virginia Woolf's *A Writer's Diary, London Magazine,* I (February 1954), 80–83.

Review of Sir Ernest Gower's *The Complete Plain Words, London Magazine,* II (February 1955), 88–91.

"An Unfinished Novel," *London Magazine,* VI (April 1959), 11–17.

* Edition quoted in the text.